Praise for *Liberty in Peril*:

"*Liberty in Peril* is an important book. It seeks to show the transformation of the underlying ideology of American government since the Revolution from commitment to the principle of individual liberty to the principle of democracy—that government should be responsive to the will of the people. It combines sophisticated—but easily readable—economics with sophisticated political science and a deep historical interpretation of changes in American politics over this period which have completed the transformation. It is an outstanding political and economic history of the U.S."

> —**George L. Priest**, Edward J. Phelps Professor of Law and Economics, Yale University

"*Liberty in Peril* is a gem. Randall Holcombe traces the inexorable growth of government through war and peace, from railroads to autos, and during prosperity and depression."

> —**Burton W. Folsom Jr.**, Distinguished Fellow, Hillsdale College; author, *New Deal or Raw Deal? How FDR's Economic Legacy Has Damaged America* and *FDR Goes to War. How Expanded Executive Power, Spiraling National Debt, and Restricted Civil Liberties Shaped Wartime America*

"The Independent Institute has been leading the way for some time in asking uncomfortable questions about a disturbing tendency: the transformation of the American government and market system toward cronyism. In his marvelous Independent book, *Liberty in Peril*, Holcombe lays bare the case in careful detail. Using the interest group model of public choice, Holcombe is able to show the slow but cumulatively catastrophic changes that have taken place, punctuated by a few crises of the type Robert Higgs has emphasized for decades. The problem, at its base, has been the erosion of the protections for liberty in favor of populist 'democracy.' I hope that this timely and well-written call to action can motivate a consideration of the limits, and the need to limit, the dangerous impulses of interest-group politics."

> —**Michael C. Munger**, Professor of Political Science, Economics and Public Policy and Director of the Philosophy, Politics, and Economics Program, Duke University

"Randall Holcombe's *Liberty in Peril* illuminates the forces that have shifted power and responsibility from individuals to government, and from local to centralized government, throughout American history. This timely reminder is must reading for all those concerned with the erosion of, and new threats to, the legal rights and liberties that form the core of a successful society."

> —**Michael J. Boskin**, former Chairman, President's Council of Economic Advisors; T. M. Friedman Professor of Economics, Stanford University; Wohlford Family Senior Fellow, Hoover Institution; Research Associate, National Bureau of Economic Research

"Every new book by Randy Holcombe is a pleasure to read. Clearly written, insightful, thought-provoking and of high importance to the state of the world, *Liberty in Peril* is no exception. The book describes how fundamentally the U.S. has changed as a political system, and how the ideals of individual liberty, limited government and separation of powers have eroded. It should be read by everyone concerned about the growth and abuse of government power, no matter whether it is done by the left, the right or the center."

> —**Peter Kurrild-Klitgaard**, Professor of Political Science, University of Copenhagen, Denmark

"In *Liberty in Peril*, Randall Holcombe dissects the commonplace assertion that democracy and liberty support one another and rejects it. His rejection is based on a careful analysis of the working properties of democratic institutions and processes. Any reader looking to find a short and readable explanation of how political democracy can erode personal liberty should read this book."

> —**Richard E. Wagner**, Holbert L. Harris Professor of Economics, George Mason University

"Liberty for individuals guided the U.S. founding fathers. Randall Holcombe gives a powerful explanation as to why over time liberty gave way to the 'will of the people' or 'democracy.' Citizens get what they think they want but do not fully appreciate the loss of liberty. *Liberty in Peril* is a welcome wake-up call about the stakes at play."

> —**Lee J. Alston**, Ostrom Chair, Professor of Economics and Law, and Director of the Ostrom Workshop at Indiana University

"Holcombe's well-written book *Liberty in Peril* provides the reader with a clearly stated explanation of how the grand American experiment, which began as a republic formed by people who prized liberty, evolved to become a highly politicized 'democratic' economy. Taking a bold political economy approach, the book is brimming with fresh constitutional comparisons and historic treatments. Woven together, they yield a coherent story of how, over the course of our history, liberty, broadly speaking, has been systematically compromised. *Liberty in Peril* is a must read for those who wish better to understand the deep roots of America's politically intertwined economy."

—**Bruce Yandle**, Alumni Distinguished Professor of Economics Emeritus and Dean Emeritus, Clemson University

"Individual liberty and democratic self-government, the twin ideals on which the United States were founded, do not co-exist in perfect harmony. Aware of this fact the Founders designed a constitutionally limited government to guard against the threat majoritarian democracy may pose to individual liberty. Holcombe's book *Liberty in Peril* is about how over time a growing role of majoritarian rule and direct popular vote worked to erode the constitutional constraints the Founders intended, resulting in continuous government expansion and spreading interest group politics. With his detailed and instructive historical account Holcombe demonstrates the causes that are behind and the mechanisms that have propelled this transformation. His sobering account of the evolution of American democracy calls for renewed inquiry into the problem the Founders sought to solve: How to limit democratic self-government by constitutional constraints that effectively protect individual liberty and keep interest-group politics in bound."

—**Viktor J. Vanberg**, Professor Emeritus of Economic Policy at Freiburg University and former Director and Senior Research Fellow of the Walter Eucken Institute

"*Liberty in Peril* is pure Holcombe, with a fine linear lucid narrative that presents the gradual disencumbering of the Federal Government from constitutional constraints as a shift from a government conceived in liberty to one emphasizing 'democracy.'"

—**Roger D. Congleton**, BB&T Professor of Economics, West Virginia University

"To protect individual liberty or to promote the general welfare—which is the proper role of government? Charting the 200-year transformation of American government from the former to the latter, Randall Holcombe's book *Liberty in Peril* is a masterful work of U.S. political-economic history. Learned and scholarly, yet fun and accessible, *Liberty in Peril* is perfect for anyone interested in 'how we got here.'"

—**Edward J. López** is Professor of Economics and BB&T Distinguished Professor of Capitalism, Western Carolina University; and Executive Director, Public Choice Society

"Randy Holcombe's book, *Liberty in Peril*, continues his intensive study of American political and economic history which he began in *From Liberty to Democracy*. In this latest work, Holcombe argues that wars and interest groups have eroded America's emphasis on liberty and replaced it with an emphasis on 'democracy.' From the Revolutionary War through the New Deal, he finds government interventions increasingly detrimental to freedom and to the American Republic. If you like thought-provoking and provocative arguments, you will certainly enjoy *Liberty in Peril*."

—**Keith L. Dougherty**, Professor of Political Science, University of Georgia

"In the valuable and accessible book *Liberty in Peril*, Randall Holcombe reminds us that a government of the people, for the people, and by the people once meant—and should once again mean—far more than just counting up the votes."

—**Richard N. Langlois**, Professor of Economics, University of Connecticut

"*Liberty in Peril* is spot on! Holcombe is right to say that we have lost so much of the liberties upon which our nation was founded. His book should be read by anyone who cares about the future of freedom from government tyranny."

—**Robert A. McGuire**, Adjunct Research Professor of Economics, The University of Akron; author, *To Form A More Perfect Union: A New Economic Interpretation of the United States Constitution*

"We often think of liberty and democracy as complements, even two sides of the same coin. Randall G. Holcombe begs to differ. Americans in the founding era championed liberty, and founded a constitutional republic to secure it. In the modern era, however, Americans champion political 'democracy' instead, which, Holcombe argues, has come at the expense of liberty. In the provocative and timely volume, *Liberty in Peril*, Holcombe confronts us with the steady loss of liberty in America, and offers a bold argument for a return to the ideals that made America the land of the free."

—**James R. Otteson Jr.**, Thomas W. Smith Presidential Chair in Business Ethics, Professor of Economics, and Executive Director of the Eudaimonia Institute, Wake Forest University

LIBERTY
IN
PERIL

Also by the Author

Political Capitalism (2018)
How Economic and Political Power Is Made and Maintained

Advanced Introduction to Public Choice (2016)

Producing Prosperity (2015)
An Inquiry into the Operation of the Market Process

The Great Austrian Economists (2015, 1999)

Advanced Introduction to the Austrian School of Economics (2014)

Liberalism and Cronyism (2013)
Two Rival Political and Economic Systems

Housing America (2009)
Building Out of a Crisis

Entrepreneurship and Economic Progress (2006)

Public Sector Economics (2005, 1987)
The Role of the Government in the American Economy

From Liberty to Democracy (2002)
The Transformation of American Government

Smarter Growth (2001)
Market-Based Strategies for Land-Use Planning in the 21st Century

Writing Off Ideas (2000)
Taxation, Foundations, and Philanthropy in America

Growth and Variability in State Tax Revenue (1997)
An Anatomy of State Fiscal Crises

Public Finance (1996)
Government Revenues and Expenditures in the United States Economy

Public Policy and the Quality of Life (1995)
Market Incentives versus Government Planning

The Economic Foundations of Government (1993)

Economic Models and Methodology (1989)

An Economic Analysis of Democracy (1985)

Public Finance and the Political Process (1983)

INDEPENDENT
I N S T I T U T E

INDEPENDENT INSTITUTE is a non-profit, non-partisan, public-policy research and educational organization that shapes ideas into profound and lasting impact. The mission of Independent is to boldly advance peaceful, prosperous, and free societies grounded in a commitment to human worth and dignity. Applying independent thinking to issues that matter, we create transformational ideas for today's most pressing social and economic challenges. The results of this work are published as books, our quarterly journal, *The Independent Review*, and other publications and form the basis for numerous conference and media programs. By connecting these ideas with organizations and networks, we seek to inspire action that can unleash an era of unparalleled human flourishing at home and around the globe.

100 Swan Way, Oakland, California 94621-1428, U.S.A.
Telephone: 510-632-1366 • Facsimile: 510-568-6040 • Email: info@independent.org • www.independent.org

RANDALL G. HOLCOMBE

LIBERTY
IN
PERIL

DEMOCRACY
AND POWER
IN AMERICAN
HISTORY

FOREWORD BY BARRY R. WEINGAST

INDEPENDENT
INSTITUTE
OAKLAND, CALIFORNIA

Liberty in Peril: Democracy and Power in American History

This revised and updated text is based on the text of *From Liberty to Democracy* which was published by the University of Michigan Press in 2002.

Copyright © 2019 by the Independent Institute
ISBN: 978-1-59813-332-5

Independent Institute
100 Swan Way
Oakland, CA 94621-1428
Telephone: 510-632-1366
Fax: 510-568-6040
Email: info@independent.org
Website: www.independent.org

Cover Design: Denise Tsui

Library of Congress Cataloging-in-Publication Data Available

To Lora, and to Ross, Emily, Mark, Bailey, Connor, Becca, and their children, with the hope that their liberty and the liberty of those in their generations can be preserved.

Contents

Foreword

by Barry R. Weingast

THE ARC DEFINING the contours of Randall Holcombe's *Liberty in Peril* is the idea that the United States has slowly been but massively transformed since the founding era. This country began with the founding of government on the guiding principle of liberty, an era characterized by the rejection of tyranny from kings or unlimited majority rule. We now have a government based on democracy in an era where citizen choice is central, quite often at the expense of liberty.

> Liberty means freedom from the powers of government, and there is no doubt that the attempt to escape from government oppression was the motivation behind the American Revolution. An ideology of liberty naturally creates a population that is suspicious of government power, that wants the government to act within strict limits, and that will be intolerant of a government that tries to expand beyond those limits. An ideology of democracy advocates furthering the will of the majority through the actions of popularly elected representatives, which removes the most severe constraints placed on those in power. (7)

How did this transformation happen?

Government, the national government in particular, is such a familiar presence in our lives that most Americans are likely to be surprised that the idea of liberty—sustainable limits on the powers of government—was so central to the founding era and America's first century. This reaction is in part caused by the very phenomena studied by Holcombe: we live in a rich, stable, and developed society and take it all for granted. Governments are typically far more malicious in developing countries. Many developing countries make no attempt to create the elements of liberty, rule of law, or elections. But even those developing countries that do make that attempt struggle mightily with the effort, and very few succeed. This logic implies that the problems confronting Americans in the late 18th century differed from those confronting them in the early 21st century.

For one, no country in the 18th century can be considered developed, the United States in particular. Prior to independence, the colonies did thrive. As Adam Smith observed in the *Wealth of Nations*, this growth reflected to an important degree of the liberty enjoyed by the colonists.

But the British changes in the governance of the Empire following the Seven Year's War (1756-63) altered American perceptions: Where elements of liberty had grown and been sustained for nearly a century, came new elements of what to Americans appeared arbitrary deviations from the implicit constitution of the British Empire. This caused Americans to think seriously about how to sustain liberty in practice. No country at that time had sustained liberty (Britain is traditionally labeled the closest). Prior to the American Revolution and, indeed, "Throughout history, citizens had been viewed as servants of their governments, and the new idea that government should be the servant of its citizens took hold and sparked the American Revolution" (8).

At the end of the 17th century, John Locke provided the philosophical basis for the American approach. "Locke's revolutionary idea was that people naturally have rights, and the ... purpose of government is to protect the rights of citizens" (9). "The idea of liberty was a bold challenge to the governance structure of the world's most advanced nations" (10). In the late 18th century, liberty was a radical idea.

The revolting colonies were among the first in modern times to put these ideas into practice. Americans made it part of their heritage by putting this logic directly into the Declaration of Independence, which, after announcing that "men" had "inalienable rights," says:

> That to secure these rights, Governments are instituted among Men, deriving their just powers from the consent of the governed,—That whenever any Form of Government becomes destructive of these ends, it is the Right of the People to alter or to abolish it, and to institute new Government, laying its foundation on such principles and organizing

its powers in such form, as to them shall seem most likely to effect their Safety and Happiness.

Holcombe explains in chapters 3 and 4 how the founders created a system to sustain liberty.

So, then, how does Holcombe explain the transformation of American ideology from liberty to democracy? His answer is two-fold. The first and lesser effect is war. Holcombe says, "Without a doubt, the single most important event in the transformation of American government was the War Between the States" (92).

The second and more important effect involves Holcombe's relentless, comprehensive application of the interest group perspective in the context of the "market intervention" paradigm. Competitive markets exist, but many groups have policy proposals to make themselves better off, say by restricting entry or a protective tariff limiting foreign competition. Because the political system is responsive to group organization, policies are biased toward those who are organized. Too often, in Holcombe's eyes, public policy represents "market intervention."

One by one and without any advanced plan, Holcombe explains, the constraints on national policymaking were dismantled, typically because these constraints prevented some policy to benefit a particular group, particularly after the Civil War or, as Holcombe calls it, the War Between the States. As evidence, he adduces a series of national regulatory acts beginning with the 1887 "Act to regulate commerce," but also including the Sherman Act and the Clayton Act of 1890 and 1914, respectively.

The transformation leading Holcombe to consider liberty in peril is seen by the following sharp contrast. Americans in the Jacksonian era believed in what we would today call a level playing field, especially an absence of privilege. They would therefore have perceived as illegitimate an attempt by an interest group to get ahead through specialized legislation. In contrast, modern Americans value precisely this democratic responsiveness. This is the arc of Holcombe's book.

Let me close with a final remark. We should be mindful that the differences in the definition of liberty in the 18th century world of Adam Smith and the American founders versus liberty in today's world, and seek to understand how the meaning of liberty has evolved (or devolved). In this regard, we should explore what factors have contributed to this transformation: the ideology of interest groups, public goods, and the integration of markets, and finally, was this transformation inevitable?

In *Liberty in Peril*, Holcombe has given us a well-constructed and much-needed volume for assessing these questions and the directions in which we should move forward.

Barry R. Weingast
Senior Fellow, Hoover Institution, and
Ward C. Krebs Family Professor of Political Science
Stanford University

Preface

IN THE TWENTY-FIRST century, Americans tend to think of their government as a democracy, in the sense that they view the proper function of government as carrying out the will of the people, as revealed through democratic elections. This differs substantially from the vision of the American Founders, who deliberately designed their government to be insulated from democratic pressures. The role of government, as they saw it, was to protect the rights of individuals, and the biggest threat to individual liberty was the government itself. So they designed a government with constitutionally limited powers, constrained to carry out only those activities specifically allowed by the Constitution. This book describes how the fundamental principle underlying American government has been transformed from protecting individual liberty to carrying out the will of the people, as revealed by a democratic decision-making process.

In a nation that views itself as a democracy, any criticism of democracy might appear anti-American. The material that follows shows that liberty, not democracy, was the principle underlying American government, and the American Founders clearly understood that unconstrained democracy can undermine liberty just as much as autocracy. The idea that government should carry out the will of the people as revealed through democratic elections may be even more dangerous, because it legitimizes the actions of democratic governments by claiming those actions were approved by the people.

This book is a revised version of my earlier book, *From Liberty to Democracy: The Transformation of American Government*, published in 2002 by the University of Michigan Press. I am grateful to them for allowing the publication of this new edition. The biggest change in this edition is the reduction in the amount of material aimed at an academic audience to make these ideas accessible to a general audience. This edition focuses on the historical events that transformed of American government, as did the earlier edition, but reduces the discussion of academic ideas and theories that would be of less interest to a general audience. The 2002 book also has many more footnotes and references, for readers who have a more academic interest in the subject.

I am very grateful to the Independent Institute and its president David J. Theroux for sponsoring this book. In undertaking the revision I have received helpful comments from Roy M. Carlisle, John Samples, and William "Bill" Shughart. Bill provided very detailed and very helpful comments, and deserves special mention. Roy has provided enthusiastic support for the book since we first discussed it and was helpful and encouraging at every step along the way. Lora, my wife, also an economist, has been uniformly supportive and encouraging. My hope is that this volume will reinforce the ideas of liberty on which the American government was founded in 1776, and which are threatened by the very government that was designed to protect them.

I

Liberty
The Revolutionary Cause

IF YOU WERE to go back to 1776 and ask typical Americans to summarize, in one word, the fundamental principle underlying their new government, that one word would have been liberty. The American Revolution was fought to establish a new government to protect the rights of its citizens, ensure their freedom, and do little else. If you were to ask typical Americans today to summarize, in one word, the fundamental principle underlying American government, that one word would be democracy. The role of the government is to carry out the will of the people, where the will of the people is determined by the preferences they express through a democratic decision-making process. This book describes how the fundamental principle underlying American government has been transformed from liberty to democracy.

When the nation was founded, Americans viewed government to be the greatest threat to their liberty. The Declaration of Independence consists mostly of a list of grievances against the King of England—a list of the ways in which he had violated their rights. The American Founders intended to design a government with limited powers that would protect their rights, but that would be constrained from violating them. The limits of the federal government's functions and powers are enumerated in the Constitution forged at Philadelphia in 1787, but because some of the Founders felt that the Constitution did not spell out the limits of the government's powers clearly enough, they added the Tenth Amendment, the last of the Bill of Rights, ratified shortly after the Constitution, which states, "The powers not delegated to the United States by the Constitution, nor prohibited by it to the States, are reserved to the States, respectively, or to the people."

By the end of the twentieth century, Americans viewed their government very differently from the vision of the nation's Founders. When the nation was founded, the federal government was viewed as a protector of individual rights, and by the end of the twentieth century, the federal government was viewed as an institution for carrying out the will of the majority, and for protecting and furthering the economic interests of its citizens. The Founders viewed government as a necessary evil. By the end of the twentieth century, government was no longer viewed as a necessary evil, but as a potential power for good. Democracy had replaced liberty as the fundamental principle of American government.[1]

This transformation of American government occurred gradually, from the time of the nation's founding. The influence of major events over the scope of American government is well-documented and undeniable. The War Between the States, two World Wars, and the Great Depression are associated with substantial changes in the size and scope of American government, but it is also true that even without these events there has been a steady move toward expanding the scope of democracy and away from the protection of individual liberties. The result has been more government power, more government programs, and more government expenditures.

The most dramatic changes have come in the twentieth century, but even as early as 1835, Alexis de Tocqueville, in his book *Democracy in America*, was able to foresee the path over which American government would evolve.[2] The constitutional limits placed on American government by the Founders have been eroded by the democratic institutions embodied in the Constitution itself. Democracy means accountability to the voting public, and this accountability gives voters the ability to demand that public policies be responsive to their interests. The constitutional challenge, the Founders clearly realized, was to limit the scope of government so that it could not be used to further the interests of particular groups over the general public interest.

---

1. "Democracy has become the battle cry of our day," proclaimed Carl J. Friedrich, professor of government at Harvard University, in the first sentence of his book, *Constitutional Government and Democracy*, rev. ed. (Boston: Ginn, 1950).

2. Alexis de Tocqueville, *Democracy in America* (New York: Alfred A. Knopf, 1963), originally published in French in 1835.

The tremendous growth of government in the twentieth century has made this challenge even more formidable. When government is small and the scope of its activities is limited, special interests have few incentives to try to use the government to advance their interests. Government has little power to do so. When government is large and when its limits are less sharply defined, potentially large gains can be had if government policies are steered in a particular way. Thus, government growth results in a government that acts more for the benefit of narrow interests and less for the benefit of the general public interest.

Today, citizens rarely question the idea that America's political status quo is merely an extension of the constitutional principles of the eighteenth century. One reason is that they are propagandized to believe it is so. Everyone from politicians to civics teachers instills patriotic messages to all willing (and some unwilling) listeners. Dissenters are heard, to be sure, but they do not have the visibility and status of those who sell the principles of democratic government. Another reason is that citizens have little incentive to consider political issues, because as individuals, they do not make policy decisions. Voters face a very limited set of political choices, and when they do cast their ballots they know that their one individual vote will not affect the final result. Voters are ignorant of politics, but rationally ignorant. Little incentive exists to become informed about issues over which one has minimal influence.

Rational Ignorance in Politics

Despite the frequently heard claim that every vote counts, and that one of the most important duties of citizens in a democratic nation is to vote—and even the admonition that if you do not vote you have no right to complain—voters realize that their one vote will not determine an election's outcome.[3] This may not be as true in local elections, where fewer voters participate, but in national elections, the probability of an individual voter casting a decisive

---

3. This idea is discussed at length by Anthony Downs, An Economic Theory of Democracy (New York: Harper & Row, 1957), which provides an insightful analysis of democratic decision-making.

vote is miniscule. In presidential elections, one is more likely to be killed in an accident driving to the polls than to cast a decisive vote.[4]

Counterarguments to the idea that one's vote does not count typically rely on the fallacy of composition, noting that all votes together determine the election outcome so each individual vote must count. "What if everybody thought that and didn't vote?" But many people do vote, so for an individual voter, the election outcome would be the same regardless of for whom that voter voted, or whether the voter abstained. Despite the reality that one vote will not change an election's outcome, many voters insist that their votes are important. Individually, they are not, but collectively they are. If turnout is very low, that takes away some of the legitimacy claimed by those who are elected. So politicians have an incentive to promote the propaganda that every vote counts, and that citizens have a patriotic duty to vote.

Because the probability of casting a decisive vote is so small, voters have little incentive to become informed about the issues. When asked, a surprisingly large percentage of people cannot even name the candidates in legislative elections, let alone tell you anything about their positions. Once elected, representatives put in full days passing legislation, and most people know nothing about most of it. This does not mean that all voters are ignorant about everything. Some people are interested in politics and become informed for their own enjoyment, just as some people are interested and very well-informed about sports. Readers of this book are likely to be more informed than most people. Ask yourself this: Is Congress in session this week? If so, what issues are they considering? What are the positions of your representatives on these issues? Consumers tend to be better informed about differences in restaurants they might choose than they are about political candidates. That makes sense because they get to choose the restaurants at which they eat. But the politicians who represent them will do so regardless of how they vote.

---

4. The original edition of this book was being written during the 2000 presidential election that was decided by fewer than 1,000 votes in Florida. There was substantial controversy regarding whether there should be a recount, and if so, how that would be accomplished. Ultimately, the issue was decided by the Supreme Court, with George W. Bush being declared the winner. This example illustrates that one vote never counts and that when elections are very close, the courts are more likely to decide the winner rather than an accurate count of the votes.

Because Americans view the fundamental principle of American government as democracy, a critical analysis of democracy seems almost anti-American. One of the themes of this book is that the Founders had no intention of creating a democracy, in the sense of a government that would be guided by popular opinion. In fact, a critical assessment of this vision of democracy fits squarely with the Founders' vision of their new government.

The Constitution describes a government of limited and enumerated powers and was designed with a system of checks and balances to control government power. Originally, the government was designed to be one-sixth democratic. Members of the House of Representatives were to be elected by the people, but Senators were to be chosen by their state legislatures, and that remained the case until the Seventeenth Amendment was ratified in 1913. The judiciary has always been appointed, insulating that branch from democratic pressures, and the president was to be chosen by an Electoral College. Chapter 3 describes how the Electoral College was designed to insulate the selection of the chief executive from democratic pressures and also how the Founders' design rapidly evolved into the system of presidential elections we have today. A government wherein three branches check and balance each other can work only if the branches are roughly equally powerful. With a president chosen by an Electoral College, an appointed judicial branch, and Senators chosen by their state legislatures, only one-half of one-third of the government was elected by the people.

Even that Constitution, ratified in 1789 and one-sixth democratic, is more democratic than the Founders originally envisioned. The Articles of Confederation, the nation's first constitution, did not allow citizen voting for any federal official. Chapter 4 gives a more detailed argument about why the replacement of the Articles of Confederation with the Constitution of the United States was an early move in the transformation of the nation's ideology from liberty to democracy.

Democracy and Ideology

Americans often have been critical of propaganda from other nations. The communist bloc nations during the Cold War and Nazi Germany stand out, but post–World War II Japan has been criticized for whitewashing its record during the war, and almost any nondemocratic nation is subject to criticism that it stifles dissent through both formal and informal means. The US government controls the flow of much information, citing national security concerns, and any dissent often is portrayed as unpatriotic. Citizens tend to support their governments and identify with their policies because of institutions that give them ideological support.

Citizens accept government's actions, even when they disagree with them, when they view those actions as legitimate. A major function of propaganda is to convince citizens that the government is acting in their interests and that its actions are supported widely by the citizenry. An important function of democratic elections is to convey legitimacy upon the decisions that are made by those who are elected.[5] If one agrees with the democratic process, even though one may disagree with some specific decisions made by the president or Congress, one still agrees that those elected representatives have the legitimate right to make those decisions for us.

The democratic ideology that creates the image of legitimacy explains why politicians always urge citizens to vote, despite the fact that most voters are very uninformed. If arriving at a good collective decision was the goal, voting would be limited to those who have both the knowledge and the motivation to best understand the alternatives, yet there has been a consistent push throughout American history to extend the franchise to everybody, including those who show little desire to even want to register to vote. As Tocqueville noted in 1835, "When a nation begins to modify the elective qualification, it may easily be foreseen that, sooner or later, that qualification will be entirely abolished. There is no more invariable rule in the history of society.... [N]o stop can be made short of universal suffrage."[6] If everybody votes, it is difficult to object to the decisions that are made by popularly elected representatives, who were chosen by the citizens to make those decisions. If turnout is low, however, elected officials will have a more difficult time claiming to be the legitimate representatives of the population.

---

5. A very insightful discussion of this idea is found in Murray Edelman, *The Symbolic Uses of Politics* (Urbana: University of Illinois Press, 1964).

6. Tocqueville, *Democracy in America*, 57.

The ideology of democracy conveys substantial powers to government, so it is easy to see why governments have an incentive to nurture it.[7] Within the American experience, it is worth emphasizing the advantages to the political leadership of the ideology of democracy over the ideology of liberty. Liberty means freedom from the powers of government, and there is no doubt that the attempt to escape from government oppression was the motivation behind the American Revolution. An ideology of liberty naturally creates a population that is suspicious of government power, that wants the government to act within strict limits, and that will be intolerant of a government that tries to expand beyond those limits. An ideology of democracy advocates furthering the will of the majority through the actions of popularly elected representatives, which removes the most severe constraints placed on those in power.

The story of the transformation of the fundamental principle of American government from liberty to democracy is compelling partly because the powers embodied in America's twenty-first-century democratic government are those that eighteenth-century Americans revolted against to escape.

The Political Philosophy of the American Revolution

At the time of the American Revolution, the concept of liberty was relatively novel. The idea of liberty, as it applies to the creation of American government, goes back to John Locke, who published his *Two Treatises of Government* in 1689; less than a century prior to the American Revolution.[8] The intellectual fathers of the American Revolution built their political philosophy on the writers of the European Enlightenment, including Locke, Montesquieu, Voltaire, and others. Revolutionary ideas were supported by pamphlets circulated extensively throughout the colonies citing Enlightenment writers, and especially Locke.

---

7. This idea has been developed by Douglass North. See, for examples, "Ideology and Political/Economic Institutions," *Cato Journal* 8 (Spring/Summer 1988): 15–28; and *Structure and Change in Economic History* (New York: W. W. Norton, 1981).

8. A good recent edition is John Locke, *Two Treatises on Government* (1689; repr., Cambridge: Cambridge University Press, 1967).

Locke's ideas on property, individual rights, and social contract provided substantial intellectual support for the American revolutionaries, and *Cato's Letters*, first published in the 1720s and extensively reprinted,[9] generated popular support for liberty as the revolutionary cause. Throughout history, citizens had been viewed as servants of their governments, and the new idea that government should be the servant of its citizens took hold and sparked the American Revolution.

A good contrast for examining the ideas of the American Revolution is found in the works of Thomas Hobbes and John Locke. Both are known for their support of the concept of a social contract, but the different rationales of the two writers give some insight into the newness of the revolutionary idea of liberty. Hobbes's famous treatise, *Leviathan*, was published in 1651, only about forty years prior to Locke's *Two Treatises of Government*, but the substantial differences in the ways they supported their ideas of the social contract show how new the idea of liberty really was at the time of the American Revolution.

Hobbes's analysis began with a vision of life in anarchy, without the protection of government. In Hobbes's view, life in anarchy would be solitary, poor, nasty, brutish, and short. Anarchy, Hobbes argued, would be a war of all against all. Hobbes believed that the only way to prevent this war of all against all was to form a government and have all citizens submit to the power of that government. Under the social contract, to quote Hobbes, every person would promise all others, "I authorise and give up my right of Governing my selfe, to this Man, or to this Assembly of men, on this condition, that thou give up thy Right to him, and Authorise all of his Actions in a like manner."[10] Hobbes makes it clear that to produce an orderly society, individuals would have only those rights that the government would allow to its citizens. Hobbes further argued that those who did not abide by this social contract could "justly be destroyed by the rest." The government that Hobbes advocates, which has absolute power over its citizens, and in which individuals possessed only those rights granted by the state, was the prevailing view of government at the time.

---

9. See John Trenchard and Thomas Gordon, *Cato's Letters, Or Essays on Liberty, Civil and Religious, and Other Important Subjects* (Indianapolis, IN: Liberty Fund, 1995).

10. Thomas Hobbes, *Leviathan* (1651; repr., New York: E.P. Dutton, 1950), 142–143.

Locke's revolutionary idea was that people naturally have rights, and the role of government is to protect their rights. The state of nature, according to Locke, was also "a state of equality, wherein all the Power and Jurisdiction is reciprocal, and no one having more power than another...without Subordination or Subjection."[11] People have a right to themselves, and therefore to their labor. From this, Locke reasons, people have a right to property. "Whatsoever then he removes out of the State that Nature hath provided, and left it in, he hath mixed his Labour with, and joined to it something that is his own, and thereby makes it his Property."[12]

Whereas Hobbes envisioned people subjecting themselves to the rules dictated by a sovereign to create an orderly society, Locke envisioned people agreeing with each other to produce a government for the purpose of protecting their natural liberties. Locke believed that citizens have the right to form and dissolve governments, and in stark contrast to Hobbes, believed that government is subservient to its citizens. The purpose of government is to protect the rights of citizens, Locke argues. Philosophically, Locke provided the foundation for liberty, property, and equality upon which the American Revolution was born.

Locke's ideas, being part of the American ideology today, are easy to take for granted, but when contrasted with Hobbes's vision of only a few decades before, the idea of liberty is startling and new. And, revolutionary. The American Revolution was nurtured by Locke's idea that people naturally have rights, that the role of government is to protect them, and that when government fails to live up to its obligations under the social contract, citizens have the right to replace their government.

While the Founders were familiar with the classical and Enlightenment writings on liberty that built the intellectual foundations of the revolutionary movement, the typical citizen became familiar with the ideas of liberty through pamphleteers and newspapers. Among the most influential of these sources were *Cato's Letters*, originally published in the *London Journal* in the 1720s and later collected and widely reprinted. The letters were signed using the name Cato, after Cato the Younger (95–46 BC), who was a defender of liberty in the

---

11. Locke, *Two Treatises of Government*, 287.

12. Locke, *Two Treatises of Government*, 306.

Roman republic and opposed Julius Caesar's rise to power. Pursued by Caesar's forces, he killed himself rather than fleeing or allowing himself to be captured, making himself a good role model for eighteenth-century defenders of liberty. The publication of the letters greatly increased the influence of the *London Journal* and popularized the ideas of liberty that had been espoused by Locke.

The ideas of natural rights and equality clearly were at odds with a society of aristocrats and monarchs, and the newspapers that published *Cato's Letters* were created as opposition newspapers to counter the official government sources. This may have broadened their appeal, but having them collected and published in book form shortly after they appeared in the newspapers made them readily available and a popular source for the ideology of liberty in America. Though the letters were written for a British audience, they considered the issue of the colonies and argued that only by preserving their liberty could a successful colonial operation continue. If a nation must resort to violence to preserve its colonies, the value of the colonies will fall to such a degree that they will not be worth keeping.

The idea of liberty was a bold challenge to the governance structure of the world's most advanced nations. In the monarchies of the day, people accepted the Hobbesian idea that they received their rights from government and were obligated to abide by the laws the sovereign imposed. Locke's idea that people have natural rights, independent of government, and that the role of government is to protect the natural rights of citizens literally is a revolutionary notion. It inspired the American Revolution and had a major influence on the design of the new American government.

Conclusion

Any government requires the ideological support of its citizens to keep its power. The ideology of liberty laid the foundation for the American Revolution both by undermining the legitimacy of British rule and by suggesting the principles by which a new government for the colonies could be formed. These ideas clearly had an impact on the government that was created when the colonies declared their independence. But while the ideology of liberty goes a long way toward indicating the freedoms that government ought to protect, it does not go very far toward explaining how governmental institutions can be designed to protect those liberties. This left the Founders to design their own constitution. History shows that they were dissatisfied with their first attempt. The Articles of Confederation, the new nation's first constitution, was replaced by the Constitution of the United States in 1789. Even then, the Constitution's authors envisioned a process of continual amendment and revision.

The principles of liberty provided a revolutionary cause but not a blueprint for designing a government that could preserve liberty. The institutions of governance evolved over time, sometimes through deliberate changes and sometimes as unintended consequences that those who advocated institutional changes did not foresee. Often, they were driven by the desires of citizens to have a louder voice in the operation of the government under which they lived. Thus began the transformation of American government from one based on the ideology of liberty to one based on the ideology of democracy.

2

Liberty and Democracy as Economic Systems

IN THE NINETEENTH century, economics and politics were studied jointly under the heading of political economy, until academic specialization split them into the two distinct disciplines of economics and political science at the end of that century. This division has created some blind spots in both disciplines. In political science, economic analysis is helpful for determining why particular pieces of legislation are proposed, how likely they are to be passed when proposed, and how they are likely to be enforced if they are passed. Meanwhile, economics was able to separate itself from political science only because economic analysis was undertaken with the (often tacit) assumption that economic activity takes place within a particular set of political institutions, which makes the political system relatively transparent to economic decision-makers.

Economic analysis is most commonly conducted under the assumptions that economic resources are allocated through voluntary exchange, and that all property rights are clearly defined and never violated. Economic agents are perfectly informed, and economic transactions are never tainted by fraud or contract violation. Theft is ruled out, so goods are acquired only by the voluntary consent of their owners. Exceptions exist, and the exceptions are often what makes the study of economics interesting. What if, within this setting, some property rights are not clearly defined? What if, within this setting, one party to a transaction has information that the other party lacks? Even when specific exceptions are studied by economists, they are done so with the assumption that the rest of the economy does not deviate from those assumptions. Even though economists often analyze government policy alternatives, the framework for analysis is exceedingly laissez-faire in its orientation. The political foundation of economic analysis rarely is analyzed explicitly, but it rests on the same structure of liberty that guided the political thought of the American Founders.

The principle of liberty suggests that first and foremost, the government's role is to protect the rights of individuals. The principle of democracy suggests that collective decisions are made according to the will of the majority. The Founders recognized that in order to preserve liberty the scope of collective decision-making—that is, the degree to which the outcomes of democratic elections could be used as a guide to public policy—would have to be limited constitutionally. The greater the allowable scope of democracy in government, the greater the threat to liberty. Another way of viewing the concepts of liberty and democracy is that they are methods of determining the way in which the allocation of economic resources will be determined. Liberty implies private ownership of resources, with the owners determining how their resources will be allocated, while democracy implies collective ownership of resources, with the will of the majority determining the allocation of resources.

Because economics and political science were separated as academic disciplines, the idea that liberty and democracy both are economic systems seems out of place. They are primarily political concepts. But all economic activity takes place within some political environment that defines the relevant property rights, and without saying so, most economic analysis takes place under the assumption of a political system of extreme liberty. By examining the political structure explicitly, it is possible to relate the political environment to the performance of the economy in a manner similar to the aims of nineteenth-century political economy.

Following the framework in which economic and political systems are viewed separately, Francis Fukuyama, in his 1992 book *The End of History and the Last Man*, argued that liberal democracy has established itself as the "final form of human government," and that the free market has established itself as the ultimate destination in the evolution of the economic system.[1] The analysis in this chapter questions Fukuyama's conclusions, by arguing first that politi-

---

1. Francis Fukuyama, *The End of History and the Last Man* (New York: Free Press, 1992).

cal systems inescapably lie at the foundation of economic systems, so that both liberal democracy and the free market simultaneously are political and economic systems—systems of political economy—and second, that inherent tensions between democracy and a free market economy exist that make it difficult to maintain a stable system. In particular, the ascendency of the concept of democracy threatens the survival of the free market economy, which is an extension of the Founders' views on liberty.

The Concepts of Liberty and Democracy

The inherent tensions between liberty and democracy may not at first be apparent, because they appear to apply to two different aspects of the political system. Democracy addresses the question of who should exercise the ultimate power of government and answers that the power of government rests ultimately with its citizens. Regardless of the identity of the holder of that ultimate power, liberty addresses the question of what should be the limits of that power and answers that the power of government must be limited so that it does not violate individual rights. The Founders attempted to create a government both that preserved liberty and that vested its ultimate power in its citizens.

The philosophy underlying the American Revolution was liberty, and the Founders explicitly wanted to avoid creating a democracy, in the sense of a government that was directed by the preferences of its citizens. Once the new government was created, somebody had to run it. The Founders wanted those in charge of government's operations to be selected by a democratic process because they believed that was the best way to keep the nation from falling under the control of a ruling elite. But the Founders also wanted to insulate those who ran the government from direct influence by its citizens, which is why the Constitution originally specified that only members of the House of Representatives would be elected by the people. Senators were to be chosen by the state legislatures, the president was to be chosen by the Electoral College, and Supreme Court justices were to be appointed.

By insulating political decision-makers from direct accountability to citizens, the government would be in a better position to adhere to its constitutionally mandated limits and would be relatively free from political pressures from the electorate. Only the House of Representatives was there to give citizens some direct check on the activities of their government. Thus, the Constitution created a limited government designed to protect liberty, not to foster democracy.

Liberty as an Economic System

The idea that liberty is an economic system finds its origins in the idea of political liberty, as John Locke explained. Prior to Locke, people accepted the notion that they obtained their rights from government. Locke's revolutionary idea was that people were endowed with natural rights, and the role of government was to protect them. Locke reasoned that from the idea of self-ownership, people owned their labor, and therefore they owned what they produced with their labor. Once property is owned, the only way that an individual legitimately can obtain that property is to engage in a mutually agreeable exchange with the property owner. Property rights are a part of people's overall rights, following Locke's reasoning.

One could not expect Locke, writing almost a century before Adam Smith, to develop a sophisticated and modern economic treatise. At the same time, one must recognize that the political philosophy espoused by Locke did more than just imply an economic system based on liberty. By describing the origin of property ownership and arguing that property rights were an integral part of the rights protected by the social contract, Locke was arguing for the institutions of laissez-faire capitalism. The means of production were property, just like any other property, which provided an argument for capitalism and against socialism more than 150 years before Marx began an intellectual movement that argued the other way. When considering democracy as an alternative to liberty, Locke's argument clearly supports a property owner's right to determine the use of property rather than reliance on any type of democratic decision-making process.

Locke's reasoning that defined the liberty the colonies were fighting for simultaneously identified an economic and political system. Indeed, the characteristics of the Lockean economic system of liberty are even clearer than the characteristics of the Lockean political system. Locke's vision of economic liberty rested on the notion of private ownership of property, a right that should be protected by government. The free market economy, with complete private ownership of property, was quite clearly a part of the concept of liberty that guided the Founders, and liberty was as much an economic system as a political system in the minds of eighteenth-century Americans.

Democracy as an Economic System

The idea that democracy is an economic system is more abstract, because many different types of democratic institutions could be designed through which democracy can guide the allocation of economic resources. Nonetheless, the dangers of democracy as an economic foundation were clearly evident to the Founders, who wanted to design a government that could keep the forces of democracy in check to preserve liberty. If liberty implies private ownership of property and allows property owners the right to determine how their property will be used, then the alternative must mean that private owners do not have the right to determine how property is to be used. Within the twentieth-century framework, capitalism, the embodiment of economic liberty, has been contrasted with socialism, in which property is not owned privately. It follows that the use of property is determined by society as a whole rather than by individual owners.

This concept of socialism leaves many ambiguities, because while one can understand how an individual might make a decision, how would a society decide? In twentieth-century socialism, the actual answer was dictatorship. In Hobbesian fashion, the dictator would determine the allocation of resources, perhaps assigning some responsibilities to an economic planning bureaucracy to operate the process. The collective decision-making process was to vest the decision-making authority in the dictator and then, in hierarchical fashion, have officials below the dictator implement the dictator's plans.

Conceptually, such a system is closer to capitalism than to socialism, although it is a type of capitalism wherein ownership of resources is vested in a single individual. Experience throughout the twentieth century has shown that economies that have called themselves socialist for the most part did not have any type of collective property ownership. Most people owned little if anything beyond their personal possessions, while the political leaders had the right to determine how resources would be allocated. Closer to the spirit of socialism would be a system in which the people, collectively, had the right to decide how resources would be allocated. This idea points toward a system of economic democracy.

Democracy as a political system implies that government's leaders are chosen through a democratic decision-making process. Democracy can also be extended to the economic system to determine the allocation of resources in addition to the selection of political leaders. Indeed, there are good reasons to believe that political democracy has a natural tendency to evolve into economic democracy, as democratically elected political leaders try to find favor with their constituents by allocating economic benefits to them.

When political decisions are made democratically, the government ultimately becomes accountable to the majority. It is easy, therefore, to see that decisions made through the political process will be more inclined to further the will of the majority than to protect economic liberty. Originally, taxes were collected for the purpose of financing the activities of government, but after two centuries of taxation the tax system has become so explicitly redistributive that no serious questions are raised about its redistributive role. At the end of the twentieth century, even individuals such as Friedrich Hayek and Milton Friedman, who were widely regarded as defenders of liberty, were supporting the use of the tax system to finance redistribution.[2]

When deciding what rights people have in the use of their property, democratic decision-making leads toward determination by the will of the majority rather than by the principles of liberty. Land use has become heavily regulated, and many characteristics of labor contracts are determined by law, including restrictions on how much must be paid to a worker, what types of benefits workers must be offered on the job, work and safety conditions, and the number of hours that can be worked. Many characteristics of the products sold in the market are controlled by government, including what sizes are allowed, what information must be displayed on the product, how products are con-

---

2. See Milton Friedman, *Capitalism and Freedom* (Chicago: University of Chicago Press, 1962), chapter 12, for his proposal to create a negative income tax. Friedrich Hayek, *The Constitution of Liberty* (Chicago: University of Chicago Press, 1960), also sees a role for using the tax system for redistribution, but through a proportional tax structure.

structed, and even extending to the prohibition of the sale of some goods and services. Economic liberty has been sacrificed to the will of the majority.

Economic democracy is a system in which the allocation of resources is determined by a democratic decision-making process. While no economies operate entirely on this principle, it is easy to see, in the American economy, a substantial component of economic democracy.

Nineteenth-Century Democracy

The Constitution of the United States was designed to create a limited government, and democracy was employed as a means to an end. The Founders had no intention of creating a democratic government in the sense that its activities would be determined by the will of the majority. Over time, the concept of democracy became more firmly established as a principle of government, starting from the nation's founding, but still, by the end of the nineteenth century, the scope of federal government remained relatively limited and the concept of liberty remained well understood as a principle of government. While democracy made inroads as a political system in the nineteenth century, the economy remained based on the principle of liberty. Thus, the study of the transformation of American government from liberty to democracy in the nineteenth century primarily is an examination of the political foundations of American society rather than its economic system. A more democratic political system laid the foundation for a more democratic economic system.

If the reach of government is measured by the money it spends, by 1913 the federal government spent only 2.5 percent of the nation's income, and as a percentage of income its expenditures had been declining steadily in the period between the War Between the States and World War I. Of course, government controls the economy in other ways, and the end of the nineteenth century had seen more growth in governmental regulatory control than in government expenditures, including the Act to Regulate Commerce (1876) and the first antitrust law ever, the Sherman Act of 1890. Nevertheless, the expansion of democracy in nineteenth-century America primarily was a political phenomenon, because the Founders deliberately tried to insulate public policy from democratic impulses.

Twentieth-Century Democracy

The situation changed substantially in the twentieth century, when democracy became much more of an economic phenomenon in addition to a political phenomenon. Early in the twentieth century, two constitutional amendments extended the political reach of democracy substantially. The Seventeenth Amendment, mandating the popular election of senators, ratified in 1913, meant that a larger part of the federal government was directly accountable to voters. Prior to 1913, the Constitution specified that state legislatures chose the state's senators, insulating them from voters and making them accountable to the state's political elite. The US Senate represented the interests of the state governments. After 1913, senators were accountable to the voters in the same way as were members of the House of Representatives. In 1920 the Nineteenth Amendment to the Constitution was ratified, granting women the right to vote in federal elections, again extending the reach of democracy to a larger fraction of the citizenry. At one time, elections might have been viewed as a method of selecting competent people to undertake a job with constitutionally specified limits. With the extension of democracy, elections increasingly became referendums on public policy.

The political extension of democracy was well underway early in the twentieth century, but the economic extension of democracy had only begun. The Sherman Act, passed in 1890, was one of the early measures taken to use the political process to redistribute economic power from those who had more of it to those who had less. Antitrust laws, by defining the limits of acceptable business activity, and even in the extreme by allowing government to dismember companies, began replacing the allocation of economic resources by voluntary contracts, mutually beneficial exchanges, and the market mechanism, with a system that allocated resources through democratic decision-making and oversight. Regulation of the railroads as well as food and drug regulation, undertaken in the late nineteenth and early twentieth centuries, were extensions of the same principle. Some economic activities became illegal even if all parties to them were in agreement, and the government mandated the conditions of some exchanges and even ruled that ownership of property was subject to government approval.

The breakup of Standard Oil, which forced John D. Rockefeller Sr., to divest himself of property that he had acquired through market activity, was the most visible example of the application of government decision-making replacing a free market economic order. Rockefeller, labeled a "robber baron," was quite unpopular in his day, and one might debate the conditions under which his Standard Oil Company was able to amass such a large share of the market. Notwithstanding standardizing the refining of kerosene and lowering its price substantially, Rockefeller eventually had to divest himself of much of his property not because of the way it was acquired but rather because he had such a large share of the market that his business was determined to be an unlawful monopoly.

Historical events show that around the turn of the twentieth century democracy was extended from a political concept and a mechanism for selecting government officials into an economic concept, with the implication that if public opinion demanded it, the government could intervene in people's economic affairs to direct the allocation of resources. This principle, although never fully articulated, continually was extended throughout the twentieth century, and government gained more latitude to intervene in people's economic affairs and even to direct the allocation of economic resources itself.

Comparative Economic Systems

In the twentieth century, following the world's political divisions, the economic analysis of comparative economic systems dealt primarily with the differences between capitalist and socialist economies, with political structures being left aside for the most part. Capitalist economies were those with private ownership of the means of production and market allocation of resources. Socialist economies were those that did not have private ownership of the means of production and allocated resources through central economic planning.

While the concept of capitalism always has been relatively easy to understand and conforms with the liberal economic order described by Locke, the concept of socialism never has been entirely clear. In a capitalist system, that somebody owns something implies that the owner has the power to determine how that resource will be used. In a socialist system wherein the means of production are not owned privately, the way in which resources are allocated amongst competing uses is left unspecified. Socialism, seen this way, is not an economic system at all. An economic system must provide a mechanism for determining how and to whom economic resources will be allocated.

Karl Marx's influential book, *Das Kapital*, was critical of the capitalist system, but it was a book that attempted to explain how capitalists exploited labor. The subject of the book, as its title implies, was capitalism, but Marx did not provide a blueprint for how a socialist economy would allocate resources. Socialist writing before the creation of the Soviet Union was critical of the operation of capitalist economies but did not explain how the socialist replacement would work or how a socialist economy would be organized. Thus, when the Soviet Union was established in 1917, its Marxist founders knew what economic institutions they wanted to abolish but did not have a clear concept of what they would create to replace them.

Within a few years of the Soviet Union's creation, Austrian economist Ludwig von Mises challenged the supporters of socialism by claiming that a socialist economy could not allocate resources rationally. Mises's claim was that without markets and market prices, the information necessary to allocate resources to their highest-valued uses would not be available to economic planners or to anyone else.[3] Economists who supported the ideas of socialism responded by developing economic models in which central planners could design a system that would mimic market pricing and market allocation of resources, but Mises and his student Friedrich Hayek argued that the supporters of socialism misunderstood their critique of socialism and that rational resource allocation through central planning was not possible even in theory.

Hayek, the most articulate critic of central economic planning, explained that markets operated by making efficient use of the decentralized knowledge that everyone in the economy had, but that could not possibly be known by a central planning authority.[4] Much of the knowledge people acquire is not of a form that can be written down or communicated to others, but comes from experience. When new circumstances arise, people can use their knowledge to make informed decisions, even though they would be unable to artic-

---

3. Ludwig von Mises, *Socialism* (New Haven, CT: Yale University Press, 1951).

4. A good example is Friedrich A. Hayek, "The Use of Knowledge in Society," *American Economic Review* 35 (September 1945): 519–30.

ulate ahead of time how that knowledge might be used. Hayek emphasized the importance of this type of tacit knowledge, in contrast to explicit scientific knowledge, and noted that it could not be articulated or passed on to central planners.

The problem is not that there is too much information to aggregate (although there may be), but that the information necessary for the rational allocation of resources cannot be communicated to others. Those who have the information are the only ones who can use it, and the market economy coordinates the aggregation and distribution of this decentralized knowledge so that it is used most effectively.

While the ideas of Mises and Hayek generally were accepted at the beginning of the twenty-first century, this was not true in the middle of the twentieth. In 1973, the year Mises died, Nobel Laureate Paul Samuelson, in his best-selling introductory textbook for college economics courses, *Economics*, argued that although the Soviet Union had a per capita income about half that of the United States, the superiority of central economic planning over the market allocation of resources gave them a faster growth rate, and Samuelson projected that the Soviet Union would catch up to the United States in per capita income perhaps as soon as 1990 but almost surely by 2010.[5]

The twentieth-century analysis of capitalism and socialism saw political and economic systems as completely separate and even viewed the issues of markets versus central planning as being independent of private versus collective ownership. Mises and Hayek took a more Lockean view of the market system, arguing that its operation rested critically on private ownership, the protection of property rights, and freedom of exchange. A market economy required liberty, as Locke defined liberty, and a movement away from liberty was a movement toward socialism. Political and economic systems are inextricably linked.

Political and Economic Systems

Following the twentieth-century taxonomy, political and economic systems are independent of one another, so the political and economic systems of countries

---

5. Paul A. Samuelson, *Economics*, 9th ed. (New York: McGraw-Hill, 1973), 883.

can be represented in a two-dimensional continuum. One dimension represents economic systems and is a continuum running from capitalism to socialism. All economies lie somewhere on this continuum, with mixed economies lying between the extreme capitalist and extreme socialist end points. Another dimension represents political systems and is a continuum from democracy to dictatorship, again with the possibility of intermediate forms of government between the extremes. Following this taxonomy, political and economic systems are unrelated, so particular nations can locate anywhere from one extreme to the other in either dimension.

In the Cold War era, the United States was an example of a capitalist democracy, and the Soviet Union an example of a socialist dictatorship, but any combination was viewed as possible. Sweden often was cited as an example of a socialist democracy, and Nazi Germany was depicted as a capitalist dictatorship. Mixed systems could be anywhere in either dimension.

Many issues might be raised with this taxonomy of political and economic systems, but a major one is that it depicts political and economic systems as independent of each other, although they are in fact very interconnected. Consider the extreme case of a pure capitalist economy. Little room exists for government of any type in this framework. The government protects individual rights and prevents citizens from using force against each other, and resources are allocated through markets as a result of voluntary exchange. In a capitalist economy either democracy or dictatorship plays a minimal role. Decisions are made by individuals, and interactions among individuals occur through voluntary agreement rather than by government mandate. Capitalism is the economic component of liberty advocated by Locke.

As one moves away from capitalism toward socialism, government allocation of resources ranges more broadly and deeply. Collective decision-making increasingly replaces individual decision-making. Thus, moving from capitalism to socialism, the potential role for both democracy and dictatorship expands. Government takes on a larger part, and those government decisions can be made democratically, or dictatorially. Moving from capitalism to socialism, one could envision both democratic and dictatorial decisions having more influence on resource allocation. Government's economic policies could respond to the will of the people through the institutions of democratic decision-making, while political leaders as well as civil servants would be in a position to unilaterally impose policies regardless of public opinion.

The alternatives are more complex than this two-dimensional view of politics and economics that people held in the twentieth century suggests, because political and economic systems are interdependent. As the ideology of the twentieth-century United States supported capitalist democracy, the ever-growing ideological shift from liberty to democracy was undermining its market economy. As the role of government increasingly was viewed as carrying out the will of the people rather than protecting their liberty, higher taxes and more regulations meant that resources increasingly were allocated by government rather than by markets. The ideology of democracy was undermining the market allocation of resources, and thereby undermining the ideology of liberty.

Conclusion

Francis Fukuyama declared that the evolution of political and economic systems has come to an end with the ascendancy of liberal democracy as a political system and the free market economy as an economic system. The analysis that follows questions the ultimate compatibility of democracy with a free market economy. The fact is that as the United States has become more democratic, it has narrowed the scope of its market economy, and if democracy is viewed as an economic system in addition to a political system, there is reason to think that the decline in economic liberty and the rise in political democracy are not independent events. The United States consistently has moved toward more democracy, and the unintended side effect has been a reduction in liberty. Political and economic systems are interdependent, and the move from liberty to democracy has substantial economic as well as political implications.

3

Consensus versus Democracy
Politics in Eighteenth-Century America

AT THE BEGINNING of the twenty-first century, democracy, embodied in the principle of majority rule, is seen so universally as the most desirable form of government that alternatives to the principle of majority rule are not often considered with any seriousness. Yet, at least in theory, decision-making by consensus is a compelling alternative to majoritarian democracy. In a political environment where democracy is accepted unquestioningly, the idea that political decisions can be made by consensus is novel, but when the American Constitution was evolving in the eighteenth century, political decision-making by consensus was acknowledged as desirable and even preferred to democracy by those who were promoting the cause of liberty in America. By the end of the eighteenth century, however, majoritarian democratic principles largely had supplanted consensus in political decision-making. Decision-making by consensus offers some clear advantages to majority rule but has some drawbacks too. Consensus decision-making played an important role in colonial American government, so it is of historical interest, and also offers some theoretical principles that can help understand contemporary constitutional democracy.

Collective decision-making can be undertaken with greater or lesser degrees of consensus. Even today, when the most common collective decision rule used in the public sector is simple majority rule, Congress still must muster a two-thirds majority to override a presidential veto, and in criminal cases juries must reach unanimous agreement—complete consensus—to render a verdict of guilty. Would it be possible to replace majority rule voting with consensus decision-making in the United States today? To do so would require some changes in political institutions and also would alter the scope and character of government. The best way to see how the nature of government would be affected is to compare majority rule and consensus decision-making from a theoretical perspective, but the best way to understand what institutional changes would be required is to examine the actual use of consensus decision-making in colonial America.

This chapter offers two main theoretical points. First, the optimal scope of government declines as the level of consensus required to make collective decisions increases. This happens because when more consensus is required, such as moving from simple majority rule to two-thirds majority, collective decisions are more difficult to make, so collective decision-making costs rise. Collective decision-making costs are the costs imposed on a group by the decision-making process itself. Higher collective decision-making costs mean that some collective activities that would have produced net benefits in the absence of decision-making costs, and that would have been undertaken with a less inclusive decision rule, no longer will produce net benefits because the added decision-making costs block collective action. For example, one-third plus one of the voters oppose a proposal; the proposal doesn't pass. Second, a requirement of more consensus in collective decision-making entails not only more agreement but institutional changes designed to facilitate the reaching of agreement. Political institutions that efficiently produce majority rule decisions will be different from political institutions under a more inclusive decision rule.

Agreement and Social Welfare

One of the fundamental ideas of economics is that a competitive market economy allocates resources in a manner that maximizes the society's welfare. The idea goes back at least to Adam Smith's monumental treatise, *The Wealth of Nations*, first published in 1776, in which Smith argues that individuals pursuing their own self-interest are led by an invisible hand to further the best interest of the whole society. The mechanism by which Smith's invisible hand operates begins in a setting where property rights are clearly defined and enforced so that people interact with each other only voluntarily. Parties to exchanges must be made better off according to their own evaluations, or they would not engage in the exchanges. Looked at from a political vantage point, the key to welfare enhancement in a market economy is that whenever any decision is made, it is made with the unanimous consent of those who participate. Agreement signifies that their welfare has increased as a result of the transaction.

If the same criterion for social welfare enhancement is applied to political decision-making, one could be sure that political decisions enhanced social welfare if everyone were required to agree. Under simple majority rule, for example, some people agree with the decision but others do not. Because no good way exists to compare the gains to the gainers against the losses to the losers, even when a majority agrees to something one cannot be confident that what they agreed to is in the public interest. In other words, under majority rule, there is no guarantee that the gains to the majority are greater than the losses to the minority.

Concepts like social welfare, or the general welfare, or the public interest, are discussed often as if some measure of the welfare of a group of people exists that goes beyond the welfare of the individual members of the group. In fact, the welfare of a group is nothing more than the aggregate of the welfare of each member of the group. It makes no sense to talk about the welfare of a group of people independently of the well-being of the group's members. A group is better off when its members are better off; it is worse off when its members are worse off. This leaves some ambiguous situations in which changes might improve the well-being of some group members while harming others, but in those cases, if one wants to say something about the group's welfare, any conclusions must be based on a comparison of the value of the gains to some people against the losses of others.

A problem arises in this case because no foolproof way is available for weighing the gains to some people against the losses of others, thereby seeing if the gainers gain more than the losers lose. Various mechanisms have been devised to try to weigh these gains and losses, but every mechanism leaves some uncertainty, because an external observer cannot measure the harm that befalls those who are made worse off as a result of a group decision.

In practice, democratic politics, which assigns each voter equal weight, is used most frequently as an approximation, but using democratic decision-making as a measure of social welfare has the obvious drawback that the average loser in the collective decision-making process may lose more than the average gainer gains. It is easy to see that group decisions made by majority rule (or any other rule short of unanimous consent) could end up leaving the group worse off, and even the most sophisticated methods that try to weigh the gains against the losses from collective action suffer from the same basic problem.

The argument in favor of collective decision-making by consensus is thus relatively straightforward. When a consensus of opinion exists, everyone is in agreement, so the collective decision is in the best interest of the group because it is in the best interest of every member of the group. One could hardly object to decisions that are made by consensus, because everybody agrees with them. The drawback is that it is often difficult to get everyone in a group to agree to anything, so a requirement for consensus can prevent groups from undertaking actions that would, on net, be beneficial. A trade-off exists, and a group is able to undertake more extensive collective action if it requires less consensus to act.[1]

Some Constitutional Principles

For many collective decisions, it may be optimal to use a less-than-unanimous decision rule, like simple majority rule or two-thirds majority, and one test of this is whether those in the decision-making group unanimously would agree to the less-inclusive rule. Imagine, for example, ten people deciding where the group will go for lunch. They all might agree that if any six members of the group agree on one place, all will go there. Thus, that hypothetical group would unanimously agree to use simple majority rule to determine their lunch location. One could imagine the same thing for a larger group: Americans might be in general agreement that simple majority rule is a good rule for electing the members of the House of Representatives. The principle is that everybody would agree to abide by a less-than-unanimous decision.

This principle divides collective decision-making into two stages. At the first stage—the constitutional stage—everyone agrees unanimously on the rules for taking collective action. Think of this as the social contract, along the lines of Locke and Hobbes in the previous chapter. At the second stage—the post-constitutional stage—the optimal decision rule for group decisions could be

---

1. This trade-off is examined in detail in James M. Buchanan and Gordon Tullock, *The Calculus of Consent* (Ann Arbor: University of Michigan Press, 1962).

less than unanimity, such as simple majority rule, if everyone agrees to this at the constitutional stage. This setup provides a framework for evaluating group decision-making, but applied to political decision-making, the framework is speculative because, in fact, few people actually have the option of agreeing to the constitutional rules by which they are governed.[2]

Thinking about consensus in collective decision-making tends to evoke an image of modern majoritarian democracy and to extend that political setting toward the requirement that decisions be made by unanimous rather than majority consent. If one thinks more broadly about consensus, better examples can be found. In medieval towns formed in the period from 1050 to 1150, it was common to have meetings where all of the residents would gather in the center of the town to affirm verbally their allegiance to the town's rules. This may be the historical antecedent to the theory of the social contract developed by Locke and Hobbes.[3] For contemporary examples, unanimous agreement in a contractual setting is more common, even when many parties are involved. For example, agreement to abide by restrictive covenants when a home is purchased means that unanimous agreement exists among all homeowners in a subdivision. The same is true of covenants governing condominium associations. All homeowners agree at the time they purchase their homes. The requirement for unanimous agreement to the rules under which people interact, while rare in contemporary political settings, is not beyond the realm of possibility and even happens with some regularity.

A problem with less than unanimous agreement is that some people can impose costs on others through the political process. The greater the degree of consensus required by a decision-making rule, the lower would be the expected costs that are imposed on nonconsenting individuals. For example, if 90 percent agreement were required for the group, then individuals in the group will be less likely to bear costs associated with being outvoted than if 51

---

2. Buchanan and Tullock, *The Calculus of Consent*, make this division between constitutional and post-constitutional decision-making. Criteria for agreement with constitutional rules are discussed in John Rawls, *A Theory of Justice* (Cambridge, MA: Belknap Press, 1971); and James M. Buchanan, *The Limits of Liberty: Between Anarchy and Leviathan* (Chicago: University of Chicago Press, 1975).

3. This history is discussed by Harold J. Berman, *Law and Revolution: The Formation of Western Legal Tradition* (Cambridge, MA: Harvard University Press, 1983).

percent of the group were required to agree. Unanimous agreement eliminates completely the possibility of costs being imposed on some members of the group by a collective decision, because the group cannot do anything without the approval of everyone.

Because a requirement for unanimous agreement gives everyone in the group veto power over collective actions, a government that took action only when everyone agreed would not be able to get much done. That is why individuals might agree unanimously to a less-than-unanimous decision rule, such as majority rule, for some decisions. For many routine government decisions, citizens may believe that sometimes they gain and sometimes they lose, but on net they are beneficiaries of government action. Thus, they could agree to majority rule decision-making and believe they are better off than if unanimity was required and the government could do almost nothing. However, under such a circumstance, citizens should demand strong constitutional constraints on the scope of government to assure that some do not pay disproportionately for benefits that go to others. Agreeing to majority rule for some decisions does not mean that government could do anything a majority would approve. Constitutions like the Constitution of the United States constrain majority rule decision-making to a limited set of government actions.

One can be assured that a group decision enhances the welfare of the group only if unanimous approval by everyone in the group is required. However, because it is difficult actually to reach unanimous agreement, a group may be better off deciding some issues with less than unanimous approval, accepting the risk that some of the group's decisions may lead to a reduction in welfare.

Decision Rules and the Scope of Collective Action

As the degree of consensus required increases, it becomes more difficult and more costly to arrive at a collective decision. Some projects that would be cost-effective under simple majority rule will not be when broader consensus is required, because the additional decision-making costs offset the benefits of collective action. Thus, the more inclusive the decision rule, the more limited will be the optimal scope of collective action. For this reason, a government requiring a high degree of consensus before taking action will have a more limited scope than will a government that can act with less collective agreement. If the demand for collective action increased, group members would have to be willing to accept having larger costs imposed on them from the collective action.

Examples include wars and depressions, where citizens believe that nations can deal with their problems more effectively though more energetic government action. Citizens will be willing to risk increased costs from collective action when they perceive that greater benefits are available by broadening the scope of governmental action.[4] If circumstances arise in which citizens believe that an expansion in government action is in the public interest, they will be willing to trade off the cost of a reduced consensus in collective decision-making to facilitate an expansion of collective activity. The more citizens want to further national goals through government action, the less consensus they will demand in the collective decision-making process. The converse also is true. If a group requires a high degree of consensus before it undertakes collective action, that will limit the scope of the group's collective action.

The Meaning of Consensus

In the framework of contemporary democracy, consensus might be viewed narrowly as the percentage of the group required to agree when undertaking specific types of collective action. Sometimes simple majority is used, at other times a two-thirds majority is required, and in other cases group action can proceed only if unanimous agreement exists. This typology depicts only the end of what might be a lengthy political bargaining process. Group decisions are facilitated by logrolling, or political exchange, in which agreement can be forged by trading off various aspects of a collective decision to reach agreement. Under a simple majority rule, logrolling is prevalent, but no reason exists for supporters of particular measures to continue bargaining for additional support once they have the support of a majority.

---

4. Robert Higgs, *Crisis and Leviathan (25th Anniversary Edition): Critical Episodes in the Growth of American Government* (Oakland, CA: Independent Institute, 2012), describes a ratchet effect in which government grows in response to a crisis and after the crisis passes retrenches, but not back to its pre-crisis level, resulting in a ratcheting up in the size and scope of government.

If a two-thirds majority rather than a simple majority were required, more bargaining would be needed to gain the support of two-thirds of the group. Various compromises would have to be made, and the two-thirds requirement would eliminate some inefficient proposals that would impose substantial costs on the minority. But the more inclusive decision rule also would eliminate some proposals that would produce net benefits, because of the higher costs involved in putting together a supporting coalition composed of two-thirds of the group. If unanimity were required, even more negotiation would be required to find measures that would command the agreement of everyone. Unanimity would guarantee that all collective action would be in the group's interest, as indicated by everyone's agreement, but the higher decision-making costs would reduce the scope of collective action that would be available to the group.

To capture all of the institutional detail in an analysis of decision-making by consensus requires taking into account not just the unanimity requirement itself, but also the logrolling and bargaining that leads up to the production of a proposal that can be accepted by everybody in the group. Achieving consensus is not just unanimous approval in a vote but rather is a negotiating process that leads up to a proposal that can achieve a consensus among group members. The difference between majority rule and unanimity is more than just a difference in the voting rule. Majority rule encourages the formation of coalitions in which the majority creates benefits for itself, perhaps at the expense of a minority. Unanimity encourages more inclusive institutions in which everyone must feel, first, that the group's goal really is in the collective interest and, second, that some people are not being exploited to further those collective goals.

As the degree of required agreement changes, the types of institutions that will minimize collective decision-making costs will change also, so many institutional changes will accompany changes in the degree to which consensus is required for collective action. If less consensus is required, political institutions designed to build consensus are less necessary. This suggests why, as more consensus is required to undertake collective action, the optimal scope of collective action falls. Furthermore, it shows that changes in the degree of consensus required for collective decisions will be accompanied by other institutional changes. The institutions that are optimal for producing agreement under majority rule will be different from those that must produce unanimous agreement, for example.

The Iroquois Constitution

This abstract discussion of principles of constitutional theory can help to clarify the changes that took place in the evolution of constitutional rules in colonial America. The Iroquois Constitution that governed the native population at the time the American colonists arrived from Europe is an interesting place to start. The Iroquois comprised a confederation of five (and later, six) native American nations established between 1000 and 1400 AD.[5] During colonial times they were the dominant power east of the Mississippi River and outnumbered the colonial population significantly. The Iroquois were united by a constitution that contains many features in common with contemporary American government, including a federal system with substantial sovereignty and independence among the five nations, a common military defense, and a collective decision-making process that allowed all of the nations to work together to produce unified policies in foreign affairs that were carried out by the central government. The collective decision-making process of the Iroquois is of particular interest within the context of the evolution of US constitutional history.

The Iroquois Constitution was not a written document. Its principles were passed down orally from generation to generation. Knowledge of the constitution was preserved on wampum belts and strings, which represented certain laws and regulations. Knowledge of specific provisions was passed along by teaching individuals face to face about the details of the provisions represented by each wampum belt. While seemingly primitive, similarities can be found between this type of law transmission and the modern common law, which is not stated directly but passed along though the particular decisions in each court case, allowing the law to evolve. The similarity to modern constitutional law is even more significant, to the extent that the actual constitution is not so much what the US Constitution literally says, but rather what the

---

5. Some historical background is found in Donald A. Grindle, *The Iroquois and the Founding of the American Nation* (San Francisco: Indian Historian Press, 1977).

Supreme Court has decided in specific cases. The articles and amendments of the Constitution are equivalent to the wampum belts, in that they provide a reminder about the meanings of various constitutional provisions, but the actual meaning of each provision might change as the Supreme Court modifies its opinion on issues or as the Iroquois oral tradition changed slowly over time. In either case, the Constitution evolves gradually, while adhering to long-standing constitutional principles.

In the case of the US Constitution, the actual document provides only the vaguest guidance to contemporary constitutional rules. To understand the rights and duties implied by constitutional law, one must look at Supreme Court decisions, not the original document. Just as US constitutional rules have evolved over time yet are constrained by the precedent of previous decisions, the wampum belts of the Iroquois representing constitutional rules would serve the same function. Each generation might interpret a wampum belt slightly differently yet always within the context of the well-known constitutional tradition represented by the wampum. The wampum belts anchored the Iroquois' constitution in the same way that the Constitution of the United States provides an anchor for contemporary US constitutional rules. Even though the Iroquois constitution was oral, it nevertheless contained clearly defined constitutional rules and a collective decision-making process that in many ways is the epitome of the normative ideal of consensus that lays a foundation for contemporary constitutional economics.

One of the normative principles implied in modern constitutional analysis is equality before the law. Using unanimity as a benchmark, all individuals are empowered equally in the ideal political decision-making process, because when unanimity is required every individual wields veto power over any collective decision. One first-hand observer of the Iroquois wrote, "The Five Nations have such absolute Notions of Liberty that they allow no kind of Superiority, one over another, and banish all servitude from their territories."[6] In modern democracy, this type of political equality is taken for granted, but it is very different from the hierarchical political structure that existed in eighteenth

---

6. Bruce E. Johansen, *Forgotten Founders: Benjamin Franklin, the Iroquois, and the Rationale for the American Revolution* (Ipswich, MA: Gambit, 1982), 33.

century Europe. Yet while the European governments from which they came were very hierarchical, the colonists did not have to imagine a political system of equality. They could see it in the example of the Iroquois.

Unanimity: The Iroquois Example

Using modern governments as a frame of reference, the use of a rule of unanimity for making collective decisions might seem like an unrealistic abstraction. As the previous discussion suggests, however, unanimity must be thought of not just as a voting rule in which everyone is required to agree but rather as a political bargaining process that is designed to build consensus. The collective decision-making procedures of the Iroquois nation in the 1700s give an idea of how unanimity might actually be used to arrive at collective decisions.

The Great Council of the Iroquois Confederacy was the Iroquois legislature and consisted of 50 tribal chiefs.[7] Two types of chiefs led the Iroquois: civil chiefs, called sachems, and war chiefs. The war chiefs, as leaders in battle, are not considered in this section. The civil chiefs acted not so much as contemporary legislators but rather as spokesmen for the councils of their own tribes. While the legislature might make some decisions on its own, important matters always were taken back to the tribal councils to be decided. Thus, the collective decision-making process began with individual tribes and their chiefs. The concept of considering some individuals to be chiefs was a projection of the European hierarchical form of government onto the Iroquois. Iroquois chiefs were not rulers in the same sense as European kings but were more like chairmen who facilitated the creation of consensus and acted as spokesmen for their councils. While some differences existed in status and ceremonial roles among council members, councils functioned as a body of equals.

Within the individual tribes, collective decision-making was a slow process that involved arriving at a consensus. A meeting would be held and issues

---

7. The most detailed discussion of the Iroquois government is found in William N. Fenton, ed., *Parker on the Iroquois* (Syracuse, NY: Syracuse University Press, 1968).

discussed until it could be agreed that the group had found a consensus opinion. This consensus opinion would then be taken to the legislature by the chief, who acted as a spokesman for the tribe's views rather than as a legislator with his own views. The chiefs, always men, were chosen by the women of the tribe. They served for indefinite terms but could be replaced if a consensus emerged that they were not representing the group. Thus, representatives had to carry out the views of those they represented, or they would be replaced.

The general principle at work in Iroquois collective decision-making was consensus, not democracy. The group would discuss issues at length until a consensus arose, which would both foster logrolling to help arrive at a mutually agreeable decision and provide the chief with not only a final outcome but a deeper understanding of the issues. Thus, the chief would be prepared effectively to represent his tribe at the legislature. In this collective decision-making process, the chief was not like a head of state who had the power to decide what he thought was best but rather was a spokesman for the group he represented. He had the power only to convey to the other members of the Great Council the decisions of the group he represented and to agree to actions that were in accordance with the decisions of his tribe. If an issue or alternative came up that the chief's tribe had not discussed, the chief was not in a position to do what he thought was best for his group; rather, he would have to go back to the group to find out their opinion before taking action. Following the logic of modern constitutional theory, the resulting decision would be more likely to represent everyone's opinion fairly and would minimize the possibility that a majority could exploit the minority through the collective decision-making process.

The Iroquois legislature was divided into three deliberative bodies based on tribal membership. The three groups discussed issues separately and then compared deliberations to see if a consensus had been reached among the three groups. If a consensus could not be found, the groups would meet individually again to try to work one out. No permanent leader managed that process. Rather, temporary spokesmen would be appointed to report the groups' conclusions. Requiring consensus like this assigns very high weight to the potential costs imposed by collective action; decision-making costs accordingly also were high. The Iroquois were willing to expend great effort to reach a consensus to avoid making a decision that went against the best interest of the group.

One effect of this type of decision-making process is that it would tend to preserve the status quo when compared to a simple majority rule system. When it is more difficult to make collective decisions, it is less likely that the collectivity will decide to do something that will change present conditions. Another effect is that decisions would be made slowly because, unlike European kings, Iroquois chiefs could not decide matters as individuals but always had to take issues back to their people. This type of decision-making does, however, provide powerful protection to minorities from political exploitation and created an Iroquois society of relative freedom and equality—two goals of interest to the colonists.

Implications of Government by Consensus

The colonists saw the Iroquois government as a slow and cumbersome process for making decisions. Indeed it was in comparison to taking a vote and going with majority opinion or allowing a representative to make a decision on behalf of the group. When the degree of consensus required for collective decisions to be made changes, other institutions must also change to be able to create consensus. The colonists would complain that when dealing with the Iroquois, the chiefs would never make a decision but would always go back to consult their people. The Iroquois requirement of consensus slowed down the collective decision-making process and tended to preserve the status quo. As a government, the Iroquois did little and had relatively little power compared with the European governments of the time.

Looked at from the European point of view, the Iroquois government was hampered by a cumbersome collective decision-making process that relied heavily on consensus. Looked at from the Iroquois point of view, the requirement of consensus limited the scope of government to allow a great deal of freedom and equality. The Iroquois government provides an example of a government run by consensus to minimize the costs that government can impose on its citizens. The high costs of collective decision-making necessarily limited the scope of government.

The European Alternative

During the 1700s the colonies, moving toward self-government, had the Iroquois confederation to use as an example of a federal system of government with limited power that preserved freedom and political equality for its citizens. European governments were organized very differently from that of the Iroquois. They were monarchies with top-down chains of decision-making rather than the bottom-up system of the Iroquois. Among European governments, Britain provided the most familiar model for limiting the power of government in America, notwithstanding that it was the British government's oppression against which the colonies revolted.

The most significant political idea to come from the British model of government was separation of powers and institutional checks and balances in government to control government power. Although Britain was a monarchy, the powers of the crown had been eroding continuously since the signing of the Magna Carta in 1215, and by the 1700s the British Parliament was bicameral, with representatives of the nobility in the House of Lords and to the rest of the population represented in the House of Commons, creating a balance of power in which the three groups (royalty, nobility, and commoners) each checked one another. The creation of an independent judiciary further assured the freedom of citizens by placing another check on the arbitrary expansion of government power.

Europe also was the origin of the Enlightenment ideas that pushed Americans toward revolution. But while writers in both Europe and America persuaded the colonists that they were entitled to be free of British rule, those writers did not lay out a blueprint for a new government. They were influential beyond measure in promoting American independence, but their influence stopped short of producing a design for American government. The British example was more influential in the design of American government than were those European writers who pushed the concept of liberty.

In matters of constitutional design, as opposed to constitutional philosophy, the American Founders had two distinct examples from which they could draw. One was the hierarchical system of European government, in which people were divided into classes with differing interests and differing abilities to influence governmental policies. The second alternative was the Iroquois system, based on consensus, which led to relative political equality and minimized the ability of government to impose costs on its citizens. The Founders took some elements from each.

The Albany Plan of Union

The Constitution of the United States was not produced *de novo* in the Constitutional Convention of 1787 but rather evolved from earlier constitutional agreements. The Articles of Confederation was the nation's first constitution, prior to the Constitutional Convention, but before that, the Albany Plan of Union had been drawn up in 1754.[8] The Albany Plan of Union was a document intended to unite the colonies. It was composed and approved by the Albany Congress, which met in Albany, New York, but never was ratified by the colonial legislatures, so it never went into effect. It was, nevertheless, an important precursor to the later constitutions that did take effect, and understanding the provisions of the Albany Plan of Union sheds some light on subsequent American constitutional development.

The Albany Plan of Union was affected in at least two important ways by the Iroquois. First, the Iroquois believed that they would benefit from encouraging the colonies to unite. One complaint the Iroquois had voiced strongly in a 1744 treaty was that they had to deal with many separate colonial governments. The Iroquois believed that the colonies could form a confederation, just as the Iroquois had done, to facilitate negotiations between the two groups. Because he published the treaty, Benjamin Franklin was well aware of the Iroquois's desire for a union among the colonies similar to their own confederacy. In 1751 Franklin asserted, "It would be a very strange thing if Six Nations of Ignorant Savages should be capable of forming a Scheme for such a Union and be able to execute it in such a manner, as that it has subsisted Ages, and appears indissoluble, and yet a like Union should be impracticable

---

8. Grindle, *The Iroquois and the Founding of the American Nation*, reprints the Albany Plan of Union in an appendix.

for ten or a dozen English colonies."[9] Franklin argued further that the English colonies should find it in their interest to form an alliance with the Iroquois, partly in the interest of mutual peace, but also partly because of the threat of French colonists. In disputes between French and British colonists, both sides felt that it was an advantage to have the Iroquois on their side.

The Iroquois influenced the Albany Plan of Union, first, because of their encouragement for a colonial union and, second, because their own union provided a model for one among independent colonies. Franklin was the most influential delegate to the Albany Congress. In his role as publisher of documents related to the Iroquois, he was familiar with the Iroquois government, and he also was an advocate for the creation of a confederation among the colonies similar to that of the Iroquois. Several Iroquois attended the Albany Congress, and the governor of New York expressed the hope that an agreement could come out it that would make a union of the colonies as powerful and prominent as the Iroquois union.

The Constitutional Structure of the Albany Plan of Union

The Albany Plan of Union was similar to the Iroquois constitution in many ways. The individual colonies would retain their own constitutions and sovereignty under the plan. Because they were colonial governments, the plan would be administered by a president general appointed by the British crown but would be governed by a Grand Council. The members of the Council would choose their own speaker. Colonies would be represented roughly in proportion to their populations, but each colony (rather than each representative) would have one vote. The Grand Council amounted to a unicameral legislature, which would use a rule of unanimity allowing any one colony to veto any collective action. All colonies had to agree before the union could act.

The Albany Plan of Union specified a single governing body whose power would be checked by the ability of the colonies to select their delegates and by the Grand Council's requirement of unanimous agreement. The Grand Coun-

---

9. Johansen, *Forgotten Founders*, 56. Johansen gives a description of the Albany Plan of Union and the convention that designed it.

cil would have the power to raise an army and navy and to build forts; the plan granted to the president general, with the advice of the Grand Council, the exclusive right to make treaties with the native population and to declare peace and war with them.

The two most notable similarities between the Iroquois government and the government proposed in the Albany Plan of Union are the federal system of government and the reliance on a decision rule of unanimity in a unicameral legislature. The unanimity requirement in the Albany Plan of Union was weaker than that in the Iroquois constitution because while the Grand Council would be chosen by the colonial governments, it would not be accountable to them to the same degree as the Iroquois chiefs were accountable to their people. Because this would reduce decision-making costs, the union's government would be able to broaden the scope and power of its government beyond that of the Iroquois.

The Albany Congress approved the Albany Plan of Union, but when it was sent to the colonial legislatures it failed to win their approval. The colonies never were governed by the Albany Plan of Union, but it is a significant and underrated part of America's constitutional history because it was the first attempt to form a union among the colonies. As such, it is interesting to note how much the collective decision-making of the colonies united under the Albany Plan of Union would have been based on consensus, as opposed to the majoritarian-democratic decision-making that eventually supplanted consensus in the United States.

The Articles of Confederation and the US Constitution

After declaring independence in 1776, the United States wrote their first constitution, the Articles of Confederation, which was approved in 1781. A clear chain of constitutional evolution proceeds from the Albany Plan of Union to the Articles of Confederation to the Constitution of the United States. Like the Albany Plan of Union, the Articles of Confederation established a unicameral legislature with no provision for executive or judicial branches of government. Each state had one vote in the legislature under the Articles, as they did in the Albany Plan of Union, but whereas the Albany Plan of

Union always required the consent of all of the state delegations, the Articles required unanimous consent only for amendments to them. This lowered decision-making costs and enabled the government to have more expansive powers, as would be expected for a government formed for the purpose of becoming independent from their colonial master by military means. That type of national crisis is the kind of event that likely would convince citizens to accept higher potential costs imposed on them through collective action in exchange for a government that could undertake more substantial collective action such as defeating the British Empire.

The Articles of Confederation did not last for long. In 1787 a convention was called for the purpose of amending the Articles, and the ultimate result was the Constitution of the United States, which was ratified in 1789. All of the changes that followed from adopting the Constitution in place of the Articles were designed, against anti-Federalist opposition, to make the US government more autonomous and less accountable to its citizens. The Constitution purposefully was designed to increase the power of the federal government, accepting the trade-off that created more opportunities for the imposition of costs by government on its citizens. The basic federal system remained, but even that began eroding early in the nation's history as the federal government enhanced its power over the states. When compared to the Articles, the Constitution gives the federal government more power and subjects it to fewer constraints. The next chapter discusses in more detail the substantial changes that were the result of replacing the Articles of Confederation with the Constitution of the United States.

Conclusion

Constitutional theory reserves a special place for the role of consensus in collective decision-making because if everyone is in agreement, the group must be better off because of the decision. With less comprehensive decision rules, a majority can impose costs on the minority, with no guarantee that the benefits to the majority outweigh the costs borne by the minority. The Iroquois Constitution, with its heavy reliance on consensus at all levels of decision-making, comes close to that constitutional ideal and provides a historical example to show that consensus, so desirable in theory, can be applied in practice. As the American Constitution evolved, it moved further from the constitutional principle of consensus. That movement is best understood as a way of reducing decision-making costs in order to expand the scope of government. These changes might have been adopted to make government more effective but might also have been adopted to further the interests of those who were rewriting the rules.[10]

The American Revolution was based on the concept of freeing citizens from the abuses of power by the British government. Eighteenth-century Americans clearly recognized that the majority in a democratic government could be just as tyrannical as any dictator and sought to protect themselves from all types of government power. The colonists saw government as the greatest threat to their liberty. In the Albany Plan of Union, freedom from that threat would have been achieved by collective decision-making through consensus, but as the American Constitution evolved from the Articles of Confederation to the Constitution of the United States, reliance on consensus progressively was replaced by democratic decision-making, and protection from government oppression was safeguarded by a system of checks and balances within the government itself. But, as the following chapter suggests, this opened the door for expanding government power and eroding liberty as it was understood by the American colonists.

The Iroquois government provides a historical example to show that it was possible to use the principle of unanimity as the standard collective decision-making rule in a real-world government. As American constitutions evolved, they relied less on consensus and more on majoritarian democracy. Certainly there are differences between modern governments and the colonial American governments of centuries ago, and it may well be true that these constitutional principles of consensus could not be applied effectively to governments with the scopes and powers of modern governments. To implement these principles, we would have to be willing to accept a government that is smaller in scope,

---

10. The personal interests of the American Founders are analyzed in Charles A. Beard, *An Economic Interpretation of the Constitution of the United States* (New York: Macmillan, 1913), a book that was controversial when it first appeared and remains as an important commentary on the Constitution more than a century after it was published.

that has less power over its citizens, that takes greater account of the views of minorities, that distributes political power more equally, and that would be less able to undertake initiatives without a genuine consensus of its citizens. If we were able to tolerate these things, then the colonial period of American constitutional history could be viewed as relevant to the evolution of current political institutions, rather than as just an interesting episode in history.

4

Constitutions as Constraints

*The Articles of Confederation and the
Constitution of the United States*

THE AMERICAN COLONIES united in 1776 to escape the oppression of the British government, and the Founders were keenly aware of the potential for the newly formed US government to oppress them in the same ways the British government had. Their solution was to try to design a constitution that would enable the government to protect the rights of citizens but that would constrain the government's power to violate their rights. The requirement of a consensus of opinion can provide a substantial constraint on government, but as the previous chapter argued, consensus also severely limits the scope of government action because the collective decision-making costs are so high. To allow a broader scope of action, the new government was designed to be able to undertake certain actions without the direct consent of its citizens, but the scope of allowable government action was restricted by constitutional constraints. The concept of constitutionally limited government, now familiar, was an innovation in the eighteenth century. The powers of government were limited only to those enumerated in the Constitution, and to act the government had to follow the Constitution's prescribed procedures. Embodying the new American philosophy, the role of a constitution was to guarantee the rights of individuals and to limit the powers of government.

Constitutional rules must be enforced to be effective. A system of checks and balances serves this role in the Constitution of the United States, but only imperfectly. Over time, the interpretation of what the words of the Constitution mean has changed substantially, which has had a significant impact on the transformation of American government. Designing a government so that different parts of government check and balance each other is in principle very different from the idea of government action being based on a consensus among those who are governed. The design of the US government illustrates the challenge of creating constitutional rules that effectively constrain the powers of government.

The Articles of Confederation were close to the constitutional principle requiring the consent of the governed. The Articles insisted on unanimous approval of the states (but not of every individual) for its adoption and required the same unanimous approval to be amended. The importance of consensus was recognized, at least in principle. The Articles enumerated the allowable powers of government and prohibited to it activities not specifically enumerated. That provision limited the federal government's ability to raise revenue and was designed so that the federal government was accountable to the states. Recognizing the dangers of government power and attempting to preserve the liberty of its citizens, the Articles of Confederation were designed to be an effective constraint on the powers of the federal government.

Within a few years many influential Americans felt that the Articles were too constraining on the new government, and they ultimately were replaced by the less-constraining Constitution of the United States. When viewed in isolation, the Constitution is rightly seen as a document that limits government. But when compared with the Articles of Confederation, the Constitution clearly is less constraining than the document it supplanted. The net effect of replacing the Articles with the Constitution was to loosen the constraints on the US government. Adopting the Constitution did not limit the powers of the government; it expanded them.

Government under the Articles of Confederation

The Articles of Confederation were submitted to the states for their approval in 1777 and finally were ratified by all 13 states in 1781. Because each state already had its own government, the Articles essentially provided for the common defense of the United States, for the citizens of each state to be accorded free movement of their persons and their property among the states, and for the states to provide the same rights to the citizens of any state as it did to its own. The Articles tried to establish a framework for the peaceful interrelationship among the states and conferred most powers for military operations and international affairs to the government of the United States.

By delegating most military and diplomatic powers to the federal government, the Articles created a single unified government with which other nations would deal. But the Articles limited the power of the new government severely. The US government had no direct authority over its citizens; it interacted with them indirectly through their states. Rather than raising an army directly, Congress petitioned the states to do so. Congress also had no power to levy taxes. Article VIII of the Articles of Confederation gave Congress the ability to requisition funds from the states in proportion to the value of property in the state, but Congress could not levy taxes directly.

After the Revolutionary War ended in 1782, the effective power of the US government began to wane. A major motivation for forming the government initially was to fight for independence, but with that matter settled the US government was not as important to its citizens as it had been. Indeed, when a similar attempt to unify the states in 1754 produced the Albany Plan of Union, it was rejected. Once the states had gained their independence after the American Revolution, little reason existed to believe that they would desire unification any more than they had back in 1754. With waning interest in the union, the US government was having trouble raising the revenues necessary to pay off its war debts. Approval of nine states was required to requisition revenues from the states. Getting approval often was difficult, and even if requisitions were approved, states frequently were delinquent in making payment. It was the responsibility of the states to levy taxes and forward the revenues to the United States, because the Articles gave Congress no power to levy taxes directly.

The conventional wisdom about the Articles of Confederation is that it had several weaknesses. It was inadequate in areas of international commerce, and commercial interests were concerned about the possibility of additional taxation or regulation of trade by the states. It provided inadequate means for the United States to raise revenue because its revenue had to come from taxpayers through their state governments. Concern about the degree to which the Articles provided for the security of the states was voiced, because Congress had little authority to raise an army on its own. This would be particularly true if quarrels erupted between states. Finally, the Articles were difficult to amend because amendment required the approval of all states. Essentially, many believed the Articles were flawed because they constrained the government too much and in too many ways. However, another view is that the Articles were drafted to provide a common face in international affairs, to provide for collective defense during times of war, and to serve as a treaty providing peaceful coexistence among the states as they already existed. In this context, severe limits make sense. The reality is that the union was formed to gain independence from Britain, and with that accomplished, one might expect that Americans would see a more limited role for a federal government.

The context under which the Articles were replaced must make one cautious of the conclusion that the Articles were flawed or that they somehow failed as an acceptable constitution. They were replaced by the Constitution of the United States, but not without considerable debate and controversy; of course, those who favored the new document were quick to point out the failures of the old one. Thus, the argument that the Articles somehow were inadequate was the justification for why the new Constitution was needed. This explanation supported the new Constitution, but that the new Constitution won out over the old one in the political arena does not necessarily make the supporting arguments true. Regardless of how government under the Articles was viewed, surely experience would have exposed defects in the original agreement. In this context, a convention was called for the purpose of trying to amend the Articles in such a way as to secure the unanimous agreement required for amending it.

The Constitutional Convention

The Constitutional Convention merits that name only with the benefit of hindsight, because at the time the convention was called, its express purpose was not to write a new constitution but to amend the Articles of Confederation. The act of Congress calling for the convention states that, "it is expedient that ... a Convention of delegates ... be held for the sole and express purpose of revising the Articles of Confederation."[1] For this reason, some delegates to the convention felt that the group was overstepping its authority by draft-

---

1. The text of the complete Act appears in Alexander Hamilton, John Jay, and James Madison, *The Federalist* (repr., Washington, DC: National Home Library, 1937). The Articles of Confederation appear in that volume as appendix 2.

ing an entirely new document. Furthermore, the convention was shrouded in secrecy, such that nobody but the delegates knew what was taking place, beyond the fact that a convention was meeting to propose revisions to the Articles of Confederation.

The idea of replacing the Articles with a new constitution, brought to the convention by Governor William Randolph of Virginia, was known as the Virginia plan. William Patterson of New Jersey proposed an alternative scheme for revising the Articles substantially without abandoning them completely, which became known as the New Jersey plan. Some proponents of the New Jersey plan favored it because they felt that the Virginia plan went beyond the authority under which the convention had been called; others opposed the Virginia plan more directly because they were afraid that it would lessen—or even eradicate altogether—the independent authority of the states.[2] While this concern is evident from reading the Tenth Amendment to the Constitution, it is important to note that Article II of the Articles of Confederation parallels the Tenth Amendment closely by affirming that the powers not expressly given to the US government remain with the states.

The New Jersey plan would have given Congress the power to levy taxes on imports, to regulate trade and commerce, to establish a US judiciary to which state court decisions could be appealed, to modify the nine-thirteenths rule for requisitioning the states (the replacement rule was not specified), to establish an executive branch of government, along with other provisions. However, the New Jersey plan's underlying philosophy was to retain a confederation of states, whereas the philosophy underlaying the Virginia plan was to establish a national government.

The New Jersey plan would have retained the unicameral legislature of the Articles, whereas the Virginia plan specified a bicameral legislature. The Virginia plan provided for representation in proportion to a state's populations in both houses but would have selected members of one house by popular vote

---

2. See Charles Warren, *The Making of the Constitution* (Cambridge, MA: Harvard University Press, 1937). A standard reference to the proceedings of the Constitutional Convention is Max Farrand, *The Records of the Federal Convention of 1787*, rev. ed. (New Haven, CT: Yale University Press, 1937), who chronicles the debate through a reconstruction of the original notes taken at the convention.

while the other would be chosen by the state legislatures. The latter provision was retained in the US Constitution, but a compromise was worked out between the large and small states on the matter of representation. Under the Articles, each state had the same power, because each state, as opposed to each representative, was given one vote. As a compromise, the new Senate, under the Constitution, retained this representation by giving each state the same number of Senators, with seats in the House of Representatives being apportioned on the basis of population.

The Constitutional Convention was not called for the purpose of drafting a new constitution, and a clear alternative to the new Constitution was on the table in the form of the New Jersey plan, which proposed revising the Articles. The reason the Constitutional Convention produced a new constitution was that the delegates in attendance preferred the new Constitution to an amended Articles of Confederation. As a matter of underlying philosophy, keeping the Articles, as amended, would have maintained a federal government as a federation of states, whereas adopting the Constitution meant establishing a national government with powers superseding those of the states. Those who favored the new Constitution did so because they felt that the Articles of Confederation were too constraining on the federal government.

The eventual adoption of the Virginia plan for the new Constitution expanded the powers of the federal government greatly, but it was not intended to establish government by democracy. Indeed, Governor Randolph, the chief proponent of the Virginia plan, wanted to avoid democratic government. At the Constitutional Convention, Randolph said, "Our chief danger arises from the democratic parts of our constitutions. It is a maxim which I hold incontrovertible, that the powers of government exercised by the people swallow up the other branches. None of the constitutions have provided sufficient checks to the democracy."[3] While the authors of the Constitution did deliberately expand the powers of the federal government, they just as deliberately tried to prevent the creation of a democratic government.

---

3. Paul Eidelbereg, *The Philosophy of the American Constitution: A Reinterpretation of the Intentions of the Founding Fathers* (New York: Free Press, 1968), 42.

The Interests of the Founders

Beyond a doubt, the Founders were public-spirited individuals who wanted to draft a constitution that would further the public interest. Just as surely, people tend to see the public interest filtered through their own lives and experiences, so the public interest, as viewed by the Founders, would tend to be slanted toward the interests of people who found themselves in circumstances similar to those of the Founders.[4] This observation must be tempered by the fact that the document would have to be ratified by state legislatures to go into effect. Under the Articles of Confederation, unanimous approval of the states would have been required, although this requirement was circumvented in two ways in the new Constitution. First, the Constitution was written to take effect when only nine states had agreed to it and, second, it was to be approved by conventions held in each state rather than by state legislatures.

Representation at the Constitutional Convention was not that broad, however. While all states were represented, the delegates at the convention were not a cross-section of the population. Rather, they were selected by the state legislatures, and most states had requirements of property ownership, wealth, and income to be a legislator. Clearly the convention was manned by individuals chosen from among the wealthier citizens who owned land and had business and commercial interests and landholdings. Attendance at the convention meant that the representatives had to leave their workplaces. Individuals who could afford to make that sacrifice had an incentive to see that the document they produced would protect their interests. The convention lasted from May 14 to September 17, 1787. It is difficult to imagine that farmers who worked their own lands could give up an entire growing season to attend; property owners who employed others to work their land could more easily afford the time away from home.

Considering the composition of the delegates, it is easy to see why the Constitution would be written to protect the interests of those in commerce and banking, of landowners, and of creditors, including those who held debt

---

4. This is the thesis of Charles A. Beard, *An Economic Interpretation of the Constitution of the United States* (New York: Macmillan, 1913).

issued by the US government. This does not mean that the Founders designed a constitution to further their interests at the expense of others, but rather that they represented those interests they knew best from firsthand experience. Property owners were afraid of losing their property to those who had ideas of a more egalitarian redistribution of property. Commercial interests were concerned about the possibility of trade barriers. Banking interests were worried about the stability of the monetary system, about the ability of the government to raise revenue, and about the ability of the government to pay the debts it already had incurred. They believed that the public interest would be served by a stronger central government with greater regulatory powers, with the power to independently raise revenue, with greater power to create legislation, with a more fully developed executive branch, and perhaps most significant, with the power to act autonomously, without the approval of the states. Those changes were embodied in the Constitution of the United States.

James Madison viewed the Constitution as a set of rules that were intended to regulate the economic interests of those governed by it, and no doubt exists that others at the Constitutional Convention saw that the Constitution could be a vehicle to protect their economic interests. In *The Federalist*, no. 10, Madison wrote:

> The most common and durable source of factions has been the various and unequal distribution of property. Those who hold and those who are without property have ever formed distinct interests in society. Those who are creditors, and those who are debtors, fall under like discrimination. A landed interest, a manufacturing interest, a mercantile interest, a moneyed interest, and many lesser interests, grow up of necessity in civilized nations and divide them into different classes, actuated by different sentiments and views. The regulation of these various and interfering interests forms the principal task of modern legislation, and involves the spirit of party and faction in the necessary and ordinary operations of government.

This passage is significant in light of the political climate of the day, in which a significant number of individuals wanted to redistribute property, wanted to tax exports, wanted to abolish the slave trade, would be content to renege on the US government's debt, and favored the easy creation of money to make it easier for debtors to pay their creditors. Quite clearly, factions already were at large in the United States, and the Founders belonged to one faction that wanted to protect its status and wealth against another more populous faction. Against such threats, all of these economic interests came to be protected in the Constitution.

The Founders succeeded in writing a constitution that created a stronger central government with the power to protect their interests. The role played by the economic interests of the Founders is controversial and has been debated extensively, but that the Constitution enhanced the power of the central government—and was intended to do so—is not in dispute. When viewed as a replacement for the Articles of Confederation, the Constitution cannot be seen as a document that limits the power of government, but rather as a vehicle for relaxing constraints on the federal government, and for establishing a larger central government that would grow through time.

The Articles of Confederation and the Constitution: A Comparison

The Constitution of the United States is a document that was created under instructions to modify the Articles of Confederation. Therefore, the effects of ratifying the Constitution were the changes that the Constitution made to the status quo embodied in the Articles. The next several sections consider five major areas in which the adoption of the Constitution enlarged the scope and power of the federal government: (1) the role of unanimity as a collective decision rule, (2) the role of state legislatures in the federal decision-making process, (3) taxation, (4) commerce, and (5) the organization and institutional structure of the federal government.

A more extensive analysis might also include changes in military organization and the disposition of western lands. The Constitution did transfer military power from the states to the US government and did open the way for new states to be admitted to the United States. Furthermore, this list leaves out some of the economic issues that were mentioned earlier. For example, Article I, Section 10 of the Constitution prevents states from issuing money, which was in the interest of creditors rather than debtors. Individuals at the time understood that the issuance of paper money by the states would lower the value of debt. While it is clear that the scope of inquiry could be widened from the five issues listed, these issues were selected because they are directly relevant to the fundamental constitutional changes that paved the way for the later changes that led to a more democratic nation.

Unanimity

The significance of the principle of consensus in collective decision-making was noted in the previous chapter. Consensus means that everyone in the decision-making group sees the advantage of the group's actions, and the political decision rule that embodies consensus is the requirement of unanimous agreement. The concept of consensus in collective decision-making was the underlying principle in the government of the Iroquois who populated colonial America, and that principle carried over to a substantial degree in the Albany Plan of Union, which was drawn up in 1754 but never implemented. The requirement of consensus was weakened by the Articles of Confederation, but was still there, and the Articles more closely conform to this criterion than does the Constitution of the United States.

The eighteenth-century constitutional history of the United States is a history of recurrent moves away from the requirement of consensus in collective decision-making. Under the Articles, unanimous approval of all state legislatures was required for that constitution to take effect, and amendment of the Articles required the unanimous consent of the states. Unanimous approval of the state legislatures is considerably less constraining than requiring unanimous agreement of all individuals, especially when considering that state legislatures hardly were representative of the general populations of their states. However, the Constitution required approval of only nine states to become effective, and amendments to it require two-thirds approval from both houses of Congress and three-quarters approval from the states.

The elimination of the unanimity requirement when the Constitution replaced the Articles was no accident. One of the defects of the Articles, as perceived by its critics, was the difficulty with which the Articles could be amended. Weakening the unanimity requirement might be justified by noting that this change was agreed to by those at the convention. This justification for weakening the unanimity rule falls short on two counts, however. First, the Articles required unanimous approval of the states to be amended, and because the Constitutional Convention originally was called to amend the Articles, one might presume that unanimous agreement of the states would be required under the existing constitution to adopt its replacement. However, a nine-thirteenths rule was written into the Constitution, in apparent violation of the existing and unanimously (at least by the states) agreed-upon rule. A unanimously agreed-upon rule of unanimity was overturned by a nine-thirteenths majority!

A second issue is that the convention did not approve the new Constitution unanimously. No delegate from one state (Rhode Island) was in attendance when the final document was ready for approval, and several individual delegates to the convention from other states declined to sign. Interestingly, the significance of the unanimity rule is recognized clearly in the new constitution, even though the exceptions just mentioned meant that the document did not receive unanimous approval. Because most members of every state delegation present signed, the Constitution reads, "Done in Convention by the Unanimous Consent of the States present." The aura of unanimity is there even though approval actually was not unanimous, even by those at the convention.

In *The Federalist*, no. 40, Madison states:

> In one particular it is admitted that the convention have departed from the tenor of their commission. Instead of reporting a plan requiring the confirmation *of the legislatures of all the States*, they have reported a plan which is to be confirmed by the *people*, and may be carried into effect by *nine states only*. It is worthy of remark that this objection, though the most plausible, has been at least urged in the publications which have swarmed against the convention. The forbearance can only have preceded from an irresistible conviction of the absurdity of subjecting the fate of twelve States to the perverseness or corruption of a thirteenth.

Thus, Madison concedes that the most plausible objection to the Constitution has nothing to do with the government that would result from it but follows from the fact that procedurally it calls for an end run against the unanimity requirement in the existing constitution (the Articles) and that it violates the commission of the convention itself. Madison's only argument for violating both the charge given to the convention and the existing constitution is that it would be absurd to abide by those rules.[5] This seems to be an especially weak argument, because it could plausibly be used against the replacement rules contained in the Constitution.

Madison's argument in *The Federalist,* no. 40, against following the constitutionally mandated unanimity rule meanwhile is couched within a broader support for unanimity. In *The Federalist,* no. 39, Madison stresses that the decision rule for ratification is not majority rule but "the *unanimous* assent of the several states that are parties to it." Article VII of the Constitution states that it will take effect in the states that have ratified it when nine states agree. Quite clearly Madison and the other Founders recognized the importance of unanimity, so much so that they were willing to invoke the concept even when the principle of unanimity clearly was violated. This move away from consensus toward democracy is one way in which the constraints placed on the federal government were relaxed when the Constitution was adopted.

The Role of the States

One of the frequently cited virtues of the Constitution is its system of checks and balances. One branch of government always stands ready to check the abuse of power by another. The constitutional constraints in the Articles were much more effective because rather than having the federal government checked by branches of itself, it was checked by the states. One important check, discussed in the next section, was that states controlled the flow of revenue into the US government. Also under the Articles, state legislatures selected their representatives to Congress rather than representatives being elected directly, which gave state governments direct control over Congress. Furthermore, the Articles gave states the power to recall and replace their delegates at any time. If a state legislature felt that its representatives in Congress were not representing the interests of the state, it could replace them immediately. The Articles attempted to guarantee that representatives in Congress

---

5. Madison reiterates this defense that "[t]o have required the unanimous ratification of the thirteen States would have subjected the essential interests of the whole to the caprice or corruption of a single member" in *The Federalist,* no. 44.

could not act in ways that did not represent the wishes of the state legislatures directly. In promoting the virtues of the new Constitution, *The Federalist*, no. 51, mentions the role of the states as additional checks on the power of the federal government but does not consider that the Constitution limits the ability of the states to control the federal government when compared with the Articles.

When Congress was not in session, the Articles provided for the Committee of the States established under it to oversee the administrative functions of the federal government. The committee was composed of one representative from each state, and such decisions as engaging in war, borrowing money, coining money, and appropriating money required the approval of nine members of the committee. The method of representation and the supermajority voting rule imposed additional constraints on the federal government.

In general, the Articles created a federal government that reported to and was run by the state legislatures, whereas the Constitution replaced that government with a national government that had more power to act on its own. Contemporary constitutional analysis sees virtue in constraining government to act within a well-defined body of rules. The Articles were more constraining than the Constitution that replaced them; indeed, a common argument for the benefits of the new Constitution was that it allowed the national government to be freer of constraints. The Articles more effectively bound the government to rules—and in particular, rules of accountability—while the Constitution of the United States provides greater opportunity for government officials to act at their own discretion.

Taxation

One of the major factors pushing the Founders to amend the Articles was that the US government had no power to raise revenue directly, but rather had to get it from the states. Because members of Congress were selected by and represented the states rather than representing individuals directly, state legislatures indirectly determined the amount that the federal government would spend and the amount of revenue it would ask states to contribute, and state legislatures approved the payment to the federal government directly.

The Articles specifically provided that states pay in proportion to the value of property in the state. One notable feature of this method of public finance is that it forces state government to take account directly of the opportunity cost of federal government spending. Any money going into the federal treasury is money that is taken directly from state treasuries, which reduces the money that state legislatures have to spend themselves.

Individuals have little chance of overturning spending legislation and would have little to gain individually even if they did. Each individual expenditure program takes only a little from each taxpayer, even though in the aggregate all expenditure programs can sum to substantial amounts. States, however, contributed large amounts of money under the Articles, making an obvious and explicit trade-off between state spending programs and federal programs. This method of federal revenue collection under the Articles provided a much better method of assessing the opportunity cost of federal spending.

One frequently cited problem with the Articles at the time was that under the requisition method of federal revenue generation the federal government chronically was short of funds and had difficulty collecting from the states. One possible explanation is that the state legislatures evaluated the benefits of federal spending and decided that their money would be better spent in their home states rather than on federal activities. Recall that the immediate motivation for forming the United States was to fight a war of independence, and once that war was over the importance of the federal government to the states declined. It is reasonable that the states would want to contribute less to an institution that now provided fewer collective benefits.

One alternative at that point would have been to modify the Articles in the other direction: to make the governing regime more like a treaty among states and dissolve the federal government, or at least weaken it substantially. However, as noted earlier, many politically powerful individuals had economic interests in retaining and strengthening the federal government. One of the most significant ways in which the powers of the federal government were enhanced by the adoption of the Constitution was that the federal government was given the power to tax its citizens directly rather than having to go to the states for revenue. Many of the Founders had loaned the federal government money to help finance the war and were bondholders concerned that their bonds would never be repaid because of the difficulty the US government had in raising revenue. This difficulty was overcome by granting the federal government the power to tax.

Commerce

Commercial interests were represented heavily in the decision to replace the Articles with the Constitution. The Commerce Clause now gives the US government virtually unlimited latitude to regulate commerce; however, that was not the Founders' original intent. The Commerce Clause was intended to facilitate the free flow of commerce among the states, not to create federal regulation that inhibits commerce. But congressional regulation and Supreme Court decisions have continued to expand the scope of federal regulation of commerce in response to interest-group pressures. In addition to the Commerce Clause, several other aspects of the Constitution relate to the commercial interests of the nation. Two issues of concern to different factions were the importation of slaves and the taxation of exports. The Constitution specifically prohibits taxes on exports and prohibits states from imposing duties on goods shipped from other states. The Constitution allowed the importation of slaves to continue until 1808. Another fear of commercial interests was that states would create paper money, which would cause inflation and transfer wealth from creditors to debtors. The Constitution prevents states from doing so.

The Articles say little about commerce, but like the Constitution, leave powers not specifically given to the federal government to the states. The Commerce Clause in the Constitution gives broad powers to the federal government—likely broader than the Founders envisioned. In yet another area, the Constitution is less constraining than the Articles had been.

Organization and Institutions

Most of the changes the Constitution makes over the Articles concern the organization of government. The number of words that could be written under this heading is nearly unlimited; indeed, much of the study of government involves analyzing how various institutional structures affect the outcomes of collective decision-making. This section considers a few of the most significant changes.

According to the conventional wisdom, one of the great achievements of the Constitution was the creation of a system of checks and balances through the establishment of three branches of government. No federal courts were provided for under the Articles, so legal decisions—except when the dispute was between states—were made by state courts. The Articles did provide for a method of dispute resolution between states at the federal level. It must be obvious to the contemporary observer that the creation of federal courts enhances the power of the federal government. With regard to the judicial system, the changes brought about by the Constitution enhance rather than limit the powers of the federal government.

The Articles did not provide for a separate executive branch of government. All government activities were undertaken under the direction of Congress. When Congress was not in session, the Committee of the States oversaw government business, but the committee essentially was an arm of Congress and had no independent power when Congress was in session. While the committee might be viewed as a sort of executive branch, it was subservient to the legislative branch. Because Congress acted as an agent of the states and had limited ability to act in ways the state governments did not approve, both the legislative and rudimentary executive branches of government under the Articles had little power to act in ways that would be unpopular with state legislatures. The establishment of an independent executive branch clearly enhanced the power of the federal government and clearly gave the federal government greater ability to make decisions that could prove unpopular with the population at large. The establishment of an executive branch of government enhanced the discretionary powers of the federal government.

Congress under the Articles was unicameral, and each state was entitled to one vote. The bicameral legislature under the Constitution consists of one house in which states are represented equally and one house in which they are represented in proportion to their populations. The Senate is more comparable to the Congress under the Articles. There are, however, significant differences between the Congress as specified in the Articles and the Senate as specified in the Constitution. The original Constitution specified that senators be chosen by the state legislatures, just as were the representatives under the Articles. However, under the Articles states could send anywhere from two to seven representatives, but each state had only one vote. The state's vote would be determined by the majority of the state's delegation. Furthermore, state representatives could be recalled and replaced at any time.

Under the Constitution, senators, although they still were chosen by the state legislatures, served six-year terms, and each senator got one vote in the Senate. Thus, senators did not have to agree on a state's position on the issues, as they would under the Articles, and any senator who voted in a manner not consistent with the desires of the state legislature could not be replaced until the expiration of his six-year term. Thus, senators under the Constitution were able to exercise much more discretion and deviate much more from the desires of state legislatures than was the case under the Articles. Senators under the Constitution were much less accountable to anyone than were the representatives chosen under the Articles. This enhanced their discretionary power and increased the power of the federal government. Again, the Constitution imposed fewer constraints on the federal government than the Articles did.

Representatives in the House of Representatives under the Constitution are elected in proportion to their state's populations, except that each state is guaranteed at least one representative. The debate between whether to have the same amount of representation per state, as is the case in the Articles, or to have states represented in proportion to their populations was really a debate between whether the new government was to be more of a federal government or a national government. A federation of states would imply that each state is represented equally, while a national government would represent each individual equally. The establishment of one house of each type is the result of a compromise, but it clearly shows that the change from the Articles to the Constitution was a movement away from a federal government and toward a national government. The establishment of a national government in place of a federation of state governments enhances the power of the central government.

The Constitution provides that members of the House of Representatives be elected by popular vote. In the Articles, all representatives were chosen by state legislatures. Thus, the popular election of legislators increases further the national character of the US government. According to the original Constitution, senators were chosen by state legislatures and the president was chosen by an Electoral College. The method of selecting the electors in the Electoral College was left up to the states. Over time the popular election of electors made the government even more national and less federal than was originally envisioned by the Constitution's authors.

This overview of the organizational and institutional changes that occurred as a result of replacing the Articles with the Constitution illustrates that adopting the Constitution produced a US government with more power and less accountability. While the Constitution is correctly viewed as a document that constrains government, it is much less constraining than the Articles of Confederation it replaced. The net effect of replacing the Articles with the Constitution was to increase the scope and power of government and to reduce its accountability for it actions.

The Growth of Government

While the adoption of the Constitution had an immediate impact, the most significant effects were not felt right away, but took place over time. The Constitution created an environment within which the US government had greater ability to grow than would have been the case under the Articles. A comparison of the Articles with the Constitution shows four important reasons why the adoption of the Constitution laid the foundation for the transformation of American government from its limited origins as a defender of liberty into a democratic government designed to further the will of the majority.

1. The Constitution gives the legislative and executive branches more discretion than did the Articles. Under the Articles, Congress was directly accountable to the state legislatures, whereas under the Constitution, Congress and the executive can act with less accountability.

2. The Constitution allows the federal government to raise revenue independently, so it is no longer accountable to the states for tax increases.

3. The powers of the federal government were more carefully enumerated under the Articles than under the Constitution. The Constitution gives the

federal government poorly specified powers, such as to coin money and to regulate commerce, and then gives a procedure for deciding how the government should act rather than clearly stating the bounds of government action, as was done in the Articles. Perhaps most significant, Section 8 of the Constitution gives Congress the power to collect taxes to promote the general welfare of the United States, without specifying at all what particular activities fall under the heading of promoting the general welfare.

A careful reading of the Constitution suggests that the intention was not to allow Congress to do anything that promotes the general welfare but rather to restrict Congress to those activities that are in the general public interest rather than to further special interests. First, the phrase clearly is linked to government's new power to levy taxes directly, rather than indirectly through the states. Second, no reason for enumerating the scope of the federal government in the Constitution would exist if the enumeration was meant to include anything that conceivably was in the general welfare. Third, the Tenth Amendment to the Constitution explicitly prohibits the government from exercising any powers not delegated to it in the Constitution. Again, no reason for such a restriction is tenable if the government were permitted to do anything it decided would promote the general welfare.

The contemporary interpretation is different, however, and gives Congress broad latitude to produce legislation because it promotes the general welfare. The vague wording in this clause has been interpreted more loosely over time as an open-ended permission for the government to promote the general welfare in any way it sees fit. This open-endedness in the activities allowed by government paves the way for expanding government activity over time.

4. The government created by the Constitution is more of a national government than a federation of states, which gives it more power over the states and provides another vehicle for growth, as power is transferred from the state governments to the central government.

When the impact of replacing the Articles with the Constitution is evaluated not only in terms of its immediate effects but also the longer-term effects, it is apparent that the new Constitution opened the door for governmental growth.

Federal Versus State Government Power

The argument in the previous section might be tempered in one way. There can be no question that the replacement of the Articles by the Constitution had the effect of enhancing the power of the federal government and laying the foundation for government growth, but while the federal government had less power under the Articles, the states were in a position to exert more power. John Jay makes a similar point in *The Federalist,* no. 2: "It is well worthy of consideration, therefore, whether it would conduce more to the interest of the people of America, that they should, to all general purposes, be one general nation, under one federal Government, than that they should divide them-selves into separate confederacies, and to give the head of each, the same kind of powers which they are advised to place in one national Government."

It may be that with many state governments, intergovernmental compe-tition would work to limit the power of the states, but there is at least room for debate as to whether individual liberty would have been better preserved under the Articles or under the Constitution. Perhaps a strong constitutionally limited federal government is a good way to constrain the power of the states, but another alternative would have been to constrain the federal government as in the Articles while revising the Articles to limit the power of the states also. The adoption of the Constitution of the United States loosened con-straints on the federal government, but when considering both the state and federal governments an argument could be made that the federal constraints on state government have resulted in a more constrained government overall.

Conclusion

The ultimate conclusion of this chapter stands at odds with the conventional wisdom on the US Constitution. The Constitution often is portrayed as a document that limits the powers of the federal government and guarantees the liberty of its citizens. When put in historical perspective, the effect of the Constitution must be evaluated in light of the status quo it replaced. When compared to the Articles of Confederation, the Constitution places less constraint on the federal government and allows those who run the government more discretion and autonomy and less accountability. The adoption of the Constitution enhanced the powers of government and laid the foundation for two centuries of government growth.

5

The Growth in Parties and Interests before the War Between the States

THE AMERICAN REVOLUTION was fought to secure the liberty of the citizens of the United States, and the nation's citizens viewed the power of government as the most serious threat to liberty. Thus, the Founders sought to craft a government that walked a fine line. They wanted a government strong enough to protect the rights of individuals, but that also was constitutionally constrained from violating them. One of the most immediate threats to liberty the Founders foresaw was the emergence of interest groups, or factions, within the polity. The Founders belonged to a political elite that governed the fledgling nation, and the first six presidents, also members of that elite, warned consistently against the rise of political parties and special interests in American politics. The election of Andrew Jackson in 1828 brought with it an abrupt change. Jackson was the first president elected with the support of an organized political party, and after his election Jackson rewarded his supporters with political favors. With the election of Jackson, American government shifted away from political elitism and toward a more democratic representation of political interests.

The development of the Democratic Party to elect Jackson to the presidency changed the political landscape significantly. Jackson amassed a substantial amount of political power because of the organized party behind him, which prompted those who opposed Jackson to create their own party. The Whig Party was born, and the two-party system that characterizes American politics today came into being. Although the Twelfth Amendment to the Constitution modified slightly the way the president was chosen, the biggest changes came not from modifications in the constitutional rules, but rather from two significant modifications in political institutions. The first, which mostly was complete by the time Jackson was elected, was the selection of presidential electors by citizen vote. The second was the creation of the party system.

The Elitist Constitution

The Constitution devised democratic processes for collective decision-making, but the Founders had no intention of designing a government that would respond to the will of the majority. Citizens had almost no direct input into the federal government as the Constitution was originally written and ratified. The federal government comprised three branches of government, each checking the others, to limit governmental power and was meant to operate within the limited bounds specified by the Constitution. At the founding, the members of the House of Representatives were the only federal officials elected by popular vote. None of the branches of government were designed to reflect the will of a hypothetical national majority, and the Constitution gave citizens only limited input into the selection of some members of one of the branches.

Supreme Court justices (and all federal judges) are appointed by the president and confirmed by the Senate, giving citizens no direct oversight or representation in the judicial branch. The president and vice president were chosen by an Electoral College; the Constitution makes no provision for direct voting for electors, leaving selection methods to be chosen by the states. The legislative branch of government was the only one in which citizens had a limited say. The Founders created a bicameral legislature in which the Senate was composed of members chosen by state legislatures. Representatives were elected by direct vote of the citizens, but even here the Constitution does not provide unlimited popular voting rights.

Article I, Section 2 of the Constitution states that when choosing members of the House of Representatives, "Electors in each State shall have the Qualifications requisite for Electors of the most numerous Branch of the State Legislature." Thus, states set their own voting qualifications, and at the time of independence every state but one had either a requirement of property ownership, some level of wealth, or both. Because of the design of the Constitution, it is apparent that the Founders did not intend for public opinion to have any influence over the federal government's policies or operations. In two of the three branches of government, the general public had no direct say, and in the third branch a subset of citizens, determined by the states, was able to vote directly for members of only one of the two legislative chambers. If the Founders had intended for this vote to convey the general public's opinions on public policy, then they would have established uniform voting requirements across states. Direct voting for representatives serving two-year terms was designed as a check on the power of the representatives, not as a vehicle for voter input into the congressional decision-making process.

If each branch of the federal government were equally powerful, as it would have to be for a system of checks and balances to be effective, and if each house of the legislature were equally powerful, then as the Constitution originally designed the federal government only one-sixth of it would have had any direct democratic oversight. In the twenty-first century, with direct election of presidential electors and senators, two-thirds of the government is elected democratically. Measuring government oversight in this way obviously is unscientific but probably understates the growing influence of democratic input. Because the Supreme Court justices are appointed by the president and confirmed by the now popularly elected Senate, greater democratic input into the legislative and executive branches undoubtedly spills over into the judicial branch.

The Constitution designed the US government to be run by a political elite and to undertake the very limited function of preserving the liberty of its citizens. It did not take long after the creation of the federal government for it to become more democratic and more broad in the scope of its operations.

The Election of Representatives

The place in which the Founders designed the government to be most directly accountable to citizens was the House of Representatives. The Constitution originally gave the states the right to determine who could vote for congressional representatives, and amendments to the Constitution have subsequently created a federal right to vote and in the process expanded the franchise. The right of citizens to vote, which became an axiom of democracy in the twentieth century, clearly was not provided in the Constitution of 1789.

By the end of the twentieth century members of the House of Representatives all were elected from single-member districts, but that method of representation is not specified in the Constitution. The most common alternative to single-member districts was general ticket representation, in which representatives were chosen in statewide elections and all voters cast ballots for all of the seats to be filled. The practice was common until 1846, when it was discouraged but not prevented by federal law. Hawaii, in 1968, was the last state to elect representatives by general ticket, but North Dakota only gave the practice up in 1962 and New Mexico continued the practice until 1966.[1]

If states gain representatives, one alternative to redistricting is to retain the same districts but elect the new representatives at large. At-large representation has been common throughout American history. In 1912, twelve states elected some at-large representatives. Three states elected at-large representatives in 1964, the last year the practice was used. Early in the nation's history, many states also adopted plural districts from which more than one representative was elected from a district. Plural districts were last used in 1840. The historical details are interesting, but the larger point is that the election of representatives from single-member districts, a firmly established political institution by the end of the twentieth century, was not the only way representatives were elected.

Congress passed many pieces of legislation to encourage single-member districts, beginning in 1842 and continuing through 1967, but all had exceptions that allowed for different methods of electing representatives. Representatives themselves have good reason to favor single-member districts because that system minimizes the chance that incumbent representatives would run against each other. Now, this happens only when redistricting occurs every ten years following one or two years after a US Census when seats in the 435-member House are reapportioned to take account of population growth and shifts either across states or within them. Single-member districts create a cartel-like arrangement in which representatives are monopolists within their own districts.

---

1. See Kenneth C. Martis, *The Historical Atlas of United States Congressional Districts: 1789–1983* (New York: Free Press, 1982), for the standard reference on the history of congressional districts.

A similar arrangement exists in the Senate, where even though two senators are elected from each state, their six-year terms are staggered so that they never face each other in the same election year. One crucial difference is that both senators represent the entire state, giving citizens two senators whom they can approach. With single-member congressional districts citizens have two senators but only one representative. These differences were not established by the Constitution, however. Senators originally represented the state legislatures, and the Constitution says nothing about single-member (or multi-member) congressional districts. Single-member districts give more power to representatives by limiting competition among incumbents, and by conferring some monopoly power on them by giving each citizen only one representative.

The Logic of Bicameralism

Article I, Section 2 of the Constitution originally specified that "[t]he Senate of the United States shall be composed of two Senators from each State, chosen by the Legislature thereof." Members of the House of Representatives were elected by those citizens of the state who were eligible to vote. The logic of this system is that the two houses of the legislature represent different constituencies with different interests, so, it is more challenging to pass legislation through both houses than it would be to get approval from either one.

The bicameral legislature was intended to represent the different interests of citizens and of state governments. Because senators were chosen by the state legislatures, any legislation that passed both houses of Congress had to be approved both by the representatives of the people and the representatives of the state governments, a more difficult test than today when both houses represent the same constituents. The design of the federal government shows that the Founders made a serious attempt to have the interests of state governments represented in federal government decision-making as a way of ensuring that the states had some power to check the activities of the federal government.

The Founders looked to the British government as the example of where liberty had been most fully developed in Europe, and a part of what they saw was a system of checks and balances in which the aristocracy, represented in the House of Lords, and the general population, represented in the House of Commons, checked each other's power. Although the Senate was not filled by aristocrats, its members were chosen by state governments and therefore represented political elites, whereas members of the House of Representatives were chosen by the general population of voters. Because the House and Senate were chosen by different constituencies, they could provide a check on each other. Legislation had to meet the approval of both the representatives of the people and the representatives of the state governments.

The passage of the Seventeenth Amendment in 1913 mandated that senators be elected by direct vote rather than chosen by the state legislatures. This institutional change had two major effects. First, it eliminated the representation of state government interests from the system of checks and balances and, second, it made the two houses of Congress more homogeneous, which made it easier to pass legislation. It also made the federal government more democratic because senators now were directly accountable to the voters, which was a significant step in transforming the underlying principle of government from liberty to democracy.

The Electoral College

The Constitution was designed so that a group of highly qualified experts would be designated to select the president and vice president. Article II, Section 1 states, "Each State shall appoint, in such a Manner as the Legislature thereof may direct, a Number of Electors, equal to the whole Number of senators and representatives to which the State may be entitled in the Congress; but no Senator or Representative, or Person holding an Office of Trust or Profit under the United States, shall be appointed as an Elector." Constitutional amendments have altered some aspects of the process by which the president is elected, but this provision remains unchanged.

The wording of the constitutional provision makes it apparent that the Founders did not intend for electors to be elected democratically, although they did not rule out the possibility; it is even more apparent, though, that however the electors were chosen it was not intended that the selection would dictate how the electors would cast their ballots for president and vice president. Otherwise, why would the Constitution rule out federal officials as electors? Article II, Section 1 of the Constitution continues, "Electors shall meet in their respective States, and vote by Ballot for two Persons, of whom one at least shall not be an Inhabitant of the same State with themselves." If one candidate received votes from a majority of the electors, that person would be elected president and the second-highest vote getter would become vice president. This provision was changed by the Twelfth Amendment in 1804, so that the president and vice president were voted on separately, but the Electoral College system remained unchanged otherwise.

The Constitution never has bound electors to vote for specific candidates, and the Constitution makes it clear that the Founders envisioned the electors as using their discretion to select the best-qualified candidates in their view. That system remains intact in the twenty-first century, and even though electors are associated with specific candidates, from time to time an elector has broken ranks to vote for someone other than the candidate chosen by the state's voters.

In practice, most presidents have won election by receiving a majority of the electoral votes, but at the time the Constitution was written the Founders anticipated that in most cases no candidate would receive votes from a majority of the electors. The Founders reasoned that most electors would prefer candidates from their own states, so the typical elector would vote for one candidate from his own state and a candidate from another state, following the constitutional requirement, and it would be unlikely that voting along state lines would produce any candidate with a majority of the votes. This state bias is reinforced by the fact that the electors are charged by the Constitution to meet in their states and then forward their votes to the president of the Senate to be counted. Much less opportunity for consensus exists under this system than under a system in which electors from all the states gather together in a common location, making it even more likely that no candidate would receive a majority.

Article II, Section 1 also specifies, "The Congress may determine the time of choosing the electors, and the day on which they shall give their votes; which shall be the same throughout the United States." Today, it is common to explain the constitutional provision that electors meet in their own states rather than gather in a common location as a result of the fact that transportation costs were much higher back then. Yet, this provision served an important function. Requiring that electors meet in different locations and cast their votes at the same time prevented them from bargaining with one another to choose a consensus candidate when no consensus was apparent. Article II, Section 1 goes on to specify that "if no Person have a Majority, then from the five highest on the List the said House shall in like manner chuse the President." The Founders envisioned that in most cases the president would end up being chosen by the House of Representatives from the list of the top five electoral vote recipients.

The Founders intended the electoral votes to be cast by electors who would be more knowledgeable than the general public rather than by popular mandate, and the Founders envisioned that in most cases the final decision would be made by the House of Representatives rather than by the electors themselves. Furthermore, there was no indication that the number of electoral votes received should carry any weight besides creating a list of the top five candidates. The House could then use its discretion to determine who on that list would make the best president. The process was not intended to be democratic, although it has evolved that way despite the fact that the constitutional provisions for selecting a president remain essentially unchanged.

As specified in the Constitution, the election process should resemble the way in which a search committee might serve to identify a slate of finalists for a high-ranking corporate (or government, or academic) administrative post. The Electoral College was intended to be the search committee that would develop a list of candidates, and the House of Representatives would make the final choice from candidates on the list. Only if a consensus emerged among electors would the choice be made by them, which the Founders viewed as unlikely. As it actually has evolved, this multistep process has been set aside in favor of popular elections.

The Electoral College system envisioned by the Founders was designed to select a chief executive for the nation from a candidate pool composed of an elite group. Successful candidates would have to be well known and viewed as highly qualified in many states to get enough electoral votes to make the final list, and they would have to have enough respect within the House of Representatives to be chosen from a list of finalists. Those involved in the selection process would be an elite group of Americans, and the process was engineered to produce a president that came from the upper echelons of the American elite. The process was not intended to be democratic.

The Selection of Presidential Electors

The current selection of electors is by a restricted general ticket, which allows voters to vote only for a bloc of electors who represent a specific candidate. This method was chosen by the states and is not specified in the Constitution. The general ticket method of selecting electors was not well-established until at least three decades after presidential elections began, and the most common method for selecting electors early in the nation's history was to have state legislatures do it. In the first presidential election, only two states, Pennsylvania and Maryland, used general ticket elections to select their presidential electors. In the second presidential election in 1792, the nation had fifteen states: three used general ticket elections, ten chose their electors in the state legislature, and two had district elections for electors. In the election of 1800, which chose Thomas Jefferson for his first term, sixteen states had been admitted to the Union; only one used a general ticket election while ten had their state legislatures choose their electors.

The selection of electors by state legislatures remained common through 1820, when James Monroe was elected to his second term of office. In that election, nine of twenty-four states chose their electors in the state legislature, while eight used general ticket elections. After 1820, the selection of electors through general ticket elections rapidly became more common. In 1824, twelve of twenty-four states used general ticket elections and only six state legislatures selected electors. By 1828, eighteen of twenty-four states used general ticket elections and only two legislatures chose electors. By 1832, only South Carolina's legislature chose its electors, one state had district elections, and the other twenty-two adopted general ticket elections. In 1836, all states but South Carolina used general ticket elections. South Carolinians did not vote directly for their electors until after the War Between the States.

The movement toward democratic elections for president in the nation's early history is striking. States used a variety of methods for selecting their electors, but until 1820 the most common method was by the state legislature, with no direct voting. By 1832, just twelve years later, direct voting had spread nearly almost nationwide. The design of the Constitution makes it apparent that the Founders did not intend to have the president elected by popular vote, but they left it up to the states to determine exactly how presidential electors would be chosen. The result was that despite the retention of the Electoral College, the president effectively is chosen by direct vote and has been since the 1820s. The movement toward the democratic election of the president also corresponds with a more democratic notion of the office itself, beginning in the 1820s.

The Elite Presidency: 1789–1829

When the Founders at the Constitutional Convention were designing the office of president, one factor underlying the discussion was the assumption that George Washington would be the first president. Washington, revered today, also commanded a huge amount of respect after the Revolution, and the office was designed in part with the thought that he would set the precedent for the details of the office on which the Constitution was silent. The institutional details of the new federal government would have been more difficult to design, and might have proceeded along different lines, had there not been such an obvious and popular candidate to become the first president.

The Founders were wary of the potential for tyranny that majorities could exert in a democratic government and tried to guard against the exploitation of a minority by a majority in several ways. The role of democratic decision-making was limited severely both by insulating the new government from popular voting and by limiting the scope of the national government. In addition, the Founders wanted to guard against the emergence of factions to prevent citizens from viewing their interests as being represented by one group of political candidates rather than by another. Especially with regard to the presidency, the system was designed to select the most qualified individual to head the executive branch of government rather than to select a candidate who represented some citizens more than others.

The Constitution makes no reference to political parties, and the methods of selecting federal officials were designed to prevent them from playing major roles. Modern sources tend to cite the party affiliations of all past presidents, but political parties in the modern sense did not assume any importance in presidential elections until 1828, when Andrew Jackson was chosen. Candidates for the office came from a political elite, and because of widespread selection of electors by state legislatures, candidates needed to garner the support of other political elites to win the presidency. Despite the rapid emergence of factions in American government, prior to 1828 parties did not campaign for presidential candidates. There was no reason to undertake campaigns aimed at citizens, as is done today, because state legislators played such an important role in selecting members of the Electoral College, and those electors were the people who voted for president.

George Washington and John Adams, the first two presidents, are associated with the Federalist party, a distinction that became crucial during Adams's term as president. Washington remained unchallenged as head of state during his two terms as president and had a solid enough following that his vice president, John Adams, was elected president when Washington chose not to serve a third term. In contrast to Washington, who was not seriously challenged during his two elections, Adams won his election by a margin of only two electoral votes over Thomas Jefferson, a member of the Democratic-Republican party, who, then, following the rules of the original Constitution, became vice president.

By the time of Adams's election in 1796 there had developed some serious philosophical differences regarding the way the federal government should evolve. At the center of much of the controversy was Alexander Hamilton, Washington's Secretary of the Treasury. Hamilton served as much more than just the Secretary of the Treasury during Washington's administration; indeed, one historian referred to him as effectively the "prime minister," partly because the Treasury Department was so large compared to the rest of the government at that time and partly because Hamilton took it upon himself to strengthen the authority of the federal government whenever the opportunity presented itself. One issue that created a considerable controversy was the creation of the first Bank of the United States as a federally chartered corporation. As Secretary of the Treasury, this was Hamilton's project, but among its significant opponents were James Madison and Jefferson. Despite that opposition, in 1791 the first Bank of the United States was given a twenty-year charter.

The Bank of the United States was but a part of Hamilton's broader vision of the role of the US government. At the Constitutional Convention, Hamilton had argued that all communities can be divided into the few who are rich and well born and the remaining mass of people. Their interests are often at odds, he argued, but the masses are seldom good judges of what is right. Thus, Hamilton wanted a constitution that would ensure the "rich and well-born their distinct, permanent share in the government." As Secretary of the Treasury, he tried to design a government that would protect and promote domestic industry. Hamilton's "Report on Manufactures," written while he was Secretary of the Treasury, advocated policies that encouraged government protection of industry, and Hamilton advocated an internal improvements program that would spend enough to maintain a national debt. Hamilton viewed the debt as creating a binding tie among the interests of financial groups, businesses, and creditors with the federal government. "A national debt, if not excessive, will be to us a national blessing," Hamilton said.[2]

James Madison, who had strongly opposed parties and factions in *The Federalist,* no. 10, revised his opinion as a reaction to the Hamiltonian expansion of the scope of government; along with Jefferson, he created the Democratic-Republican party to try to counter the growing power of the federal government that they viewed as occurring in the Washington administration. After Adams was elected president in a close race against Jefferson, Jefferson was able to create an unpleasant political environment for Adams, who was the first one-term president and was unseated by Jefferson in the election of 1800. The problems created by having a president and vice president from different parties laid the foundation for the Twelfth Amendment, which established separate electoral balloting for the offices of president and vice president.

Jefferson's two terms were followed by his fellow Democratic-Republicans Madison and Monroe. While their political alignments emerged originally in opposition to Hamilton's vision of an energetic US government that would promote elite commercial and business interests, their policies drifted toward Hamilton's. For example, despite Madison's leadership of the opposition to the first Bank of the United States, whose charter ran out in 1811, the Second Bank of the United States was chartered in 1816, also for twenty years, during Madison's presidency. What in hindsight appeared to be a fissure between

---

2. Quoted from Arthur M. Schlesinger Jr., *The Age of Jackson* (Boston: Little, Brown and Company, 1945), 11.

factions that created the Democratic-Republican party did not produce a great political division, especially in comparison of those that would appear within a few decades.

The first six presidents were members of America's political elite, chosen by America's political elite. After a close election for his first term, Jefferson received 162 out of 176 electoral votes to win his second term, in the first election in which the president and vice president were selected from separate ballots. Madison and Monroe, the fourth and fifth presidents, each won two terms in office with electoral landslides, making the elite nature of the office uncontroversial. Outside of George Washington, Monroe might lay claim to the title of the least partisan of all American presidents. But controversy erupted in the election of 1824, when John Quincy Adams was selected by the House of Representatives to be the nation's sixth president.

Four candidates received electoral votes for president in 1824. Andrew Jackson received the largest number of electoral votes with 99, followed by John Quincy Adams with 84, William H. Crawford with 41, and Henry Clay with 37. Because no candidate received a majority, following the rules modified by the Twelfth Amendment, the House of Representatives had to choose the president from the top three electoral vote recipients. Rather than choose Jackson, a war hero but a political outsider, they chose Adams, the son of the nation's second president and a member of the political elite. Adams's election followed the rules, but Jackson's supporters were outraged by the choice, believing that Adams was chosen only because of a "corrupt bargain" between him and Henry Clay in which Clay was appointed Secretary of State in exchange for Clay's support of Adams's candidacy.

The Formation of the Democratic Party

The dissatisfaction of Jackson's supporters is consistent with the rising democratization of American government at the time. Presidential elections increasingly were being decided by popular vote, with the big transition occurring in the 1820s. The diffusion of democratic election methods underlay the formation of the Democratic Party, which was organized for the specific purpose of electing Jackson to the presidency. Jackson's supporters, led by Martin Van

Buren, formed the Democratic Party after the election of 1824 to ensure that four years hence Jackson would garner a majority of the electoral votes and could not be denied the presidency by an elitist House of Representatives.

The efforts of Jackson's supporters to form the Democratic Party began even before John Quincy Adams was inaugurated as president. Although Adams's bargain to appoint Clay as Secretary of State seemed reasonable to Adams, and Clay was eminently qualified, Van Buren was quick to paint Adams as undertaking partisan activity. In contrast to presidents over the previous two decades, Adams had a very narrow base of political support, which in itself created political opposition and enhanced the appearance of factionalism. Adams could appeal only to his supporters to accomplish anything while in office, enhancing the appearance of governance by a political elite. Although the "corrupt bargain" between Adams and Clay produced the immediate reward of Adams's presidency, it also initiated the process that unseated Adams four years later, and greatly accelerated the movement of the United States toward democracy as its fundamental governing principle.

Well-defined factions had existed within American government for decades. It was in Washington's administration, after all, that Jefferson and Madison formed their political party to oppose what they viewed as an unwarranted Hamiltonian expansion of government power. In contrast to the elitist notion of party that had characterized American politics and that had placed John Quincy Adams in the White House, Van Buren began to promote a new and more positive view of political parties. His idea was that "[p]arties should be democratic associations, run by the majority of their membership."[3]

Van Buren was well aware of the American tradition opposing factional political parties, whose origins could be traced back to *The Federalist,* no. 10, and which was supported in word by all six of the first presidents. But Van Buren, a senator from New York, perceived legitimate political differences among politicians that could be expressed along party lines. More significantly, he viewed the opposition that incumbents had to organized parties as support for the continuance of political dominance by America's aristocratic elite. Without organized opposition, elites could continue to dominate American

---

3. Ralph Ketcham, *Presidents Above Party: The First American Presidency: 1789–1829* (Chapel Hill: University of North Carolina Press, 1984), 141.

government indefinitely. Parties served the legitimate interest of organizing political opposition, resisting the concentration of power in an elite group, and providing a broader representation of the political views of most Americans.

Van Buren did not misperceive the role that his new Democratic Party would play. Indeed, the Founders tried to insulate the government from democratic control for what they believed were good reasons and had no notion that the president would be chosen by the popular votes of American citizens. Yet the Democratic Party had formed to do just that. The efforts of Van Buren and the Democrats were an unqualified success, and Jackson won the presidency in 1828, defeating the incumbent president by an electoral vote total of 178 to 83. The modern party system was born, as both the Democrats and their opponents recognized that after Jackson's election, a party organization would be necessary to win the presidency. After Jackson's two terms as president, Van Buren was elected president for one term, but was unseated by his Whig challenger, William Henry Harrison, in 1840. The American two-party system has evolved since then, but has not changed fundamentally.

Jacksonian Policy

Andrew Jackson viewed himself as following a Jeffersonian tradition, both in opposing the status quo of the previous administration and in trying to limit the powers of the federal government and loosen the grip of political elites over American governance. Jackson perceived that under his predecessors the scope and power of the federal government had slowly but steadily been growing and was controlled by elites, giving the broader population little say in the operation of their governing institutions. Jackson wanted to reverse those trends, to limit the powers of the federal government and to move from government by elites to government by democracy. The Founders had intended for the federal government to be controlled by elites rather than to respond to the masses, placing Jackson's populist ideas at odds with them, but the Founders just as clearly intended the federal government to be limited strictly in scope, making Jackson's ideas along those lines more in harmony with the Founders.

One issue Jackson pursued was the Second Bank of the United States, which he opposed as an institution that centralized power and shackled the

American economy's growth.[4] Jackson believed that the policies of the Second Bank perpetuated monopoly in the banking industry, giving privilege to the few at the expense of the many. Despite an attempt by Congress to extend the bank's charter, Jackson was able to veto the bank, and it passed out of existence in 1836, the last year of Jackson's second term. Jackson's philosophy of government arose from a group of successful businessmen who pushed laissez-faire ideas. While monopolistic business practices could prove harmful, the Jacksonians, following Adam Smith, believed that government was more often the source of monopolistic practices rather than the solution to them. Rather than try to get the government involved in the economy, Jackson attempted to pull back, in the case of the Second Bank and in the case of government regulation and support of the economy more generally.

Jackson wanted to dilute the economic power wielded by America's business elites and he viewed that much of that power was driven by government policy, including incorporation policies. In Jackson's day, banks were state-chartered corporations that wielded considerable economic power, and he wanted to eliminate private bank note issues and move to a system of hard money to remove some of the banks' power. Banks were only one part of the incorporation problem, however. Corporate charters often were granted for projects that conferred some monopoly power, such as the building of toll roads and bridges, and Jackson wanted to extend the ability to incorporate so that anybody would be allowed to create a corporation following general laws rather than have to be granted a special corporate charter for a specific business purpose. General incorporation laws at the state level, following the Jacksonian idea, began to spread before the War Between the States and became universal afterward. Corporate forms of business enterprise are so common today that it is difficult to imagine commerce without it, but the modern corporate form is a direct legacy of Jacksonian democracy.

Another important issue for Jackson was the federal funding of "internal improvements," mainly roads, bridges, and other infrastructure. Jackson was against it, not just as a matter of policy but on constitutional grounds.

---

4. Arthur A. Schlesinger Jr., *The Age of Jackson* (Boston: Little, Brown and Company, 1945), 74–114, discusses the debate between Jackson and the supporters of the Second Bank in detail.

Jackson saw no allowance within the Constitution for the federal government to engage in public works and believed that if the people wanted the government to be involved, they should either petition their state governments to undertake the projects they desired or amend the Constitution.[5] That was an issue on which Jackson stood in stark contrast to John Quincy Adams, who in his first State of the Union address proposed a stunning array of public works, including roads and canals, a national university, and federal support for the exploration of the western territories. Those activities should be undertaken for the good of the nation, regardless of popular opinion, Adams argued. Adams inadvertently had given Jackson two issues that differentiated the two men sharply and created a clear policymaking contrast for the presidential election of 1828. The first issue directly was related to the federal government's involvement in public works, but the second larger issue was the role of popular opinion as a guide to government policy.

Jackson's first major move against public works was his Maysville veto in 1830, cast against a bill that would have provided federal funding for a road that was to be built entirely within the state of Kentucky. The bill's supporters argued that the road would be an important link in the federal transportation system, but Jackson viewed that argument as irrelevant. The federal government had no constitutional authority to finance internal improvements, regardless of whether they were national or local in character.

Jackson also believed that the courts, and the law itself, were too inaccessible to most citizens and favored codification and simplification of law to weaken some of the courts' power. Jackson would not have prevented the courts from interpreting laws, but believed that the Supreme Court was substantially overstepping its constitutional bounds whenever it attempted to divine the true meaning of ambiguous parts of the Constitution. To do so made the actions of the other branches subordinate to the interpretations of the judiciary, which was contrary to Jackson's understanding of the Constitution's design.

---

5. Donald B. Cole, *The Presidency of Andrew Jackson* (Lawrence: University of Kansas Press, 1993), 63–65.

In contrast to Hamilton's view, Jackson opposed the national debt and by 1835 had retired it entirely, an accomplishment for which he took pride. He also wanted the federal government to cede ownership of public lands. Jackson claimed to be a Jeffersonian republican, committed to the idea of limited government and determined to turn around what in his opinion was an unwarranted expansion of federal government power under his predecessors. His policies consistently were laissez-faire, and he left his mark on the nation by successfully limiting the scope of government in many ways. At the same time, Jackson viewed the federal government as a necessary check on the power of state governments and believed that a balance between the two was necessary to preserve liberty. He opposed the attempts of states to try to nullify federal law within their borders, and when South Carolina threatened secession in 1833, Jackson made it perfectly clear that he would use military force, if necessary, to preserve the Union, setting a precedent that President Lincoln called upon less than three decades later.

Jacksonian Democracy

The public policy positions adopted by Andrew Jackson consistently were aimed at narrowing the scope and reducing the power of the federal government, but in addition to these policy ends Jackson also believed in democracy as a means of controlling the federal government. The top federal government officials should be elected directly, Jackson believed, including senators and the president, to make them more accountable to the people, and once elected they should heed the electorate's wishes. Through democratic principles, Jackson wanted to remove the federal government from control of the political elite that had overseen it since the approval of the Constitution.

As an outsider, a war hero, and a person who had worked his way to national prominence rather than having been born into privilege, Jackson found a sympathetic audience in the electorate. Jackson's ideas were not the product of thoughtful scholarship or an in-depth understanding of political theory, but rather were a reaction to his perception that a government established to protect the liberty of its citizens had been accumulating power in the hands of political elites. Democracy was the mechanism Jackson favored for redistributing power away from this elite and returning it to the people.

Interests in Jackson's Administration

Within the context of the growth of federal government power, Jackson's presidency had two opposing effects. Jackson consistently favored a smaller federal government with less power, and this return to Jeffersonian principles had the immediate effect of reducing the size and scope of the federal government. Pulling in the other direction, however, was Jackson's desire for more democratic representation in the federal government and his assigning of federal government positions on the basis of political patronage. Jackson did away with the fledgling civil service system that existed when he was elected. Prior to Jackson's administration the notion was widespread that civil servants who performed their duties well were entitled to keep their jobs. Jackson saw things differently. He believed that the jobs were not so demanding that people of reasonable intelligence could not perform them and argued that more was lost by giving people a guarantee of continuing employment than was gained by retaining an experienced workforce. Thus, Jackson replaced many government workers after his election.

Jackson's argument about giving government workers an incentive to perform has some merit and found a sympathetic audience in his day, but one byproduct of Jackson's actions was the transformation of government jobs into political patronage awards. Jackson's political supporters ended up getting government jobs and had an incentive to continue supporting Jackson if they wanted to keep their jobs. Political appointments have a certain logic behind them, because if government workers perform poorly then incumbent politicians are more likely to lose the next election and those workers are likely to lose their jobs. Thus, political appointees have an incentive to make government look good. But it was also apparent that many government employees had their jobs only because they supported the Democratic Party. Thus, Jacksonian democracy brought with it political patronage and reinforced the idea that in political competition, to the victor belongs the spoils. The nation had taken another step away from liberty and toward democracy.

The scope of the federal government during Jackson's administration was limited, which meant that few opportunities existed for political interests to receive government benefits. Most of the nation's revenues came from tariffs, and this was one area that attracted interest-group activity. The southern states felt that tariffs worked against them and wanted low tariffs, but especially favored low tariffs on manufactured goods. Southerners believed that because tariffs were imposed on imports but not on exports by constitutional design, the South, which imported manufactured goods but sent much in the way of raw materials to the North for manufacture and export, bore the brunt of tariffs. Southerners paid tariffs on their imported manufactured goods and exported raw materials to the North. Northerners, therefore, did not pay tariffs on their imports from the South and were able to export their manufactured goods duty-free.

The tariff was a major issue, and while Jackson philosophically favored lower tariffs, he also wanted to keep tariff revenue flowing into the Treasury to retire the federal debt. In 1828 Jackson sought to maintain political support by adjusting tariff rates of different goods, producing a tariff with so many distinctive rates tailored to benefit special interests that it has since been called the "tariff of abominations." Federal tariff policy became one of the issues over which the southern states argued they should secede from the union. In 1832 most of the "abominations" were eliminated from the tariff and rates were reduced. Still, the tariff was one of the earliest issues in which interest groups became involved in distributive politics.

While Jackson viewed himself as aligned with Jeffersonian political ideals, his election campaign had little to do with issues and everything to do with personalities. The Democratic Party was formed to elect Jackson, and for that Jackson owed a debt to his supports. Jackson repaid supporters with federal government positions. Jackson's avowed motives aligned with the tenets of his Democratic Party. He believed that replacing a complacent elite group of federal employees with a new group of citizens would enhance the democratic nature of government and would improve the efficiency of its operation. The result was to establish political patronage as a method of rewarding those individuals and groups who supported victorious politicians.

After Jackson, Before the War

Jackson remained a popular president, and one result was his ability to pick Martin Van Buren, the architect of the Democratic Party, to succeed him in office. After Jackson's administration, it was apparent that any candidate for the presidency would have to have the support of an actively campaigning political party to claim the White House. The presidents following Jackson were considerably less popular than he was. The next president re-elected to a second term was Abraham Lincoln. The Whig Party had arisen to counter the Democrats, and Whig candidate William Henry Harrison unseated Van Buren, only to die in office a month after his inauguration. Vice President John Tyler was sworn into office, but the Whigs nominated Henry Clay as their candidate in 1844 and Clay lost to Democrat James Polk. Because of the succession of one-term presidents and the overriding issues that led to the War Between the States, the presidential terms between those of Jackson and Lincoln saw a relative lull in the evolution of American democracy.

Interests and the Post Office

The Constitution delegated few functions to the federal government, but one was to establish a post office. Running the Post Office was a revenue-generating operation until 1851, when, after much debate in Congress, an act was passed that greatly overhauled the nature of mail delivery. The 1851 act lowered postal rates to three cents for letters for delivery up to 3,000 miles and six cents beyond that limit, and by 1863 all letters were delivered at the same price. The 1851 act also specified that "[n]o post office now in existence shall be discontinued, nor shall the mail service on any mail route in any of the states or territories, be discontinued or diminished in consequence of any diminution of revenues that may result from this Act,"[6] marking the act as the transition of the post office from a profitable public enterprise into a subsidized activity that transferred benefits from taxpayers in general to the recipients of subsidized mail delivery.

The main beneficiaries were residents on the Pacific coast. In 1857 and 1858, the post office established new routes to the West Coast that showed expenses of more than $2 million, but raised only $339,000 in revenues. In 1865, the Post Office established new routes between Utah and California with an annual cost of $750,000, which yielded revenues of only $23,900. The guiding principle of the Post Office became the provision of service without regard to the revenue it generated. The result was that additional extensions

---

6. Clyde Kelly, *United States Postal Policy* (New York: D. Appleton, 1932), 32.

of service became the subject of congressional debate, pitting West Coast interests against those in the more populous East.

The use of the Post Office as a mechanism for transferring benefits to a subset of the population is not as important for the subsidies it created as for the precedent it set. The transfer element of Post Office operations established the precedent that federal programs could use general tax dollars to benefit identifiable subgroups of the population.

Conclusion

The government of the United States was significantly different by the mid-1800s than its creators envisioned. The US government was not intended to be a democracy. The Founders went to great lengths to see that public policies were not beholden to the will of the majority, whose tyranny they feared above all. Andrew Jackson was the most important figure in promoting democracy prior to the War Between the States. Even before his election, however, the nation had moved significantly down the road to democracy, especially in the area of presidential elections. Because popular voting for president increasingly became common, and because Thomas Jefferson, James Madison, and James Monroe won their elections by such significant margins, Americans had several decades of experience leading them to believe that the presidential candidate most popular with the voters would become president. Thus, despite the fact that John Quincy Adams's selection as president by the House of Representatives was done according to both the letter and the spirit of the Constitution, it created the appearance of impropriety and led to the establishment of the Democratic Party for the specific purpose of guaranteeing Jackson an electoral majority in the next presidential election.

Jackson's Democratic Party was named appropriately, because Jackson believed that liberty could be protected only by allowing the people to govern through majority rule. The expanded scope of democratic oversight over American government was something Jackson favored. He favored popular election of the president and US senators and even favored democratic oversight of the Supreme Court. Jackson saw democracy and liberty as self-reinforcing, because democratic oversight of the government would guard against its being taken over by a political elite and would prevent government from pursuing policies that would benefit the elite few at the expense of the masses. The Founders felt otherwise, for two reasons. First, they did not believe that most people had the capacity to make thoughtful and informed decisions about their government. Second, they believed that rule by majority could be just as tyrannical as rule by a king or by any elite group. Thus, they designed the government to be run by a political elite, but constrained in its actions by the Constitution.

Jackson fought for democracy as a method of limiting the scope and power of the federal government, but, ironically, the result of making the nation's government more democratic has been to expand the scope and power of government in response to popular demands for government programs. This was a result the Founders foresaw and tried to guard against by limiting the role of democracy in their new government. Jackson was a strong president and was able to accomplish many of his immediate goals while in office, but the results of his presidency do not look as good, judged by his own goals, over a longer time horizon. Although Jackson wanted to limit the powers of the federal government and succeeded in doing so during his own administration, the more democratic government that he created laid the foundation for future government growth. The growth of government as a direct result of Jacksonian democracy after Jackson left office more than offset the reductions in the scope of government that Jackson presided over during his eight years in the White House.

6

The Impact of the War
Between the States

WITHOUT A DOUBT, the single most important event in the transformation of American government was the War Between the States. Prior to that war, state governments were viewed as the nation's primary governing bodies and the federal government was viewed, as its name implies, as a federation of governments. After the war, no doubt existed that the federal government was supreme and that the state governments were subservient to the federal government. Prior to the War Between the States, the United States was used as a plural term. Because of their differences, the United States were headed for the most destructive war in their history; after the war they were more firmly under the power of the federal government, and in many ways more divided than ever.

Abraham Lincoln referred to the War Between the States as a civil war in his Gettysburg Address, and while the term has the advantage of being more concise than the War Between the States, it describes the conflict inaccurately. Civil war normally refers to a conflict in which different factions are fighting for control over a nation's government, whereas in this case one part of the nation was trying to gain independence from another part. Had the Confederate States of America been victorious, the war surely would have been remembered as the war of Confederate independence, much as the Revolutionary War is remembered as the American war of independence.

The major issue that led to the war was slavery, and the freeing of the slaves was a major victory for the principle of liberty on which the nation was founded. Earlier chapters noted the importance of that principle to the Founders and discussed the way they designed the government to preserve the liberty of America's citizens. But slaves were not counted among those citizens, and not only was their liberty not protected, the Constitution explicitly permitted slavery, noting in Article I, Section 2 that, for purposes of a census they be counted as three-fifths of a person, and in Article I, Section 9 that a prohibition on the importation of slaves was prevented until 1808. The abolishment of slavery was the most significant event for the advancement of liberty in the history of the nation.

To view the War Between the States simply as a crusade to eliminate slavery is a major oversimplification of the impact of the war. In addition to emancipating the slaves, the War Between the States left a lasting legacy of more firmly entrenched federal government power as the federal government established itself as dominant over the states and enlarged its authority in many other ways. Liberty was advanced substantially by the freeing of the slaves, but in many other ways, the result of the war was to compromise liberty and to transform government policies more toward favoring special interests. While recognizing that slavery is antithetical to the Founders' commitment to individual liberty, and acknowledging the moral significance of emancipation, this chapter examines other issues related to the war to show that the result of the war was to compromise the principle of liberty. Perhaps the most obvious place to start is with the issue of secession itself.

Secession

The issue of secession had been considered long before Lincoln's election and long before the creation of the Republican Party. South Carolina had considered seceding during the Jackson administration, and there was discussion of secession among the Northern states because of their opposition to slavery. In 1840, John Quincy Adams argued that if Texas, which allowed slavery, became a state, the event would justify the dissolution of the United States, and other Northerners argued that Southern slavery was able to survive only because of costly enforcement measures imposed on Northern states. The nation's Fugitive Slave Law required nonslave states to patrol their territories for fugitive slaves and return them to their owners. Opponents of slavery argued that if the North seceded and no longer had to enforce the South's laws, slaves could then escape to the North and Southern slavery would rapidly collapse. The point is that secession was considered as a serious possibility by both Northerners and Southerners and was even declared justified (under certain conditions) by John Quincy Adams, a former US president. Secession was not a new idea in 1860.[1]

One constitutional issue is whether secession is allowed under the Constitution that united the states in the first place. Article VII of the Constitution states, "The Ratification of the Conventions of nine States, shall be sufficient for the Establishment of this Constitution between the States so ratifying the Same." With thirteen states unified and governed by the Articles of Confederation, that article provides for the secession of up to four states if nine agree to the new Constitution. Thus, any state that did not want to be governed by the Constitution was given the option of leaving the Union. The Constitution explicitly allows states to secede in Article VII, so the Constitution was written envisioning the possibility that some states might want to leave the Union if they did not agree with the decisions of others in this specific circumstance.

The Tenth Amendment to the Constitution reads, "The powers not delegated to the United States by the Constitution, nor prohibited by it to the States, are reserved to the States respectively, or to the people." The Constitution does not give the United States the power to prevent states from seceding and even explicitly allows secession under the conditions specified in Article VII, so the United States does not have the constitutional power to prevent states from leaving the Union. The power of secession by states is not prohibited by the Constitution, so that power therefore is reserved to the states, following the Tenth Amendment. A literal reading of the Constitution does not prevent secession and in one case specifically allows it.

Secession had been contemplated in both the North and the South for decades before the Confederate States actually seceded. It appeared to be accepted as a possible remedy for the rift that had grown between the Northern and Southern states, and it appeared to be constitutionally allowable. One result of the War Between the States was to establish by force that states did not have the right to secede, and this, by itself, vested the federal government with more power. If states can secede, that gives them a check on the power of the federal government. After the war, it was clear that states did not have the

---

1. Jeffrey Rogers Hummel, *Emancipating Slaves, Enslaving Free Men: A History of the American Civil War* (Chicago: Open Court Press, 1996), discusses various arguments by both Northerners and Southerners for secession.

option of withdrawing from the Union if they viewed the costs of membership to be greater than the benefits. Secession did appear to be possible before the war, and this change alone gave the federal government much more leverage in its dealings with the states.

Slavery and Emancipation

Slavery was, of course, the overriding issue that led to the division between the North and South and ultimately precipitated the war. However, Lincoln's aim was to preserve the Union, and he was willing to tolerate slavery to do so. In his inaugural address in 1861, Lincoln stated, "I have no purpose directly or indirectly to interfere with the institution of slavery in the United States where it exists. ... I believe I have no lawful right to do so, and I have no inclination to do so."[2] Lincoln reiterated this opinion in 1862, shortly before issuing his Emancipation Proclamation: "My paramount objective in this struggle *is* to save the Union, and is *not* either to save or destroy slavery. If I could save the Union without freeing *any* slave I would do it, and if I could save it by freeing *all* the slaves I would do it; and if I could save it by freeing some and leaving others alone I would also do that."[3]

The Emancipation Proclamation, issued on September 22, 1862, gave the Confederate States until the end of that year to end the fighting and rejoin the Union. Then, "within any State [or] part of a State [that had not rejoined the Union], all persons held as slaves ... shall be then, and thenceforward, forever free."[4] For states that met the deadline, Lincoln proposed compensating slave owners and resettling former slaves, perhaps in Central America. The Emancipation Proclamation did not apply to the four border states of Delaware, Maryland, Kentucky, and Missouri, which were all under Union control at that time, or to those areas of Tennessee, Virginia, and Louisiana that had fallen under Union control. Thus, the Emancipation Proclamation applied only to slaves in those areas that continued to fight for their independence from the

---

2. Charles Robert Lee Jr., *The Confederate Constitutions* (Chapel Hill: University of North Carolina Press, 1963), 203.

3. Hummel, *Emancipating Slaves*, 207–208.

4. Hummel, *Emancipating Slaves*, 210.

United States. Slaves located in areas controlled by the Union were not freed by the Emancipation Proclamation, further reinforcing Lincoln's claim that his only motive in interfering with slavery was to save the Union. Lincoln was opposed to slavery, beyond a doubt, but that was not the principle under which he was fighting the war.

Lincoln's Emancipation Proclamation was a huge leap in the exercise of presidential power. The Constitution at that time explicitly recognized the institution of slavery, yet Lincoln, in complete disregard for the Constitution, proclaimed some slaves to be free, not based on any moral argument but as a retaliatory measure against states that did not give up their war for independence. The slaves that Lincoln proclaimed freed were not in the areas controlled by the Union, so the Emancipation Proclamation did not actually free any slaves. Slaves in areas that were under the control of Lincoln's government were not freed because the Emancipation Proclamation did not cover them, and slaves outside those areas were not freed because Lincoln's government did not control them.

Reconstruction

"Reconstruction" refers to the period of time from the end of the war until 1877, during which federal troops occupied the Southern states. The occupation began during the war, when Union troops took control of specific Confederate territories, such as New Orleans and Vicksburg, Mississippi, the latter of which fell to General U. S. Grant's troops on the same day Robert E. Lee's armies began withdrawing from the battlefield at Gettysburg, Pennsylvania, so complete occupation was an extension of the process that occurred during the war. As a part of his war powers, Lincoln appointed military governors to the captured territories. While occupied by federal troops, the former Confederate states found themselves in political limbo. Both President Lincoln and, after him, President Andrew Johnson recognized the states, but Congress refused to seat their representatives. The Thirteenth Amendment, outlawing slavery, received its required two-thirds majorities of both houses of Congress in the absence of representation from the Southern states, yet they were recognized as states for the purpose of counting the three-fourths of the states needed for ratification; the amendment was ratified only because ten of the eleven former Confederate states voted for it.

Union troops closely supervised Southern elections, disallowing many white voters as Confederate sympathizers unless they signed loyalty oaths, while encouraging the registration of blacks. This led to many black office-holders and temporarily enhanced the strength of the Republican Party in the South. With Republicans in control of both chambers of Congress and the White House, one can see the advantages of such policies to those who created them. From a constitutional standpoint, during Reconstruction the War Between the States was viewed as the result of actions of individuals who were disloyal to the federal government rather than of actions of the states themselves. Thus, states always were recognized as part the Union, even if their citizens were not.[5]

While the black population did temporarily gain political standing, after Reconstruction blacks effectively were disenfranchised and the South became solidly Democratic. No lasting legacy of black voting rights emerged from the episode, but Reconstruction did permanently expand the size of federal military forces and established the precedent, unimaginable before the War Between the States, of having federal troops enforce federal laws within the nation's borders.

It goes without saying that Reconstruction had a huge impact on the post-war South and was instrumental in shaping the next century of American politics. It also had a huge impact on the scope of federal governmental power over the states. Southern whites were not in a hurry to end occupation because with so many whites disenfranchised because they were considered traitors to the Union, an end to the occupation would result in the election of many blacks, and Southern whites often preferred the military rule of Northern whites to that of Southern blacks. The political power of blacks eroded quickly after Reconstruction ended and whites regained voting rights.

One consequence of the political environment the North imposed on the South was that because Southerners did not object strenuously to the military

---

5. David Donald, *The Politics of Reconstruction: 1863–1867* (Baton Rouge: Louisiana State University Press, 1965).

occupation of their states, the scope of government power that citizens viewed as legitimate expanded considerably. The federal government originally was formed as a federation of states to undertake activities in their mutual interests. In less than a century, it had become a central government that would use military force to ensure compliance with its laws, even to the extent of directing the operations of state governments.

The Fourteenth Amendment

The ratification of the Fourteenth Amendment to the Constitution in 1868 signaled a major change in the way states interacted with the federal government and brought with it a major advance in the powers of the federal government. While many factors have conspired to increase the scope and power of the federal government over its history, no amendment to the Constitution has conferred more power to the federal government than the Fourteenth. The Thirteenth Amendment, abolishing slavery, was ratified in 1865, but it became apparent to Northern observers that while slavery per se may have been abolished, states were enacting a number of laws restricting the rights of former slaves. Most Southern states denied blacks the right to bear arms or to assemble after sunset, policies that had been implemented during Reconstruction. Mississippi prevented blacks from renting homes or leasing land outside of cities. This led to the Civil Rights Act of 1866, which guaranteed blacks the right to enter into contracts and to buy and rent property and more generally provided blacks with the same rights as whites. However, the question remained as to whether the federal government had the constitutional power to enforce the law, which led to a demand for a constitutional amendment.

The constitutional question turned on what was implied by the Thirteenth Amendment. The first section of the amendment abolished slavery, and the second gave Congress "power to enforce this article by appropriate legislation." One interpretation of the Thirteenth Amendment was that it simply severed the bond between slaves and their owners but established no new rights. Following this interpretation, the Civil Rights Act was on shaky ground because it was designed to extend the rights of blacks. Another interpretation of the Thirteenth Amendment was that it was intended to extend to everyone the same rights enjoyed by whites. Those issues were not limited to Southern states. In Indiana, for example, blacks were not allowed to enter into contracts, to own real estate, to sit on juries, or to marry whites. If the Thirteenth Amendment was meant simply to free the slaves, it would have no effect on state laws such as those in Indiana. If it was meant to prevent states from discriminating amongst races, its effects would be more far-reaching. The passage of the Fourteenth Amendment made the question moot by preventing this type of discrimination explicitly.

Prior to ratification of the Fourteenth Amendment, it was presumed that the Constitution placed limits on the actions of the federal government, but that it did not bind the states. The Fourteenth Amendment for the first time explicitly extends federal power to cover the actions of the states. The proponents of the Civil Rights Act questioned the degree to which it could be enforced. It plainly would prevent the federal government from discriminating against blacks, but the question remained about whether the federal courts would view state laws as falling under their jurisdiction or whether enforcement at the state level was a power constitutionally reserved to the state governments. The Fourteenth Amendment deals explicitly with the issue by obligating state governments to abide by federal law, which led to a permanent increase in federal government power. The move to enhance the power of the federal government over the states was intentional and was an extension of the movement within the Republican Party, begun by Lincoln, to establish firmly the supremacy of the federal government over the states.

Constitutional scholars at the time believed that Congress overstepped its constitutional authority when trying to enforce the right of Southern blacks to vote, because enforcement of such laws—and even the determination of who had the right to vote—fell clearly within the powers reserved to the states. Article I, Section 2 of the Constitution explicitly gave states the power to determine eligibility to vote in federal elections. Thus, any federal law establishing individuals' voting rights was questionable on constitutional grounds. The Fifteenth Amendment, which reads, "The right of citizens of the United States to vote shall not be denied or abridged by the United States or by any state on account of race, color, or previous condition of servitude" deals with that issue.

The Fourteenth and Fifteenth Amendments expanded federal power by giving the federal government constitutional authority over state government activity.

In the context of twenty-first century America, it is easy to focus on the Fourteenth Amendment's effect of extending rights to all citizens. It is also easy to overlook the fact that the amendment fundamentally altered the relationship of the states to the federal government, massively expanding the federal government's powers by establishing that federal laws have supremacy over state laws.

The National Banking Act

One major impact of the War Between the States was the re-establishment of the federal government's authority over the banking industry. The United States always had had a relatively small presence in banking, and in their heydays the First and Second Banks of the United States were sources of controversy. When the charter of the Second Bank of the United States expired at the end of Jackson's presidency in 1836—as a direct result of Jackson's opposition to the bank—the nation entered an era of free banking, during which the federal government had nothing whatsoever to do with the nation's banking system. That was consistent with Jackson's laissez-faire philosophy and with the philosophy of the Democratic Party through the end of the nineteenth century.

From 1836 until 1861, banks issued their own bank notes, redeemable in gold, with no federal oversight. The US Treasury did mint coins, but money minted by foreign governments and private mints circulated alongside government-minted coins and privately issued bank notes. Critics of the free banking era cite frequent problems with the monetary system, such as banks going out of business or the notes of questionable banks trading below par against notes from other more reputable banks. Still, the free-banking era survived unthreatened for 25 years, and the American economy continued to prosper. What brought the free-banking era to an end had nothing to do with the merits of free banking as a monetary system, but rather with the demands that war finance placed on the US government.

In 1861, the US Treasury sold $150 million in bonds to Northern banks to help finance the Union's war expenditures. When people began to conjecture that the war would be long and costly, the ability of the federal government to redeem the bonds came into question; they then began falling in value. Because banks were holding these bonds as assets, depositors began doubting whether their own banks would be able to redeem the notes they issued and started turning in bank notes for gold. As a result, the federal government suspended note redemption in 1861 to help avert a banking panic. Then, in 1862, the federal government began issuing its own currency, declaring that it was legal tender but not backing it with gold. Those bills, green in color, became known as "greenbacks" because they were not backed by anything else. Although the redemption of private bank notes had been suspended, their issuers were still obligated to redeem them once the suspension was lifted. Greenbacks carried no such promise.

An increase in the quantity of money leads to inflation, and the issuance of greenbacks into the nation's money supply was no exception. Because private bank notes did carry at least some promise of eventual redemption in gold, greenbacks began trading at a discount to bank money. In response, Congress passed the National Banking Act of 1863, which created federally chartered banks and imposed a 10-percent tax on transactions that used private bank notes. The idea was that this would drive all state-chartered banks out of business or make them apply for federal charters, thus replacing the existing system of state-chartered banks with a national banking system. This idea did not work exactly as planned because state banks began to use demand deposits—checking accounts—more widely and were able to survive. The National Banking Act was intended to replace state-chartered banks with federally chartered banks, but state banks survived and the current dual system of state-chartered and federally chartered banks remains intact.

By 1865, about 75 percent of the money in circulation in the United States consisted of greenbacks and other US notes that were not backed in any other way.[6] One result of the War Between the States is that the US government had replaced the 25-year-old system of free banking with a system of federally

---

6. Michael R. Baye and Dennis W. Jansen, *Money, Banking, and Financial Markets* (Boston: Houghton Mifflin, 1995), 411.

issued currency, had begun federal regulation of the banking system, and had taken control of the money supply. This is another area in which federal power was enhanced as a direct result of the war and also is an area in which state government power was transferred to the federal government.

Distributive Politics before the War Between the States

One of the Madisonian ideals for American government was to create a government free of factions, such that the apparatus of government was insulated from interest-group politics. However, American government before the War Between the States increasingly became factionalized. The first major split occurred when President Thomas Jefferson explicitly wanted to reverse the growth that he saw in the Washington and Adams administrations, spearheaded by Secretary of the Treasury Alexander Hamilton. The creation of the Democratic Party and the introduction of the spoils system into federal politics by Jackson marked another milestone. The divisions that led to the War Between the States factionalized the nation further and led individuals and groups all along the ideological spectrum to see the federal government as a vehicle for furthering their own interests. Interest-group politics, an accepted part of the political process in the twenty-first century, was something the Founders recognized as a danger and tried to prevent.

Prior to the twentieth century, the Democrats were the party of limited government and states' rights, and the Republicans were the party of protectionist tariffs, governmental growth, and federal government dominance. This characterization is roughly accurate until the election of Woodrow Wilson and was reversed completely with the election of Franklin Delano Roosevelt (FDR). Even up through the 1970s Southern Democrats retained the legacy of limited government and states' rights, in contrast to the tectonic shift in the Democratic Party that came with the New Deal.

The ideas of limited government found their way into the Confederate Constitution, which shows the concern those in the Confederate states had with the influence of factions and special interests in American government. The Confederate Constitution was a slightly modified version of the US Constitution, and the most significant modifications were intended to rectify the problems emerging from the rise of interest-group politics.

The Confederate Constitution

In outline and language, the Confederate Constitution follows the Constitution of the United States almost exactly.[7] It uses the same language unless its authors believed that an obvious improvement could be made. Furthermore, the Confederate Constitution follows the same outline as the Constitution of the United States, except when an obvious reason to deviate was apparent. Thus, for example, Article I, Section 8 of both documents describes the powers of Congress, and both use the same wording except when the Confederate Constitution intends to change the meaning or interpretation of that section deliberately. The similarities between the two documents make the differences stand out as areas the Confederates perceived as problems with the US Constitution after more than seven decades of experience with it.

One difference is that the Confederate Constitution explicitly states, "No bill of attainer, ex post facto law, or law denying or impairing the right of property in negro slaves shall be passed." But the explicit provision in the Confederate Constitution simply preserved the status quo that had existed under the Constitution of the United States. So the treatment of slavery—obviously a key issue behind the war—did not deviate substantially from what was in the US Constitution.

A very significant difference exists between the two constitutions with regard to the purposeful omission of a few words. The Confederate Constitution does not refer to the general welfare. The US Constitution gives Congress the power "[t]o lay and collect Taxes, Duties, Imposts, and Excises, to pay the Debts and provide for the common Defence and general Welfare of the United States," while the parallel passage in the Confederate Constitution gives Congress the power "To lay and collect taxes, duties, imposts, and excises, for revenue necessary to pay the debts, provide for the common defense, and carry on the Government of the Confederate States." Quite clearly, reference to the general welfare already was viewed as a potential open door for any type of government activity.

---

7. Lee, *The Confederate Constitutions,* gives a complete history of the Confederate Constitution and also prints the Confederate Constitution and the Constitution of the United States side-by-side to facilitate a comparison.

It would seem that the proper interpretation of the "general welfare" in the US Constitution would be to prevent government financing of activities that benefited particular groups or individuals rather than the nation as a whole. The term "general welfare" is inserted into the sentence referring to taxation. Furthermore, if the intent was to have the government in general try to promote the general welfare, there would be no reason for the Constitution to enumerate the allowable activities of the federal government, because those activities would be in addition to anything else Congress thought would promote the general welfare. And it would be contradictory to restrict the government, as in the Tenth Amendment, to those activities enumerated in the Constitution if one of those activities was to promote the general welfare in whatever way Congress saw fit.

Immediately following that clause in the Confederate Constitution is a clause that has no parallel in the US Constitution: "But no bounties shall be granted from the Treasury; nor shall any duties or taxes on importations from foreign nations be laid to promote or foster any branch of industry." The Confederate Constitution also prevents Congress from appropriating money "for any internal improvement intended to facilitate commerce" except for improvements to facilitate waterway navigation, but "in all such cases, such duties shall be laid on the navigation facilitated thereby, as may be necessary to pay for the costs and expenses thereof." In several places the Confederate Constitution explicitly prohibits general revenues from being spent for the benefit of special interests.

While reference to the general welfare in the US Constitution might have an ambiguous interpretation, the changes in the Confederate Constitution make clear the interpretation the Confederates hoped to avoid. The Confederate Constitution's altered wording plainly states that tax revenues are to be spent only on programs that benefit everyone, not programs that benefit a specific segment of the population, and that in those instances where allowed expenditures are targeted at a specific segment of the population or branch of industry, taxes to pay for those expenditures must be targeted at the same specific sector. The problems of narrow special interests being able to use democratic government for their own private purposes were well-recognized by the mid-twentieth century, but the differences between the Confederate Constitution and the US Constitution show that the problem existed, and was recognized, before the War Between the States, and, moreover, that the Confederate states tried to construct their constitution in such a way as to reduce the influence of special interests.

The Post Office was one area in which special interests had influenced the US government, and the Confederate Constitution specified that the Post Office had to be financially self-sufficient. The Confederate Constitution gave the president line-item veto authority with regard to appropriations, stating, "The president may approve any appropriation and disapprove any other appropriation in the same bill." Another important difference was that under many circumstances a two-thirds majority of the legislature rather than a simple majority was needed for appropriations. "Congress shall appropriate no money from the Treasury, except by a vote of two thirds of both Houses, taken by yeas and nays, unless it be asked and estimated for by some one of the heads of departments, and submitted to Congress by the President."

Another provision in the Confederate Constitution reads, "All bills appropriating money shall specify, in Federal currency, the exact amount of each appropriation, and the purposes for which it is made, and Congress shall grant no extra compensation to any public contractor, officer, agent, or servant, after such a contract shall have been made or such service rendered." The Confederate Constitution tried to ensure against open-ended commitments and no entitlement programs in the Confederate states. All expenditure bills would specify a fixed amount of money, and another bill would be needed to exceed the initial appropriation. All of these differences in appropriations procedures between the United States and Confederate States were aimed at controlling the ability of special interests to use the government for their benefit.

The Relevance of the Confederate Constitution

An analysis of the Constitution of the Confederate States of America provides a great deal of insight into the workings of the Constitution of the United States before the War Between the States. The authors of the Confederate Constitution had enough respect for the US Constitution that they were willing to adopt almost all of its general form and language, modifying only those areas in which they believed clear improvement could be made. Thus, an analysis of the differences can pinpoint specific problems that the founders of the

Confederacy thought existed in the US Constitution's design. Despite the hostilities between the North and South, at least one Northern source, the *New York Herald*, argued on March 19, 1861, that the Confederate Constitution was an improvement over the US Constitution and that whatever the outcome of the war the Union could benefit from adopting some Confederate ideas.[8]

Seen in this light, it is interesting to note that the problems that the authors of the Confederate Constitution actually did address were overwhelmingly associated with the use of legislative powers to impose costs on the general public to provide benefits to narrow constituencies. The problems of interest-group politics and the expansion of the federal government beyond what some perceived to be its constitutionally limited boundaries already were apparent by 1860. The Confederate Constitution tried to address those issues, but the aftermath of the War Between the States created a bigger, more powerful federal government that more clearly could dictate its policies to the states rather than the more limited government that the Confederates had envisioned.

Conclusion

The purpose of this chapter is not to glorify the Confederacy or argue that in some sense it was better than the Union. Strong arguments can be raised to the contrary, the most obvious being the Confederate government's attempt to forever perpetuate slavery. Furthermore, even in its quest for independence, the Confederate government compromised the liberty of its citizens at least as much as the Union did. Both sides relied on a military draft for a substantial part of their manpower, but unlike the Union, which allowed soldiers to return home after serving their time, the Confederacy often required their soldiers to remain in service indefinitely. Both sides increased taxes greatly, but unlike the Union, the Confederacy imposed taxes in kind on farms and required farmers to sell to the government at fixed prices well below market prices, which amounted to a confiscation of agricultural products by the Confederate government. One Confederate farmer even suggested that he was better off having the Union nearby, despite the potential destruction, than the

---

8. This is reported by Russell Hoover Quynn, *The Constitutions of Abraham Lincoln and Jefferson Davis* (New York: Exposition, 1959), 297–299.

Confederate army, which was sure to take everything he had produced.[9] Both the Confederate and Union governments oversaw an expansion in the scopes of their powers well beyond anything that had been known in the United States previously.

An analysis of the differences in the constitutions of the Confederate States and the United States shows that even during that period sentiment was widespread that the federal government was too powerful and that it was too easy for interest groups to gain benefits from the federal government at the expense of the general public. The evolution from liberty to democracy was well underway prior to the War Between the States. The Confederate Constitution, which was really only an amended version of the US Constitution, would have pushed the nation back in the direction of liberty. Instead, the aftermath of the war left a much more powerful, centralized federal government in place, paving the way for future interest-group activity and additional government expansion.

There is a tendency to view the outcome of the War Between the States as freeing the slaves, but while that was a clear victory for liberty, in most other respects liberty was sacrificed and the power of government was enhanced. By establishing the right of the federal government to draft citizens to fight the war, to place federal troops in the states to enforce the law under Reconstruction, and to regulate the banking and monetary system, the US government clearly expanded its scope of power. Lincoln's Emancipation Proclamation represented a substantial increase in the exercise of presidential power. The passage of the Fourteenth and Fifteenth Amendments changed the fundamental relationship between the federal government and the states. Prior to the war, the US Constitution was viewed as a constraint on the federal government, but not on the states. The Fourteenth Amendment allowed federal law to be imposed on the states. With the Fifteenth Amendment the federal government was given the power to determine the qualifications for the right to vote, a power formerly belonging solely to the states, which further pushed the fundamental principle of American government toward democracy. The war created a more powerful federal government and firmly established the supremacy of the federal government over the states.

---

9. Hummel, *Emancipating Slaves*, 230.

7

Interest Groups and the Transition to Government Growth

1870–1915

IF ONE LOOKS only at expenditures, federal government growth really did not begin until the twentieth century. Prior to World War I, federal expenditures were only about 2 percent of the nation's income and had actually been shrinking as a percentage of income for decades, but by 1983, they had risen to more than 22 percent of gross domestic product (GDP). After a slight decline toward the end of the twentieth century, federal expenditures exceeded 24 percent of GDP in 2009. After more than a century of low federal expenditures and almost no growth until World War I, the remainder of the twentieth century showed substantial growth through the early twenty-first century. The substantial growth in federal expenditures through the twentieth century and into the twenty-first contrasts sharply with the relatively unchanging expenditures over the course of the nineteenth century. While federal expenditures did not rise during the period between the War Between the States and World War I, the activities of political interest groups laid the foundation for the transition to government growth during that period.

Since the American Revolution, which was fought for the cause of liberty, American political institutions have evolved continually away from the principle of liberty toward the principle of democracy. Leaders like Andrew Jackson viewed liberty and democracy as mutually reinforcing, but much of the impetus behind democracy was the push by interest groups to use the democratic political process to further their own narrow interests. The War Between the States had increased the power of the federal government greatly, which brought with it the opportunity for interest groups to use that power for their own ends. The activities of special interests after the War

Between the States until the beginning of the twentieth century transformed the relationship between the government and its citizens and laid the foundation for the massive government expenditure growth of the twentieth century.

In 1870, following the War Between the States, federal expenditures were 4 percent of the nation's income and fell to 2.4 percent by 1880. By 1915, federal expenditures fell further to 1.9 percent of income. From the end of the War Between the States to the beginning of World War I federal expenditures roughly were the same in inflation-adjusted dollars and had declined substantially as a percentage of income, because income was growing while federal expenditures were not. This contrasts sharply with the period of growth after World War I and demonstrates that twentieth-century federal government growth was a phenomenon in itself, not just an extension of the trends of the previous century.[1]

The transition to government growth came at the end of the Progressive Era, which commonly is dated from 1900 until the start of World War I, which provides a possible explanation for the growth. The Progressive ideology supported bigger government, and a government more oriented toward furthering the economic interests of citizens, so the cumulative acceptance of this Progressive ideology might be responsible for growing government. A conclusion that government growth was caused by a change in ideology ultimately is unsatisfying, however, because people do not change their ways of thinking for no reason. A complete explanation should reveal why a change in ideology materialized.

One can cite many institutional changes around that time as reasons for government growth. The most prominent of those was the Sixteenth Amendment to the Constitution, ratified in 1913, which allowed the federal government to collect income taxes. While it is indisputably true that the federal government could not have grown as much as it did without the income tax, the passage of the income tax must be viewed as a result of changing preferences for the size of government, and it was added to the Constitution to fund the greater demand for government expenditures. Why was the income tax amendment not passed sooner? Indeed, the United States used a temporary

---

1. Federal expenditures and GDP were calculated from data in *Historical Statistics of the United States from Colonial Times to 1970* (Washington, DC: Department of Commerce, 1976).

income tax from 1861 to 1871 to help finance the War Between the States, but repealed it. The income tax amendment did not cause the government to grow. It was passed in response to a demand for more revenues to feed a growing government.

Three major factors underlie the transition to government growth following the War Between the States: (1) An expanding economy produced a budget surplus, which in turn created opportunities for interest groups to lobby for federal transfers. Veterans were an organized interest group already receiving federal support, and during the transition veterans groups organized to become the first rent-seeking special interest to capture major transfer payments from the federal government. (2) The scope of the federal government's activities continued to be broadened from the protection of individual rights to include the promotion of the economic interests of its citizens. This is most clearly seen in the increase in federal regulatory activities. (3) The federal bureaucracy was transformed from a group of political appointees who owed their jobs and loyalties to the current administration (the "spoils system") into a "professional" civil service in which jobs were assigned objectively based on civil service examinations and where principles of scientific management were used to create a long-term workforce of career public sector employees. Each of these changes led to the strengthening of interest groups that demanded a larger government to further their economic interests.

Throughout most of the nineteenth century the transition from liberty to democracy as the fundamental principle underlying American government was a political phenomenon, not an economic one, because the government at that time had relatively little impact on people's lives. It protected their rights but taxed them relatively little, spent relatively little, and engaged in little regulation. In 1860, government involvement in the economy was small and in many areas declining. Government intervention into banking was minimal, especially at the federal level, after the 1836 demise of the Second Bank of the United States; government regulation of medical care was smaller than it ever had been; and in most other areas people's activities were only affected peripherally by government. That changed substantially in the period from 1870 to 1915, when American democracy moved from being primarily a feature of the political system into being a significant feature of the economic system as well.

The Federal Budget Between the Wars

The rise in federal government expenditures is only a small part of the transition to government growth, and even with regard to expenditures the most significant factor is not the level of expenditures but rather the way in which a powerful interest group was able to gain enough political clout to produce a major increase in direct monetary transfers to group members. Veterans established a precedent that would be emulated by other interest groups as the government grew, changing the character of government expenditures. Some background on the federal budget after the War Between the States is useful to see how veterans' groups were able to organize to capture those transfers.

The War Between the States had a profound effect on the federal budget between that war and World War I for several reasons. First, the magnitude of postwar expenditures was at least double prewar outlays. A substantial amount of this increase was war-related, however. Subtracting out the war-related expenditures, including the expenditures on federal troops occupying the South during Reconstruction, expenditures on other items in the 1870s were roughly the same as they had been before the war. The apparent ratcheting up of federal expenditures after the War Between the States was primarily the result of additional expenditures that were directly related to the war.

Federal outlays remained relatively stable until the late 1870s, when they began to rise substantially. The rate of expenditure growth increased even more in the mid-to-late 1880s, but around the beginning of the twentieth century expenditures leveled off. After the War Between the States and up through the mid-1890s the federal government ran a substantial budget surplus, which aided in repaying its war debts but also provided the resources for rising federal expenditures. The substantial increases in federal expenditures stopped at about the time the federal budget was balanced. Faced with this revenue constraint, federal expenditures had to stop growing until more revenues could be found. If the growth prior to the mid-1890s reflects the demand for greater federal spending, that pressure would explain the derived demand for a federal income tax that would allow continued growth. Substantial surpluses in the mid-1880s eroded rapidly as expenditures increased, so that by the mid-1890s the budget was balanced, which temporarily halted the growth in federal spending until the income tax amendment was ratified in 1913.

Veterans' Expenditures Between the Wars

After the War Between the States, military expenditures rose faster than non-military budgetary line items, but the most remarkable aspect of the federal budget was a tripling of expenditures on veterans from 1870 into the mid-1890s. While the substantial growth in veterans' expenditures is significant in itself, it is more significant because it represents the most substantial interest-group expenditure undertaken by the federal government prior to the twentieth century.[2] The growth of veterans' benefits was entirely the result of organized interests working through the political system to produce payments to their members, and paved the road for the dominant role of interest groups in modern American government.

Veterans made up more than 5 percent of the total population after the War Between the States, but because of the restricted franchise they made up a much larger fraction of the voting population. The presidential election of 1864 pitted Lincoln, running for reelection, against Democrat George Mc-Clellan, an army general whom Lincoln had removed from command, and both sides fervently pursued the vote of soldiers as a group. After the war, there was little in the way of assistance for veterans, but in 1865 a group called the United States Soldiers and Sailors Protective Society was formed for the purpose of aiding veterans. This nonpolitical group hoped to further the interests of veterans through "mutual confidence and mutual help."

The next year, in 1866, Union veteran Dr. Benjamin Stephenson founded a more formidable veterans group called the Grand Army of the Republic (GAR), which explicitly was set up to be a political group. The GAR was not organized along military lines but was more like a political party, with precincts and statewide headquarters, and rapidly became a substantial special-interest pressure group.[3]

Federal benefits to veterans of the War Between the States were defined by acts of Congress in 1865 and 1866. Payments went to disabled veterans and

---

2. The growth in veterans' expenditures is described in Randall G. Holcombe, "Veterans Interests and the Transition to Government Growth: 1870–1915," *Public Choice* 99, nos. 3/4 (June 1999): 311–26.

3. Richard Severo and Lewis Milford, *The Wages of War: When America's Soldiers Came Home—From Valley Forge to Vietnam* (New York: Simon & Schuster, 1989).

surviving widows and children of those killed in the war according to specific schedules. Veterans who survived the war uninjured were not entitled to pensions. To try to control expenditures on pensions, an act in 1868 specified that to be eligible for a disability pension, the disability had to have occurred in the line of duty. Soldiers injured while in the army, but not injured in the line of duty, were not entitled to pensions. Pensions had to be applied for within five years of the disabling injury for the claim to be valid, although there was an appeals process that allowed exceptions to the five-year limit.[4] Veterans' benefits at the end of the 1860s were intended to help the soldiers who were injured or killed in the war and their dependents, and those who were disabled in the war, but eventually recovered, were expected to give up their pensions.

Veterans made up a substantial interest group, and with the political organization provided by the GAR they became a potent political force. In 1872, there were 1.8 million veterans and 6.5 million votes cast in the presidential election. Without veteran voter turnout data it is difficult to say what percentage of voters were veterans, but veterans divided by voters yields 28 percent, suggesting the substantial political power of veterans. The GAR was instrumental in establishing Memorial Day as a national holiday in 1869, despite widespread sentiment that the holiday would hinder the reunification of the nation, but the GAR's broader agenda was increasing federal veterans' benefits for its members. Instrumental in that effort was the influence of a substantial number of attorneys in the GAR who became quite active in pursuing pension cases for individual veterans.

Relatively little veterans legislation was enacted through most of the 1870s, but encouraged by pension attorneys, veterans continued to apply for disability pensions through the appeals process (because the five-year time limit for applications had expired). As the commissioner of pensions noted in 1871, when an appeal was filed it often was difficult to tell whether the disabling injury was actually a result of the war. Furthermore, veterans whose injuries had healed continued to collect pensions in violation of the law, but violations were difficult to detect, and it was often a subjective determination as to whether the veteran actually had recovered from his injuries.

---

4. William Henry Glasson, *History of Military Pension Legislation in the United States* (New York: Columbia University Press, 1900).

The Arrears Act of 1879 was a major turning point for veterans' benefits. Prior to the Arrears Act, veterans would begin receiving pension benefits at the time of their application. After passage of the act, benefits commenced from the time of discharge from the army, or, for dependents, from the time of the veteran's death. Those already receiving pensions were due arrears, but what is more significant is that new applicants would also receive arrears if their appeals were successful. This policy substantially increased the value of appealing to receive a pension, increasing the number of applications tremendously and also increasing the number of fraudulent applications. Prior to the passage of the Arrears Act about 1,600 pensions claims were filed each month. After the act became the law of the land, new claims rose to more than 10,000 per month. The average arrears payment was about $1,000, which was a substantial sum because at that time the average annual earnings of nonfarm workers in the United States was about $400. As a result, federal expenditures on veterans skyrocketed in the 1880s.[5]

Veterans who were denied pensions or who were not disabled could pursue another route to receive a pension—through a special bill requiring the approval of the president. Grover Cleveland, first elected as president in 1884, signed 1,453 such bills in his first term, making him popular with veterans. Nevertheless, when in 1887 he vetoed the Dependent Pension Bill, which would have provided pensions to all disabled veterans regardless of whether their disabilities were war-related, he lost his bid for reelection, in no small part because of opposition from the GAR.

When considering the GAR specifically, and veterans in general, as an interest group, one must recognize the link between veterans' interests and the Republican Party. The Republicans, the party of Lincoln, victorious in the War Between the States, maintained their political strength in the North, whereas the South was a Democratic stronghold. If this was not enough to create regional differences in party strengths, Confederate veterans were not eligible for federal pensions, meaning that veterans' benefits were a transfer from taxpayers in general to recipients in Northern states. Thus, a natural alliance arose between the veterans groups and the Republican Party. In the twentieth century, the Democratic Party was often viewed as having close ties

5. Theda Skocpol, *Protecting Soldiers and Mothers: The Political Origins of Social Policy in the United States* (Cambridge, MA: Belknap, 1992).

with organized labor, but the natural bonds that linked organized veterans groups with the Republican Party in the late nineteenth century were considerably stronger. The Republican Party relied on veterans for electoral support and paid off their supporters with increasingly generous veterans' benefits.

Benjamin Harrison, the Republican who defeated Cleveland, understood the importance of veterans' support. One of the leading figures in the GAR was James Tanner, commander of the GAR's New York department. Tanner campaigned for Harrison, and his support in helping Harrison win the presidential election was repaid when Harrison appointed Tanner to the post of pension commissioner. Harrison instructed Tanner to "Be liberal with the boys," to which Tanner replied, "I will drive a six-mule team through the Treasury."[6] In 1890, veterans' benefits were broadened further to provide benefits to disabled veterans and survivors' benefits to widows of veterans, regardless of whether they were injured in the war and regardless of need. Thus, a veteran who became mentally or physically disabled after the war was entitled to a pension, as was any widow of a veteran. In practice, few claims were denied, and large numbers of persons, seemingly normal in health, discovered in themselves ailments that would have passed unnoticed but for the pension laws.

Benefits to veterans of the War Between the States became a major political issue as Tanner managed to transfer increasingly large sums from the Treasury to veterans. Charles William Eliot, president of Harvard College, argued in a speech,

> I hold it to be a hideous wrong inflicted upon the republic that the pension system instituted for the benefit of the soldiers and sailors of the United States has been prostituted and degraded by a whole series of Republican administrations. As things are, gentlemen, one cannot tell whether a pensioner of the United States received an honorable wound in battle or contracted a chronic catarrh twenty years after the war.[7]

Late in the nineteenth century, the conventional wisdom was that during normal times the government should run a budget surplus to offset deficits that would inevitably occur during wars and other emergencies. By 1893, the

---

6. Severo and Milford, *Wages of War*, 178.
7. Severo and Milford, *Wages of War*, 180–181.

budget surplus had been completely wiped out, and one Republican loyalist lamented, "If Tanner does not go soon, the surplus will—and the Republican party after it." [8] Tanner's successes on behalf of the veterans were not uniformly appreciated by the general public, as the preceding quotation indicates, and Cleveland, defeated in 1888 by Harrison after one term, ran again and won in 1892. That event is especially noteworthy because after the election of Lincoln, the first Republican president in 1860, Cleveland was the only Democrat elected to the White House until Woodrow Wilson in 1914.

Veterans as an Interest Group

The historical details illustrate how veterans' interests became so successful after the War Between the States. The details support a straightforward interest-group story. After the war, veterans made up a substantial share of the voting population, and because of the political entrepreneurship of Benjamin Stephenson, they became a well-organized political force through the GAR. A natural alliance emerged between the GAR and the Republican Party because the political strengths of both were concentrated geographically in the North. The GAR supported the Republican Party and in exchange was paid off with increasingly generous pensions during a period of Republican domination. Another enabling factor was that owing to the federal budget surplus, funds were available, allowing Republicans to compensate veterans in exchange for their support. Veterans were an organized group and were prepared to argue their case. The surplus provided an opportunity for them to succeed.

While maintaining the budget surplus was viewed as prudent public policy, it was unclear exactly how much of a surplus it would be prudent to keep. Eventually, increasingly generous veterans' benefits eroded the surplus completely. As long as a budget surplus existed, veterans were able to garner ever more generous transfers, but once the surplus was gone, the growth in veterans benefits ended, too.

The veterans' lobby after the War Between the States was the first large-scale special-interest group in the United States, and it paved the way for future interest-group activity. As the history of the period shows, benefits were viewed

---

8. Severo and Milford, *Wages of War*, 180.

as payments to an interest group rather than as activity furthering the common good or "general welfare." Substantial political debate surrounded the issue, and political campaigns consciously considered the payment of veterans' benefits as a way of buying the support of that voting bloc.

Lobbying, today accepted as a normal part of the political process, was not viewed that way in the nineteenth century. Veterans, with the GAR as their political organization, set the stage for large-scale lobbying by openly promoting additional benefits for the members of the group. Seeing that example, other groups who wanted benefits from Congress could hardly resist following their lead. Rather than being reserved for certain well-defined public purposes, the federal budget was being transformed into a pork pie, and if some groups did not want to try to compete for shares of it, the budget would be spent by others.

Regulation

Interest-group activity did not begin with veterans from the War Between the States, of course. Individuals attempted to use government to further their own private interests well prior to the War Between the States, and in many ways the scope of federal government activity in the United States began expanding from the time the nation was founded.[9] But the War Between the States obviously strengthened the power of the federal government because it established its primacy over the states. While the monetary transfers garnered by veterans benefited them as an interest group, the transfers did not change the overall nature of the federal government's activities. In contrast, the federal government's regulatory actions in the late nineteenth century surely did.

In the 1877 case of *Munn v. Illinois*, the Supreme Court ruled that the State of Illinois had the right to regulate grain elevator rates. Prior to *Munn*, individuals engaging in market transactions did so on terms agreed upon by the transacting parties. That 1877 case gave government the right to set the terms of private transactions. The regulation, which was intended to protect farmers from the economic power of grain elevator operators, was designed to

---

9. Jonathan R. T. Hughes, *The Governmental Habit: Economic Controls from Colonial Times to the Present* (New York: Basic Books, 1977).

further the economic well-being of one group of people, albeit at the expense of another. This was an early expression of the Progressive idea that the role of government is not only to protect people's rights, but also to look out for their individual economic interests.[10]

This landmark case allowing transfer through regulation came at the same time that the growth in veterans' benefits established the legitimacy of transferring income directly from the Treasury to a subgroup of the population. The *Munn v. Illinois* case gave a state government the right to balance the economic interests of citizens against one another, and it was not long before the federal government became more significantly involved in such activities, changing the way in which citizens interacted with their governments. Perhaps the most significant area in which government grew prior to World War I was in economic regulation, and the most heavily regulated area of the economy was rail transportation.

As the rail network grew in the second half of the nineteenth century, pushes for regulation came from two major directions. First, shippers, who were mainly farmers trying to move their products to market, wanted rate regulation to protect their economic interests from the potential monopoly power of the railroads. Second, the railroads themselves were concerned about excessive competition and wanted regulation as a way of protecting their economic interests against competitive market forces. While these two goals may appear contradictory, it is indeed possible that local shippers might fall prey to a local branch-line monopolist, while on trunk lines there could be substantial competition. The more significant feature to note in both cases, however, is that individuals wanted regulation not to protect their liberties or to secure their property, but to further their economic interests.

State governments, in support of farming interests, passed legislation to try to encourage competition among railroads, to prevent price discrimination, and to try to keep shipping rates low. The most significant action at the state level was the creation of the Illinois Railroad and Warehouse Commission in 1873. While state legislatures previously had passed legislation to aid shippers, this was the first case in which an independent commission was established for

---

10. Terry L. Anderson and Peter J. Hill, *The Birth of a Transfer Society* (Stanford, CA: Hoover Institution Press, 1980).

that purpose; the Illinois commission served as a model for the creation of the Interstate Commerce Commission (ICC) in 1887. While farmers supported railroad regulation, New York City shippers were the strongest interest group favoring regulation to try to preserve the status of the port of New York as America's dominant corridor through which goods came to and from European markets.

The railroads themselves saw advantages to regulation. Unstable prices, disliked by rail customers, could also be detrimental to the railroads. A recession in 1884 led to the failure of a number of railroads, and the railroads wanted to undertake pooling arrangements for their mutual profitability. Thus, the railroad industry, which was very competitive, wanted the ICC to stabilize rates, regulate routes, and protect their profitability. Essentially, the ICC cartelized the industry, allowing it to be more profitable than it could have been in a more competitive unregulated environment. At the beginning of the twenty-first century it is well-recognized that private businesses can use government regulation to enhance and stabilize their profits. This same idea applied to the railroad industry in the late 1800s.[11]

Interest groups on both sides of the market wanted regulation to further their own economic well-being. Regulatory interventions as a result of interest group politics represent an expansion of the role of government to further individuals' interests, as the federal government for the first time showed itself willing to intervene to further the economic welfare of specific groups rather than merely to protect their rights. In addition, the establishment of the ICC as a separate commission transferred the responsibility for regulation from Congress to a separate administrative agency within the executive branch of government. This marked a significant change in the way interest groups were able to interact with their governments.

The Supreme Court decision in *Wabash, St. Louis, and Pacific Railway Co. v. Illinois*, delivered in October 1866, also pushed Congress toward the establishment of the ICC. In *Wabash*, the Court ruled that state regulatory

---

11. See Richard White, *Railroaded: The Transcontinentals and the Making of Modern America* (New York: W. W. Norton, 2011); and Gabriel Kolko, *Railroads and Regulation: 1877–1916* (Princeton, NJ: Princeton University Press, 1965).

agencies could not impose restrictions on interstate commerce without an act of Congress, pushing Congress toward the national regulation of commerce through the ICC.[12]

The ICC was a natural place for the federal government to begin regulation of the economy, because Article I, Section 8 of the Constitution explicitly gives Congress the right "[t]o regulate Commerce... among the several States," and the ICC was the beginning of a major push for federal involvement in people's economic affairs. In 1890, the Sherman Act was passed, explicitly for the benefit of a subset of the population. The Pure Food and Drug Act was passed in 1906, the Federal Reserve was created in 1913, and the Federal Trade Commission was organized in 1914. Throughout that period, major amendments to the Interstate Commerce Act were passed, and additional legislation was enacted explicitly to further the economic well-being of specific interest groups.

At the beginning of the twenty-first century, such regulatory interventions are taken for granted as a part of the government's natural role, but at the end of the nineteenth century this was a radical departure, as a government that historically had been constitutionally limited to protecting the rights of its citizens began acting to further their economic interests as well. A change in philosophy and also a change in method as Congress, starting with the ICC, emerged as the legislature that established regulatory agencies independent of the legislative branch of government to further the economic interests of its citizens.

At the beginning of the twenty-first century, when government at all levels spends in excess of 35 percent of GDP, transfers of money and goods in kind, such as public housing and government healthcare, are common, but without a large supply of tax revenues to draw on, regulation can serve as a form of taxation by forcing individuals to provide benefits to others at their own expense. It is certainly clear that measuring the size of government by its expenditures without considering the impact of regulation substantially underestimates government's impact on the allocation of economic resources. The Interstate

---

12. Stephen Skowronek, *Building a New American State: The Expansion of National Administrative Capabilities, 1877–1920* (New York: Cambridge University Press, 1982), 147–148.

Commerce Act of 1887 was the beginning of a new paradigm in government regulation.

Civil Service and the Science of Public Administration

The evolution of the federal government was marked not only by the growth of interest groups, a radical change in the scope of government through regulation, and the participation of the legislature and the courts in designing these changes, but also included fundamental changes in the administrative nature of government. While the idea of scientific management, both in the public and private sectors, was gaining currency throughout the second half of the nineteenth century, the watershed event was the passage of the Civil Service Act of 1883, which established career civil service with formal criteria for hiring and a hierarchical professional structure for federal employees.

Civil service reform began in 1871, with a law that gave the president the authority to establish rules governing the hiring of and performance standards for government employees. With the Republican Party dominating the White House, many observers felt that civil service jobs were made on partisan political grounds, and appointments at the New York Customhouse were especially visible and especially criticized for their partisan nature. The New York Customhouse was significant because it accounted for more than half of the federal government's revenues in the 1870s. Ohio Democrat George Pendleton proposed legislation that would award civil service jobs based on the results of competitive examinations, and while the legislation was not initially given much chance of passing, Republicans sensed their vulnerability on the issue, and the measure belatedly was passed in Chester Arthur's administration in 1883.[13] Still, it was not enough to prevent the defeat of Arthur by Cleveland in 1884, making Cleveland the first Democrat elected to the presidency since 1856.

Administrative reform, focused on cutting excesses from wartime government and increasing the efficiency of government, was referred to as "retrench-

---

13. Skowronek, *Building a New American State*, 64–68. Skowronek gives an excellent history of the development of the civil service in the second half of the 1800s.

ment." However, 53,000 civilians were employed by the federal government in 1871, and by 1901 civilian federal employment had grown to 256,000, so looking at the actual evolution of federal employment during the time, retrenchment is not the first word that might come to mind.

Civil service reform in 1883 created a system whereby federal employees were hired in a nonpartisan way, based on objective test results. Throughout the remainder of the century, an ever larger share of federal employees found themselves under the new system, and therefore more and more of them did not owe their jobs to the current administration. More substantial change came after the turn of the century when President Theodore Roosevelt created more nonpatronage positions out of positions formerly available as political appointments. He also passed stringent rules to create a "neutral" civil service that had stronger ties to the executive branch of government and whose ties to Congress and political parties were severed. The civil service became more independent from political influences during Roosevelt's administration, and more substantial change occurred during the Taft administration, when, in 1911, the Lloyd-LaFollette Act gave civil servants the right to organize and to petition Congress for their own interests and also set up a civil service procedure to evaluate the performances of civil servants.

The period from the late 1870s until the beginning of World War I saw civil service transformed from a system of political patronage, controlled by party interests, into a system ostensibly insulated from politics to a large degree. The new system was insulated because hiring and promotions were determined from within, following an objective set of rules, and federal workers gained the right to unionize. Whereas prior to this time civil servants could expect their interests to be closely tied to the current administration, afterward a permanent civil service was created whose members could not be fired and could outlast administrations. This gave the civil service more autonomy in setting personnel policies and the ability to disregard the interests of the current administration. Government bureaucrats could then become an interest group themselves, having stakes in the ongoing growth of the federal government rather than having their interests tied closely to the success of incumbent politicians. Thus, a close link exists between civil service reform and the incentives for those in government to act as an interest group that would promote growth in government expenditures.

The Army

After having explained how veterans became the first major interest group to redirect substantial federal transfers their way and how civil servants were able to transform federal employees from being dependent on the administration in power into being an autonomous and powerful element in federal government, the army during this period stands as an interesting contrast. As a clue in trying to answer the question of how government was transformed in the late 1800s, the army is like the dog that did not bark. Prior to the War Between the States, most soldiers served in locally organized militias, which remained the case after the war as well. While a federal superstructure existed above the local organizations, and while those in the US War Department wanted an increasingly professionalized army, such reform did not happen until the twentieth century.[14]

The reason that this reform did not happen earlier is because local militias, with local leaders and local members, were more powerful as an interest group than their counterparts at the federal level. If soldiers had been federal employees, like civil servants, military reforms similar to the civil service reforms might have occurred. Interest-group politics leaned the other way, however, and the principles of scientific management that had permeated civil service were unable to produce meaningful reform in the armed forces. Only in the twentieth century did international conflicts lead to a centralized and bureaucratic federal military establishment that would parallel the development of civil service.

The foundations for twentieth-century growth in military expenditures were laid in the late nineteenth century, with the purchase of ships for the navy that presaged the twentieth-century military-industrial complex. Shipbuilders became an interest group that favored more military spending and a more organized military force. However, aggregate military spending data show that their main successes had to await the twentieth century. Following the Spanish-American War in 1898, the US Military Academy at West Point stepped up its effort to professionalize the army, but the real transformation in the military did not come until World War I.

---

14. Skowronek, *Building a New American State*, chapter 4, discusses military reform.

The Post Office

One can see that conditions after the War Between the States led to the growth of interest group expenditures, but the problem of special-interest politics was recognized prior to the war. One area in which the government began providing benefits to special interests prior to the War Between the States was the Post Office. Mail delivery was one of the few activities of the federal government explicitly provided for in the Constitution, but before 1851 the Post Office was run as a revenue-generating operation. That changed in 1851, when after much debate in Congress a law was passed that greatly overhauled the nature of mail delivery.

After the 1851 Act, mail delivery to western states was subsidized, but postal rates were not sufficient for profits from service in the East to cover the subsidy, so Congress appropriated money to cover the deficit. This meant that additional extensions of service became the subject of congressional debate and pitted West Coast interests against those in the more populous East. Politics also entered the picture in the Lincoln administration in a big way when local postmasters were chosen under the patronage system. The Republicans were a new political party, and party loyalists were anxious for political favors. As a result, in the 1860s the only qualification needed to be appointed as a local postmaster was the recommendation of a Republican Member of Congress. In fact, to reduce the political pressures he had to face, Postmaster General Montgomery Blair, who was appointed by Lincoln, openly recommended that applicants for local postmaster positions apply directly to their Member of Congress rather than to the Post Office Department.[15]

While interest-group activity accelerated tremendously after the War Between the States, experiences at the Post Office show that the beginnings of interest-group politics surfaced before the war. Once the principle was established that postal services would be offered at low prices regardless of the cost of the service, the opportunity for rent-seeking presented itself, and western states availed themselves of the opportunity to obtain services at less than full cost. The special-interest nature of the Post Office was aggravated by openly political appointments during the Lincoln administration. While the new

---

15. Gerald Cullinan, *The Post Office Department* (New York: Praeger, 1968), 79.

policies dated back to only 1851, the Confederate States clearly saw the problems and attempted to correct them in their constitution. The Confederate Constitution specified, as did the US Constitution, that Congress would have the power "to establish post office and post roads" but added that the cost "shall be paid out of its own revenue." The 1851 law may not have been intended to open the door of the federal Treasury to special interests, but it had that effect and provided a foundation on which veterans could build after the War Between the States.

Interest-Group Politics and the Transition to Government Growth

When the nation was founded, the federal government primarily was a defender of the rights of its citizens, and the types of transfer programs that are taken for granted in the twenty-first century were regarded as improper government activities in the nineteenth century. Seeing the federal government turn increasingly toward the provision of special-interest benefits, in 1887 President Cleveland argued, "A prevalent tendency to disregard the limited mission of [the government's] power and duty should be steadfastly resisted, to the end that the lesson should be constantly enforced that, though the people support the Government, the Government should not support the people."[16] The problem that Cleveland saw, anticipated by Tocqueville, was that in a democracy people have the political power to vote benefits to themselves. As the franchise expanded in the United States, more people were admitted to the group that could vote themselves benefits. As Tocqueville noted, "When a nation begins to modify the elective qualification, it may easily be foreseen that, sooner or later, that qualification will be entirely abolished. There is no more invariable rule in the history of society.... [N]o stop can be made short of universal suffrage."[17]

---

16. Quoted in Robert Higgs, *Crisis and Leviathan (25th Anniversary Edition): Critical Episodes in the Growth of American Government* (Oakland, CA: Independent Institute, 2012), 84.

17. Alexis de Tocqueville, *Democracy in America* (1835; repr., New York: Alfred A. Knopf, 1963), 57.

The expansion of the franchise also is linked to the metamorphosis of government from an institution that protects individual rights to an organization that enhances the economic well-being of its citizens. As interest groups such as veterans, farmers, rail shippers, and the customers and competitors of trusts are more able to use their political power for their economic benefit, it increasingly becomes important for economic interests to be represented in the political process. Likewise, as the franchise expands, it becomes more important for elected representatives to be cognizant of the economic interests of their constituents. When the franchise is limited, nobody would think that those who have the right to vote also have the right to transfer income from nonvoters to themselves. When everybody has the right to vote, that argument disappears.

Interest-group politics plays a key role in the history of the transition to government growth. The emergence of significant economic interests in the political process increased the demand for government expenditures and government regulation and laid the foundation for the Progressive Era reforms that caused federal expenditures to transition from being relatively stable to continually increasing. The War Between the States produced a well-organized interest group that seemed to have some legitimate claim to the treasury's assets, and a budget surplus brought on by economic growth gave them resources to claim. Those historical events, coupled with the propensity of factions to develop, transformed a stable, limited government into an ever-expanding one.

Conclusion

The 1870–1915 period saw a major transformation not only in the size and scope of government but also in the government's relationship to the economy. The changes in the scope of government mostly had to do with people's economic interactions with government, in seeking direct transfers, in seeking regulatory protection, and in the overall philosophy that democracy has a role to play in the allocation of resources. If government is protecting people from economic power through antitrust laws and business regulation, and if government is providing benefits to some—whether postal patrons or war veterans—at the expense of others, somehow it must decide how these benefits are distributed. Civil service reform was intended to provide a more objective and less political way of allocating benefits, but ultimately the allocation of benefits would be made democratically. Thus, democracy grew in importance as a method of allocating economic resources in addition to its role in political decision-making. Early in the nineteenth century, the implications of democratic government were almost entirely political. By the end of the nineteenth century, democracy had become more of an economic system.

8

Populism and Progressivism

AMERICANS HAVE ALWAYS had high expectations of their government. What, exactly, they have expected has changed considerably over more than two centuries, and how those changes have manifested themselves is the story of the transformation from liberty to democracy as the underlying ideology of American government. The high expectations that Americans have had came from the fundamental philosophy of the American Revolution. That philosophy, revolutionary at the time, asserted that individuals have inalienable rights and that the role of the government is to serve the citizens by protecting these rights. Prior to the American Revolution, political institutions divided people into the rulers and the ruled, and the rights of citizens were those that government granted. Americans were familiar with political systems dating back to ancient Greece in which governmental decisions were made democratically and in which a great deal of equality existed among those granted citizenship, but even in those cases the people served the government rather than the government serving the people. The new American government was revolutionary because it was intended to reverse that relationship, and this revolutionary idea raised the expectations of Americans.

The idea that the government should serve the people has become ingrained as a part of the American ideology. Government employees are referred to as civil servants, although the implications of that term rarely are contemplated in depth. Public policies are intended to serve the public interest, not the interests of the crown. This American ideology helps promote the interests of the government by making compliant citizens, regardless of whether the government's interests are congruent with the public interest, but it also sets up expectations that government policy will further the public's interest. Initially the public interest was viewed simply as liberty—freedom from government oppression. Andrew Jackson saw democracy as a means to an end and as a method of controlling government to keep it from gaining too much power. By the end of the nineteenth century, however, Jacksonian democracy had evolved to the point where democracy was an end in itself, and the appropriate role for government was viewed as protecting the interests of its citizens, whatever those interests might be, rather than just guarding their liberty. Democracy became the method by which the interests of the nation's citizens were revealed.

Toward the end of the nineteenth century and leading into the twentieth, Populism and Progressivism were two major political movements that exerted crucial impacts on the way Americans viewed their government and the way government should interact with its citizens. Briefly described, Populism was a movement to take control of the government away from elites and provide citizens with more direct control over their government. Progressivism was a movement to provide more government control over the nation's economy and to use government policy to enhance the economic well-being of its citizens. A more detailed look at Populist and Progressive ideas can shed more light on the political transformation of American government leading up to World War I.

Populism

Political movements can have ideological foundations, but they cannot gain enough support to have an impact on the political landscape unless interest groups are behind them who believe that if the movement's political principles are adopted, those in the interest group will be better off. Populism drew its support from agricultural interests in the South and West. The United States was undergoing a massive economic transformation in the late 1800s, as the primarily agrarian economy was being eroded by a rapidly expanding industrial sector. Manufacturing was growing at a breakneck pace, and the banking and financial sectors of the economy were prospering as a result. Railroads began linking the nation, providing transportation for both industrial and agricultural goods. As most of the economy prospered, however, farmers felt that they were being left behind.

In 1877, two major events changed the political climate in the United States. Only a few months after his election, President Rutherford B. Hayes announced the end of Reconstruction and withdrew federal troops from the South, more than 15 years after they had first entered and occupied the Confederate states. Then, only a few months later, President Hayes sent troops to Martinsburg, West Virginia, in an attempt to try to end a railroad strike. Federal troops were withdrawn from the enforcement of political rights in the South, but the precedent was established for using them to protect the economic interests of powerful industrialists in the North. Meanwhile, that same year several fledgling agricultural groups began to organize to try to protect their interests against moneyed industrialists.[1]

Farm productivity was increasing in the late 1800s, but at the same time the prices of agricultural products were declining sharply, especially after 1880. Farmers were familiar with the theory that prices were falling because of overproduction, but they did not believe it. The demand for farm products was increasing, but the percentage of the population engaged in agriculture was declining steadily as the economy industrialized. Farmers believed that the culprits were the railroads.[2] The nation's westward expansion in the second half of the 1800s could not have occurred without the railroads, and western farmers were completely dependent upon the railroads to bring their products to market. The railroads were able to expand because of federal land grants and often were subsidized heavily by local governments that wanted a railroad to run through their towns. Furthermore, railroad attorneys often had direct control of the local political apparatus, especially in western states. The intervention of federal troops in the 1877 rail strike make it clear that the federal government would even go so far as to use federal troops to support economic interests.

Farmers also were affected directly by the grain elevators that many of them had to deal with if they wanted to sell their produce, but they thought that anything they bought for their own use—from farm implements to clothing—

1. More detail on late nineteenth-century populism appears in Robert C. McMath Jr., *American Populism: A Social History, 1877–1898* (New York: Hill & Wang, 1993).
2. John D. Hicks, *The Populist Revolt: A Story of the Farmers' Alliance and the People's Party* (Minneapolis: University of Minnesota Press, 1931).

was controlled by trusts that were able to monopolize their segments of the market and take advantage of the economically weaker farmers. The *Farmer's Alliance* of February 28, 1891, editorialized that the price fixing that victimized farmers was the "logical result of the individual freedom which we have always considered the pride of our system."[3] Yet another old issue was the tariff, which agricultural interests had always viewed as favoring industrial interests over agriculture. Farmers also were concerned about deflation. The withdrawal of greenbacks from circulation and a movement to a true gold standard caused the value of money to rise, which hurt farmers who had taken out mortgages and had to repay them with more valuable dollars than they had borrowed.

Agricultural interests faced many problems, and the most direct way to deal with them was to take control of the government away from elite interests and return it to the people. In the tradition of Jackson, the Populists saw their salvation in more popular control of the government. Government, after all, was behind many of the problems anyway, whether it was because of its support of the railroads, its reliance on the tariff, or its control of the money supply.

Populist Organizations

Farm interests manifested themselves in a number of ways in the political arena. Several political parties established in the late 1800s gained the sympathy and support of farmers, including the People's Antimonopoly Party and the National Greenback Party. The interests of those parties and more were encompassed within the National Farmer's Alliance, which was not a political party per se, but rather was intended to be a political mouthpiece through which the interests of farmers could be heard. The National Farmer's Alliance spawned a number of derivative organizations representing smaller groups, sometimes organized by state and other times by region or other divisions, such as the Northern Alliance, the Southern Alliance, and the Colored Alliance. The key point is that Populist groups had begun organizing for the explicit purpose of influencing political decision-making for their own economic benefit.

The People's Antimonopoly Party's presidential candidate James B. Weaver garnered 22 electoral votes in the 1892 presidential election, enough to have

---

3. Quoted from Hicks, *Populist Revolt*, 79.

possibly facilitated the election of Grover Cleveland, but the Populists were more successful in state government politics than at the national level. Their sympathies with the Democratic Party relative to the Republicans led them to be absorbed into the former by the end of the 1890s. Their most popular issue at the national level ultimately was monetary reform, which remained a major point of contention.

The Money Issue

In the late 1800s, the world moved toward a gold standard, and the United States moved with it. A gold standard prevents the money supply from being inflated and prices from rising. If those who issue money must redeem it in gold, the amount of money that can circulate is limited by the quantity of gold that is available to back the money supply. If the government issued too much money, people would want to redeem it for gold, which would reduce the national gold stock and potentially could even deplete it entirely. Under a gold standard, the value of gold and the value of money remained in balance. People with gold who wanted money could exchange their gold for money, increasing the money supply, and people with money who wanted gold could redeem their money, reducing the money supply. In this manner, the quantity of gold regulated the money supply in the late 1800s.

Rapid economic growth led to a greater demand for money, increasing its value and creating a steady deflation. From 1870 to 1900, average prices in the United States declined by 34 percent. This was good for those wealthy individuals who had money and for creditors who were repaid in money more valuable than the money they lent, but for debtors, such as farmers with mortgages, the burden of repayment became heavier as deflation increased the value of money.

With the gold standard restricting the growth of the money supply, the popular opinion was that there was a shortage of money and that financial reform was needed to make more money available for the repayment of debts and for the expansion of commerce. Because the federal government now controlled the money supply, this was clearly an issue of federal policy. The Greenback Party pushed the issue by trying to get the government to print more paper money, but it was an issue for all of the minor parties. The popular belief was that the financial system was controlled by the same group of elite businessmen who increasingly dominated the entire economy. The solution was more democratic control of the money supply.

A major step was taken with the creation of the Federal Reserve System in 1913, and under the Federal Reserve monetary institutions continued to evolve over the twentieth century. In 1933, President Roosevelt continued the dismantling of the gold standard, and by 1971 President Nixon had severed the dollar's last tie with gold. The nation's monetary institutions evolved slowly, but a century after it had been formed, the Greenback Party's platform was realized in full.

Popular Elections

One of the lasting byproducts of the Populist movement is a greater ability for direct citizen voting in American politics. Popular voting for president had been virtually completed by the 1820s, but one area in which this aspect of the Populist movement manifested itself was in the ability of citizens to place referendums on state ballots by citizen initiative. Citizens have often been asked to approve new state constitutions (or amendments to them) through popular referendums, and government through New England town meetings and similar institutions has provided forums through which citizens can have direct input into their governments. However, citizen initiatives to amend state laws and state constitutions did not exist until South Dakota allowed it in 1898, as a byproduct of the Populist movement. Eighteen more states adopted citizen initiatives over the next three decades, allowing citizens direct control over the laws under which they are governed. As Populism faded from the political landscape, so did the demand for citizen initiatives, and only three states have implemented the citizen initiative process since 1918.

The Direct Election of Senators

The US Constitution originally specified that senators be chosen by state legislatures. Choosing members of the House and Senate by two different bodies of electors places an additional constraint on the types of legislation that can be passed. Under the old system, any legislation would have to meet the approval of both the representatives of the people and the representatives of the state legislatures. When senators are elected directly, both the House and the Senate represent the same interests. The selection of senators by state legislatures violated the Populist idea of direct citizen control over their government, and the Populists pushed for the direct election of senators. Their ultimate success on the issue came in 1913, when the Seventeenth Amendment to the Constitution was ratified, mandating direct election of senators.

Progressivism

As the Populist movement was losing momentum in the 1890s, the foundations of Progressivism were being built. The Progressive ideology is based on the idea that public policy should be used to protect and enhance the economic well-being of the nation's citizens in addition to just protecting their basic rights. Populism and Progressivism were distinct political movements, yet many of their objectives were consistent and overlapping. One distinction was that Populism was spearheaded by agricultural interests, whereas the leaders of the Progressive movement tended to be independent business people, lawyers, or newspaper editors. Yet both movements shared the common goal of wanting to use government to control the economic power of big business.

While Populists believed that they were being exploited by the monopoly power of railroads and overcharged for manufactured goods by big business, and therefore wanted those economic abuses controlled, Progressives saw more fundamental problems that had arisen as the American economy industrialized. Industrialization increasingly brought with it concentrated economic power and produced a few men who had amassed fortunes that would have been unimaginable only a few years before. The generally held view was that their wealth came from exploiting others. Even a century later they are often referred to as robber barons.

Part of the problem, Progressives believed, stemmed from the unavoidable evils of concentrated economic power. The Sherman Act, passed in 1890, was the first in a long series of laws that intended not just to have government regulate and control big business, but also to limit the sizes and economic powers of private commercial enterprises. The problem was not solely with business, however. The Progressives also believed that government tended to be corrupt, that it was too often controlled by party bosses, especially at the local level, and that government policies actually helped business to exploit the general public. The solution was to have a stronger federal government, national in scope, to control businesses that by then had become national in scope.

The Progressives, recognizing the problems flowing from the influence of special interests over public policy and the effects of the spoils system in which interest groups supported politicians in exchange for political support of those interests, understood that a more powerful federal government would have to be controlled to benefit its citizens generally rather than politically powerful interests. They sought control in two ways. First, they wanted to reform the civil service to create a more professional government workforce, one chosen by merit rather than by political connections and one that would be relatively independent of electoral politics. Second, they wanted the government to become more democratic and therefore more accountable to the voters.[4]

The democratic impulses of the Progressives were no different from those of the Populists, and the Seventeenth Amendment is as much a part of the Progressive agenda as it is a part of the Populist agenda. The same could be said of the regulation of railroads and more generally, of business. But the Progressives had a more comprehensive view of government control over the economy and explicitly recognized that their agenda departed from the past. Their democratic impulses might be viewed as an extension of Populism and, in turn, an extension of Jacksonian democracy. But Jackson viewed democracy as a means to produce the limited government advocated by Jefferson, whereas the Progressives viewed democracy as a method of controlling a Hamiltonian government that, out of necessity, departed sharply from the Jeffersonian vision.

In a broad sense, one might argue that only two basic ideas have influenced political platforms in the United States and that all others are merely derivative of those two basic philosophies. One philosophy is that of liberty, which went essentially unchallenged for more than a century. The competing philosophy

---

4. William Allen White, *The Old Order Changeth: A View of American Democracy* (New York: Macmillan, 1910), discusses the role of democracy in the Progressive movement.

is that of Progressivism, perhaps beginning with Hamilton and which began to be more forcefully articulated in the 1800s. How was Progressivism able to transform itself into an ideology that displaced the revolutionary cause of liberty? One reason was public reaction to the growth of the trusts and the creation of an economic elite unlike anything the world had known previously. Prior to the rise of the American industrialists, economic power and political power went hand-in-hand. American government was run by those who always had known wealth and privilege. In the Progressive movement, the general public saw government as an institution that could protect them from exploitation, but at the same time those with political power saw the growth in economic power as a threat to their status. For the first time, those with the greatest economic power in the nation were not among the political elite. Thus, politicians used their power to counter economic power partly to retain their own status. They were joined by an elite group of individuals with old wealth and professionals who found their status and influence waning in the face of the giant and growing fortunes of the new industrialists and financiers.

Another reason that Progressivism was able to develop into an ideology with national scope was that the press became an effective opponent of those with economic power. Just as pamphleteers had a substantial influence over the Revolution, so muckraking journalists had a substantial influence over the creation of the Progressive ideology. The rapid urbanization of America created new markets for newspapers. The United States had 574 daily newspapers in 1870, and that number grew to 1,610 by 1899, and to 2,600 by 1909.[5] With larger circulations and more revenues, editors began envisioning larger roles for themselves that went beyond reporting the news to doing investigative reporting, commentary, and analysis. Similarly, magazines with national circulations paid thousands of dollars to authors who wrote exposés of abuses of power in both the public and private sectors. The captains of industry provided convenient targets for which writers could gain a sympathetic readership. Thus, public opinion was turned toward an ideology that favored government control of the abuses and excesses of concentrated economic power.

---

5. Richard Hofstadter, *The Age of Reform: From Bryan to F.D.R.* (New York: Alfred A. Knopf, 1969), 187.

Regulation of Economic Power

During the first half of the nineteenth century, the trend was to reduce government intervention into private economic activity. A reversal of that trend, toward more government intervention in the economy, came with Progressivism. Big changes occurred in areas where industrialization was having big impacts. In the watershed case of *Munn v. Illinois* (1877), the Supreme Court decided that the State of Illinois could regulate private grain elevator rates.[6] The case was important because for the first time the Court declared that it was legal for the government to set the terms of a private exchange between two individuals. The demand for regulation came from the expansion of the railroads and the resulting power that it gave to grain elevator operators over farmers from whom they bought grain. From that point forward, it was a relatively modest extension of the principle to create the Interstate Commerce Commission in 1887 to regulate railroads more generally.

The Sherman Act of 1890, the nation's (and world's) first antitrust law, was intended to prevent the abuses of monopolies by giving the government the power to break them up into smaller competing companies, and such enforcement authority expanded in scope as the years went by. The Clayton Act, passed in 1914, enhanced the scope of antitrust action not just to existing monopoly power but to the prevention of actions that could lead to future monopoly power. In 1903, the Department of Commerce was created at the urging of President Roosevelt and contained a Bureau of Corporations, which helped Roosevelt earn his reputation as a trustbuster. The Bureau of Corporations increasingly gained influence as an antibusiness bureaucracy and laid the groundwork for the government's antitrust suit that broke up Standard Oil a decade later. It continued in existence until 1914, when it was superseded by the Federal Trade Commission. The Pure Food and Drug Act was passed in 1906, eventually leading to the creation of the Food and Drug Administration in 1938. All bureaus clearly were aimed at regulating the market economy and controlling the economic power of the new captains of American industry.[7]

---

6. Terry L. Anderson and Peter J. Hill, *The Birth of a Transfer Society* (Stanford, CA: Hoover Institution Press, 1980).

7. Lewis L. Gould, *Reform and Regulation: American Politics from Roosevelt to Wilson*, 2nd ed. (New York: Alfred A. Knopf, 1986).

Progressives believed that their push to expand the role of government to protect the economic interests of its citizens was necessary because of the expansion of concentrated economic power. When the nation was founded, individuals could deal with each other under a situation of relative equality, but with the rise of corporations, because of both their size and their monopolization of certain markets, people could no longer deal with them as equals. The concentrated economic power of corporations required more power concentrated in the hands of the general public (i.e., the federal government) to maintain the balance. In Jefferson's time, the tyranny of government was the largest threat to individual freedom, but the Progressives believed that, a century later, Americans were more threatened by economic power than by political power.

The Civil Service

Civil Service reform was integral to the Progressive movement. Jackson brought the spoils system to federal civil service without apology, arguing the merits of turnover in civil service jobs. By the late 1800s, however, other nations were undertaking civil service reform, and the general idea was that better personnel management practices, already proving themselves in business, could also be applied to government. In addition, blatant political favoritism was the frequent target of political attack, prompting reform as a defensive measure. Reform began in the late 1870s in the New York Customhouse, to which Theodore Roosevelt had been appointed and which was the largest source of federal revenues by far in the days before the income tax. Increasingly, jobs began being awarded on merit rather than as political favors, culminating in the Pendleton Civil Service Act of 1883. The Pendleton Act codified the merit system and also outlawed the requirement of compulsory political contributions from federal workers (although voluntary contributions were still allowed). The act also prevented government workers from soliciting political contributions on government property (although it placed no restrictions on their activities elsewhere).

The spoils system was not eliminated altogether. In 1884, only 11 percent of federal jobs required civil service examinations for appointment, but by 1900, 46 percent were covered by civil service guidelines. This left ample room for continued political patronage but at the same time built a base of permanent civil service employees who were more insulated from the political process. Theodore Roosevelt was a leader of the reform effort. In 1889, he was appointed to the Civil Service Commission by the newly elected president Benjamin Harrison, where he pushed for changes, and after his ascendency to the presidency in 1901 he actively shifted federal jobs from patronage to merit appointment. When the process of civil service reform began in the late 1870s, the federal government was relatively limited in scope, making its impact felt most heavily in customs and postal workers, but it laid the foundation for a civil service more independent of the current administration by the beginning of the twentieth century, when the federal government was poised for rapid expansion.

The need for civil service reform in the Progressive agenda was apparent. If the government was to expand its role to look out for the economic well-being of its citizens, the government workforce had to be free of the influence of special-interest groups that were politically connected to the current administration. The problems that potentially could arise otherwise already were apparent in the way Republican administrations had catered to veterans' interests after the War Between the States. Union vets who were disabled as they fought to defend the Union obviously were deserving of both sympathy and support, but patronage and the political power of their interests transformed veterans' pensions from payments to deserving individuals into a wholesale transfer program that was criticized widely by both Republicans and Democrats. If the federal government was really to get more involved in the economic welfare of its citizens—which was a controversial idea in the late 1800s—it would have to find a way to insulate government programs from politics, and civil service reform was viewed as the key.

Progressivism brought with it a complete transformation in the relationship between federal employees and their employer. The spoils system of political patronage evolved into a professional bureaucracy, chosen by merit and given job security beyond the tenure of the current administration. The professional interests of civil servants evolved from being completely tied up in the success of the current administration to being a function of the funding available to the federal government generally and their own agencies specifically. As a result, civil servants became more interested in the budget allocations of their own agencies, because their personal interests became more congruent with their agencies' budgets. Thus, civil service became another interest group with a personal economic stake in larger government. The change in the incentive structure is a result of the creation of a federal bureaucracy largely independent of the elected officials who nominally run the government.

Interest Groups and Progressivism

Progressivism explicitly extended public policy not only to protect the rights of citizens but also to enhance their economic well-being. Under the old ideology, it obviously was inappropriate for one group to seek economic benefits at the expense of others, but Progressivism meant using the government to enhance people's economic well-being and sometimes that would mean providing some people with economic benefits at the expense of others. The regulation of railroads and antitrust legislation clearly were targeted at enhancing economic opportunities for some at the expense of others. These measures undoubtedly seemed fair to most people because the intended beneficiaries were far more numerous than the few industrialists who held and wielded the concentrated economic power that ostensibly was the target of such legislation. This is the way democracy in its purest form works. The majority has more political clout than the minority.

The Founders intended for constitutional constraints to keep this type of democracy from determining public policy, but even without constitutional constraints democratic institutions do not always favor the side with the greatest numbers. Although the influence of special interests was well known in the late 1800s, the extent to which interest groups influenced public policy shocked the general public when a series of newspaper articles on lobbying appeared in the *New York World* in 1913.[8] Professional lobbying at that time was an "open secret," but it was secret no more when a former lobbyist discussed how he had been paid by the National Association of Manufacturers to lobby on their behalf. The general public was outraged, but a number of senators denied any knowledge of lobbying. Constituents, including businesses, had always argued their interests, but the idea that a third party would lobby solely

---

8. Grant McConnell, *Private Power and American Democracy* (New York: Alfred A. Knopf, 1966).

for financial gain, much as lawyers make the best arguments for their clients, was quite disturbing. Times change, however, and in the twenty-first century lobbying is considered integral to the political process.

One might question what the role of interest groups ought to be under a Progressive government. Government provision of economic benefits steps well beyond the ideology of liberty but appears quite consistent with the ideology of Progressivism, and in a democratic government it may be that the best way to discover the economic interests of citizens is to let them state their cases directly, or to hire professionals to state those cases for them. If public policy is intended to enhance the economic well-being of the nation's citizens, interest-group politics, which so concerned James Madison and the other Founding Fathers, would seem to be a part of a new set of institutions that would replace outmoded Jeffersonian ideals. One apparent problem is that often it is those with economic power who have the resources available to lobby effectively for benefits, so the interests who actually do receive economic benefits from government may not be those whom the Progressives had in mind. It is unlikely that such outrage would have been stirred in 1913 if it had been agricultural interests rather than the National Association of Manufacturers who had hired lobbyists.

Progressivism and Democracy

Progressivism and democracy are not the same things, and democracy does not necessarily further Progressivism because democratic decision-making too often furthers narrow special interests rather than the general public interest. Progressives favored more democratic oversight of the government, not as a method for furthering the will of the majority but as a method of providing oversight to prevent politicians from using their power to further the interests of those who already had economic power. Without democratic oversight, Progressives feared that those who had economic power would be able to buy government support of their agendas, and experience had borne them out. If they wanted the government to be more active in furthering the economic well-being of the general public, they believed that government officials would have to be accountable to the general public.

As events unfolded, however, democracy supplanted Progressivism as the political ideology that survived the twentieth century, at least partly because of Progressive support. Herbert Croly, a prominent Progressive writer, argued that Progressivism implied a strong role for the president. He likened presidential elections to referendums of popular opinion and argued that strong executive leadership is necessary to implement Progressive policy. Croly viewed the president as more than just a passive conduit of public opinion, however, and saw the president's role at least partly as that of an opinion maker.[9] Democracy was an integral part of the Progressive ideology and together with the notion that the government should work to further the economic well-being of its citizens hastened the transition of American ideology from liberty to democracy.

Democracy cannot lay claim to being the foundation for an ideology in the same way that liberty and Progressivism can. The idea of liberty places the protection of the rights of individuals at the foundation of government, and the idea of Progressivism places the protection of the economic well-being of individuals at the foundation. Democracy, by itself, means abiding by the will of the majority but offers no indication regarding what type of public policy the majority might favor. Progressives favored more democratic oversight of government as a means to control a government that would have more power and more discretion, but they did not believe that appropriate public policy was whatever the majority wanted. Indeed, Progressivism had clear ideas about what types of public policies were appropriate to the political and economic realities at the beginning of the twentieth century. Yet by the end of the twentieth century, Progressive ideas had faded into the background. Progressivism clearly was evident in Lyndon Johnson's Great Society, but had slipped from view during the Reagan revolution and the moderate presidency of Bill Clinton. It reappeared in Barack Obama's presidency, but while the Progressive ideology has risen and fallen, the ideology of democracy—the idea that the role of government is to carry out the will of the people—has only strengthened.

---

9. Herbert Croly, *Progressive Democracy* (New York: Macmillan, 1915).

Congressional Committees and Government Growth

When the federal government was more limited in scope, Congress had a limited set of policy issues with which to deal, and the Senate rightfully could be called a deliberative body. As the scope of the federal government expanded throughout the nineteenth century, more business needed to be taken care of and, consequently, there was less time for thoughtful deliberation. The problem was exacerbated by the growth of the committee system. Rather than Congress dealing with issues as a whole, matters increasingly began being delegated to specialized committees. While bills reported out of various committees could be amended, the job of the entire body became more one of evaluating the work of committees rather than undertaking legislation as a whole group.

The rise of the committee system had the effect of reducing the efficiency and accountability of legislation passed in Congress for several reasons. First, it allowed members to sort themselves into committees in such a way that they could find seats on committees overseeing areas for which their constituents had strong interests and they themselves had a high demand for government intervention (e.g., members from farm states want to be on committees responsible for agricultural policy). Bills that emerged from committee would then likely call for more government intervention than the median member of Congress would prefer, but as the system was designed, the body was placed in an all-or-nothing situation, where it could either take the bill as designed by the committee or reject it and hope for something better next time. In this situation, Congress would be likely to settle for something a little more interventionist from the committee than if the whole body had drawn up the legislation together.

A second factor is that because proposed legislation is coming from a committee, which contains only a minority of the members of the entire chamber, but requires majority support to become law, committee members can engage in vote trading to get legislation they like passed. "I'll vote for your bill if you'll vote for mine." Such "compromise" is the way legislation gets passed, and because legislators are likely to be more strongly in support of legislation that gives them benefits than they will be opposed to legislation that gives benefits to someone else, the result is that through vote trading a series of bills can pass into law as a group when no one individual bill could get the support of a majority by itself. Again, bigger government is the result. One of the causes of the growth of the federal government has been the growth of the committee system.

The committee system had another effect, which was to lessen the influence of third-party members of Congress. When Congress made more decisions as a whole, and was more of a deliberative body, every member would have a chance to become a part of the debate on legislation and to have an influence on the outcome. The committee system passed more control to party leaders, who could determine who served on and chaired committees. As a result, members of third parties saw their influence dwindle in Congress. Members of third parties have been relatively rare in the twentieth and twenty-first centuries, but from 1890 to 1900 the People's Party elected 39 members to the House of Representatives, who served a total of 58 terms. They also elected nine senators. Their influence was limited, however, because of the dominance of the Republicans and Democrats.

One advantage that the Republicans had in establishing themselves as a national party prior to the War Between the States was that because the committee system was not developed at that time, Republican senators and representatives could play a prominent role in national politics. Representatives from third parties could not enjoy that same prominence under the current system, because congressional work is dominated by committees.

Conclusion

The Founders attempted to preserve liberty by creating a government with strict constitutional limits on its activities. If the limits the Founders had envisioned had survived until the end of the nineteenth century, Progressive public policy would not have been possible because the Constitution would have prevented it. The issues go back to the nation's earliest days, when Jefferson ran for the presidency in 1800 in opposition to Hamilton's vision of a federal government with a broader scope of activities. Jackson again raised the issue, running as a Jeffersonian trying to rein in the expansion of the federal government.

Changes in the role of the federal government were slight in the first half of the nineteenth century but accelerated later on and have continued to do so. The federal government's relationship to the states was changed irrevocably by the War Between the States. Reconstruction created a precedent for the federal government to direct the activities of state governments when they conflicted with federal policy, and the rise of interest-group activity at the federal level after the war created the expectation that interest groups could hope to receive economic benefits from the federal government at the expense of other groups, and from taxpayers in general.

As the role of the federal government evolved, giving it the ability to exercise more power, the nation's economy also evolved, producing concentrated economic power that created a demand for more government control of the economy. That demand arose from farmers, who wanted protection from the economic power of the railroads, the grain elevators, and the firms from whom they purchased manufactured goods. That demand arose from workers, who wanted protection from the monopoly power of their employers. That demand arose from small business people and professionals, who found their economic status increasingly threatened by big corporations. That demand also came from politicians, who found their political power threatened by the substantial economic power of those who ran big business. Thus, the Jeffersonian ideology of a government strictly limited to the protection of individual rights gave way to the Hamiltonian ideology of a more active federal government that could use its power to help secure the economic well-being of the nation's citizens.

Americans already were well aware of the political power that special interests could wield, and a more active government had to deal with the threat that its political power could be directed for the benefit of those who had economic power. Thus, Progressivism brought with it changes in the way the federal government was run. It created a more professional civil service, insulated to a large degree from the political pressures faced by elected officials, but not from the pressures exerted on it by well-organized special interests. Progressivism brought with it the federal income tax to finance government expansion. The income tax might be viewed as the means that allowed such substantial growth in government expenditures in the twentieth century, but it would be more accurate to see the income tax as the result of the Progressive demand for more government expenditures rather than the cause.

Progressivism also brought with it the ideology of democracy. The Founders intentionally provided a minor role for democratic input from America's citizens when they wrote the Constitution. The leaders of government should not be directly accountable to the citizenry, the Founders believed, and they designed a government in which only members of the House of Representatives, half of one of the three branches of government, would have to answer directly to the voters. This was done intentionally to allow citizens some check on the activities of government, but having the other five-sixths of government selected in a different manner was also adopted intentionally. Jackson's major challenge to the Founders' vision of the role of democracy was echoed by the Populists and the Progressives, who saw accountability to the electorate as the best way to give the power of government to its citizens, rather than vesting it in a handful of elites.

The enhanced role of voters in American democracy makes sense in the context of the Progressive agenda. When the government's role is limited to protecting the rights of individuals, democratic input from the masses is not necessary and perhaps counterproductive because it threatens liberty. Rather, to the extent that it is used, democracy is a means to an end—a way to select the people who carry on the business of government and to remove them from office if they prove incompetent. When the role of government is expanded to furthering the economic interests of the population, democratic representation becomes crucial. Even at the beginning of the Progressive movement, the economic interests of some were pitted against the economic interests of others through the institution of economic regulation, and if citizens are to have any hope that the government will choose to further their interests they must have power over those in government. The idea that government could further the economic well-being of special-interest groups already was clear, and citizens needed a way to ensure that the government would further their interests, not somebody else's. Political incentives imply that government will look out for the interests of those to whom it is accountable.

In the Progressive Era, where the common vision was that big business stood against the common man, democracy meant that people would be represented in proportion to their numbers rather than their wealth. Thus, democracy, which served a limited role in the government that the Founders had envisioned, became an indispensable part of Progressive government. Concerning economic interests, the lines were not as clearly drawn at the beginning of the twenty-first century as they were at the beginning of the twentieth. Contrast the popularity of Bill Gates, the world's wealthiest man at the beginning of the twenty-first century, with the unpopularity of John D. Rockefeller, the world's wealthiest man a century earlier. The ideals of Progressivism have lost some of their focus, replaced by the concept of democracy as the fundamental principle underlying American government. At the same time, democracy has evolved from a method for making group decisions to a method for allocating economic resources. Public policy increasingly means providing economic benefits to some individuals and groups at the expense of others, and who gives and who gets is determined by majority rule. At the beginning of the twenty-first century public policy is guided by popular opinion rather than by principle, and the general public accepts the idea that a government policy is legitimate if most people are in favor of it. This is the lasting legacy of Progressivism.

9

The Growth of the
Federal Government in the 1920s

THE GROWTH IN federal government expenditures in the
United States began in the early twentieth century. In 1913, just prior to World
War I, federal government expenditures represented 2.5 percent of gross national product (GNP), but by 1990 that figure had risen to 22.5 percent, and it
hit 24.4 percent in 2009. The relatively small size of federal expenditures prior
to World War I shows that they exhibited minimal growth in the nineteenth
century, in stark contrast with the tremendous growth in the twentieth century. Looking at expenditures alone presents an incomplete picture of federal
government growth in the nineteenth century because of the federal government's wider scope of regulatory power and because of its greater power over
the state governments. But while the scope of the federal government expanded
throughout the nineteenth century, the growth of federal expenditures was
limited by revenue constraints. The passage of the Sixteenth Amendment,
allowing the creation of a federal income tax, was a response to the demand
for a larger federal government, and the figures cited at the beginning of this
paragraph show the dramatic result.

The decade of the 1920s deserves special attention as a part of the history
of the growth of the federal government for two reasons. First, government
expenditure growth in the 1920s was less than in any subsequent decade, so
any light shed on the growth of government in the 1920s can help illuminate
the entire process of government growth. Second, the decade of the 1920s
falls between two well-known eras of government growth: the Progressive
Era prior to World War I and the New Deal of the 1930s. One is tempted to
view the 1920s as an era of government retrenchment that, perhaps, would

have produced a repeat of the nineteenth century had it not been for the Great Depression and the New Deal.[1]

The presidents of the 1920s—Harding, Coolidge, and Hoover—often viewed as proponents of limited government, were considerably more sympathetic toward the growth of government programs and expenditures than general opinion suggests. Popular opinion often credits (or blames) Franklin Delano Roosevelt's New Deal for the major increase in federal government growth. The foundations of the New Deal go back to the 1920s and before, and Roosevelt's initiatives were not a crucial turning point in the growth of American government. As an extension of the trends begun during the Progressive Era, the 1920s is not a key decade in the growth of American government, but understanding the government growth of the 1920s is a key element in understanding the process of growth during the twentieth century.

The Administrations of Harding, Coolidge, and Hoover

At first glance, it might appear that the three Republican administrations of the 1920s, sandwiched in between the Democratic administrations of Woodrow Wilson (1913–1921) and Franklin Delano Roosevelt (FDR) (1933–1945), brought with them a period of conservatism, in much the same way that Reagan's election in 1980 might be viewed as a reaction against the expansion of government in the 1960s and 1970s. However, before FDR's administration, the Republicans were the party of government activism and the Democrats the party of conservatism, which weakens the analogy. Furthermore, except for Wilson's election, which was the result of a temporary fracture of the Republican Party into Republicans and Progressives, the Republicans, along with Republican ideas, had dominated the White House since Lincoln's election in 1860. After Lincoln's presidency, Wilson and Grover Cleveland were the only Democrats to hold the presidency until FDR. The ideas of Progressivism, found mostly in the Republican Party, provided the intellectual foundation for the substantial growth of twentieth-century American government.

---

1. This chapter draws heavily on Randall G. Holcombe, "The Growth of the Federal Government in the 1920s," *Cato Journal* 16, no. 2 (Fall 1996): 175–99.

Another factor relevant to the political environment in the 1920s was the balance of power between the president and Congress. During World War I, the balance of power tipped considerably toward the presidency, but the 1920s brought less power to the presidency and more power to the Republican-dominated Congress. After the 1920 elections, Republicans held majorities of 303 to 131 seats in the House and 60 to 36 in the Senate, and, particularly when compared to the previous two decades, the political agenda was controlled more by Congress than by the presidency.[2]

Without strong presidential leadership or an aggressive presidential agenda, political initiatives from Congress became more oriented toward special-interest programs that generated economic benefits for clearly identified groups, which involved an expansion of governmental scope and power. While some war-oriented programs were eliminated after the Armistice was signed, many were not, and the orientation of federal government activities changed substantially. The scope of government, which expanded substantially during the Progressive Era and World War I, continued expanding in the 1920s. A look at the details shows that it was not a period of retrenchment or even stabilized government activity.

The theme of the Harding administration was a return to normalcy, which must have sounded especially desirable after World War I. This theme was adopted immediately by Calvin Coolidge after Warren Harding's death in 1923. One feature of this return, and an indicator of the conservatism of the Harding and Coolidge administrations, was the slashing of income tax rates, which provoked considerable congressional debate. When the federal income tax was established in 1913, the highest marginal tax rate was 7 percent and applied to one taxpayer only (John D. Rockefeller Sr.), but it rose to 77 percent in 1916 to help finance the war. The top rate was reduced to as low as 25 percent in 1925, which was still substantially higher than the 7 percent prewar rate, and the income levels that defined the brackets also were lowered substantially from their prewar levels. The "normalcy" of the 1920s incorporated considerably higher levels of federal spending and taxes than those of the Progressive Era prior to World War I.

---

2. Robert K. Murray, *The Politics of Normalcy: Government in Theory and Practice in the Harding-Coolidge Era* (New York: W. W. Norton, 1973), discusses the balance of power between the president and Congress at this time.

The Progressive movement and the Progressive Party remained vital throughout the 1920s, the difference being that the Republicans had been able to regain the support of the Progressives. In 1924, the Progressive Party ran Robert LaFollette, a Republican senator from Wisconsin, as its presidential candidate, who gained a respectable 13 percent of the popular vote. Despite the three-way race, Coolidge still won a 54-percent majority, which contrasts sharply with the 1912 election, in which the Progressive Party split the Republican vote, leading to the defeat of Republican incumbent William Howard Taft as Theodore Roosevelt pulled votes away from Taft. Normalcy, in the Harding-Coolidge sense, meant peace and prosperity, but it also meant a continuation of the principles of Progressivism, which enabled the Republican Party to regain the support of its Progressive element.

Despite the popular view of the 1920s as a retreat from Progressivism, by any measure the federal government was more firmly entrenched as a part of the American economy in 1925 than in 1915 and was continuing to grow. Harding and Coolidge were viewed as pro-business, and there may be a tendency to equate this pro-business sentiment with anti-Progressivism. The advance of Progressivism during their two administrations may have been slower than before the war or during the New Deal, but a slower advance is not a retreat.

The Hoover administration, from 1929 to 1933, must be analyzed differently because of the onset of the Great Depression. Compared to his immediate predecessors, though, it is much easier to make the case that Hoover was an active supporter of greater government intervention into the economy. Hoover served under Wilson as head of the United States Food Administration, beginning in 1917, and throughout the Harding-Coolidge presidencies, he served as Secretary of Commerce and was the most active cabinet member in pursuing more expansive governmental involvement in the private economy. During Hoover's presidency, real per capita federal expenditures rose by 88 percent. Under FDR's administration, from 1933 to 1940, just prior to World War II, they increased only by 74 percent. Although Hoover started from a smaller baseline, in percentage terms expenditures under Hoover increased more in four years than they did during the next seven New Deal years. If a case can be made that federal policies under the Harding and Coolidge administrations represented a solidification and extension of Progressive principles, the case is made more easily for Hoover's administration.

The Growth in Federal Spending

Federal government expenditures during the 1920s were substantially higher than they were prior to World War I. Per capita expenditures were $95 in 1915 (measured in constant 1990 dollars) and, after ratcheting up to $1,330 in 1919, fell to a low of $181 in 1927. The "normalcy" of the Harding-Coolidge years brought with it expenditures exceeding their prewar levels by a substantial margin. By 1933, when Hoover left office, federal expenditures had risen to $368 per person, roughly doubling since 1927. Those figures show that, first, federal expenditures were much higher during the 1920s than during the Progressive Era prior to World War I and, second, that the conventional wisdom of Hoover standing idly by as the nation plunged into the Great Depression is not correct. Hoover increased government spending rapidly in response to the economic downturn, just as Keynesian economists a decade later argued was the appropriate budgetary response. And, given the level of expenditures throughout the 1920s, compared to prior to the war, the 1920s cannot be characterized as a lull in federal government growth. Federal expenditures per person had doubled in a decade.

The details of the federal budget reveal that some areas of the budget saw substantial increases during the 1920s.[3] Law enforcement expenditures were almost five times larger in 1930 as they had been in 1920, largely related to Prohibition. Agricultural spending grew at an annual average rate of 11.4% in the 1920s. Immigration and naturalization expenditures more than tripled, partly representing greater selectivity in admitting immigrants. Immigration was down sharply in 1915 owing to World War I, and legislation passed in 1917 restricted immigration after the war. In 1924, immigration quotas were established for the first time, further adding to spending on immigration and naturalization.

Federal expenditures on public education also increased substantially during the 1920s, funding programs such as land-grant colleges and federal subsidies for vocational education. Two features of educational expenditures are relevant to the consideration of federal growth in the 1920s. First, education, which even in the early twenty-first century normally would be considered

---

3. The data are analyzed in some detail by Carroll H. Woddy, *The Growth of the Federal Government: 1915–1932* (New York: McGraw-Hill, 1934).

to be an activity undertaken primarily by the states, witnessed considerable and rapidly growing federal involvement in the 1920s. Second, much of the federal government's expenditures were in the form of grants to the states, leading to more federal financing and more federal control in areas traditionally administered by state governments.

The Department of Commerce, headed by Herbert Hoover through the Harding and Coolidge administrations, witnessed a remarkable 13 percent average annual growth rate throughout the 1920s, more than tripling in size. By 1930, about one-third of federal commerce expenditures were allocated to aviation, but that still leaves a substantial fraction of the budget for non-aviation-related activities. The expenditures of the Patent Office increased substantially, as did those for the Bureau of Foreign and Domestic Commerce, which had as one of its main goals the promotion of sales of American goods to foreign purchasers. Expenditures more than doubled for the Radio Commission (the Federal Communication Commission's precursor) and for the Tariff Commission. Those spending increases simply may reflect the growth of commerce during that prosperous decade, but recalling that Herbert Hoover was Secretary of Commerce lends some insight into Hoover's vision of government that is apt for evaluating his presidential administration.

Overall, federal spending looks relatively flat during the 1920s, but aggregate spending is misleading because the 1920s saw a major winding down of World War I–related expenditures. Looking at the details of federal expenditures reveals that the decline in war-related spending masked major increases in domestic spending. Far from representing a retreat from Progressivism, the 1920s extended the now-established Progressive ideology.

Government-Owned Corporations

One of the methods by which the federal government expanded beyond its traditional bounds in the twentieth century was by way of the establishment of government-owned corporations. The first wholly owned federal corporation was the Bank of the United States, chartered by an act of Congress in 1791. But after the charter of the Second Bank of the United States expired in 1836, another federally owned corporation was not formed until 1904, to build the Panama Canal.

The next federally owned corporation was the Merchant Fleet Corporation, established in 1917 as a part of the war effort. The Merchant Fleet Corporation remained in business throughout the Great Depression, losing a phenomenal amount of money over the 1920s. Throughout the 1920s, protests from Members of Congress charged that the corporation was being run inefficiently, was unnecessary, and was a government-subsidized competitor to privately owned US shippers. The corporation nevertheless remained in business.

Also in 1917, the Food Administration Grain Corporation was established to help finance the sale of American wheat to Europe and pushed the frontiers of public corporations because its purpose was to aid private businesses (in this case, farms) in selling their products, although admittedly in a manner connected to the war effort. In 1918, the War Finance Corporation was established to help key industries borrow funds and thereby pushed the frontiers even further. The War Finance Corporation aided businesses more generally, and, in 1921, well after the war, its charter was extended so that it could undertake more general types of lending activity, including the making of agricultural loans. The War Finance Corporation continued in business until the end of 1931.

Federally owned corporations, a rarity only a few years beforehand, began to proliferate in the late 1910s. The Federal Land Bank was established in 1917, and the Sugar Equalization Board, the United States Housing Corporation, and the Spruce Production Corporation were created in 1918. The war effort provided some impetus to those corporations, although many had tenuous connections to the war. World War I ended in 1918. If the corporations truly were intended to help win World War I, they could have been dismantled afterwards, but they persisted and supplied models for government growth that continued in the 1920s.

In 1923, the Agricultural Credits Act created twelve federally-owned banks to make agricultural loans. The Inland Waterways Corporation was created in 1924 to operate boats and barges on the Mississippi River. In 1929, the Federal Farm Board was established to support the prices of agricultural products above market-determined levels. The use of public corporations to further the federal government's goals did not begin during World War I, but the late 1910s were transition years during which the government created more federally owned corporations than had been created previously. For the most part, they were not dismantled after the war, but rather remained in business and became models for additional federally owned corporations established in the 1920s.

The goals of those corporations are significant. They were not formed to enhance national security or to protect the rights of individuals, but to provide economic assistance to a subset of the US population. The programs were small in scale when compared to the New Deal, but they were large in comparison to federal programs before World War I. They were built on the philosophy that the federal government has a direct role to play in enhancing the economic well-being of its citizens. The New Deal changed the scale of federal programs relative to those of the 1920s but did not transform their underlying philosophies.

The Post Office

The establishment of post offices and post roads is one of the activities of the federal government explicitly authorized by the Constitution. By charging for its services, the Post Office has been able to operate in a relatively businesslike manner, even though it was not, until recently, a publicly owned corporation. Through 1851, the Post Office operated under an implied balanced budget constraint, but legislation in 1851 specifically prevented the Post Office from cutting or eliminating any of its existing services, while encouraging its continued expansion. The 1850s marked the beginning of a postal policy designed to keep rates low, which it was able to do thanks to the backing of the US Treasury.[4]

While postal budget deficits were not uncommon, in the years prior to World War I, the Post Office was able roughly to balance its budget and during the war years even reported a substantial surplus. The apparent financial success of the Post Office during the war years was bolstered by two factors. First, much mail was carried by the military during the war, and, second, postal rates rose during the war. But military assistance in carrying the mail never reduced the Post Office's expenditures. In 1915, the Post Office spent $299 million, and with increases every year, expenditures were $454 million in

<hr>

4. Clyde Kelly, *United States Postal Policy* (New York: D. Appleton, 1932).

1920. Despite some cost advantages owing to the war, the Post Office delivered all mail of military personnel without postage and added to its responsibilities by selling war-savings certificates in 1917. More than 80 percent of these war-savings certificates were sold through the Post Office.

In the Wilson administration, Postmaster General Albert Burleson, appointed in 1913, ruled the Post Office with a heavy hand, trying to do away with labor unions and to increase the efficiency of the Post Office by controlling costs. Burleson's explicit goal was to have the Post Office operate at a surplus, and he succeeded. In 1917, postage for first-class mail increased to 3 cents and for post cards to 2 cents, which added to Post Office revenues. In 1919, however, those postage increases were rescinded, creating substantial losses for the Post Office.

Postmaster Burleson was not popular with postal employees. After being elected, Harding appointed several postmasters general, all of whom were considerably more sympathetic to postal employees than Burleson. But under Harding, postal expenditures rose tremendously. Expenditures of $454 million in 1920 were followed by expenditures of $621 in 1921, and a huge postal deficit. While expenditures fell back to $546 million in 1922, they were still 20 percent larger than two years earlier; the Post Office reported a budget deficit every year after 1919, when rates were lowered to prewar levels.

Despite lower postage rates, in 1920 the salaries of letter carriers were raised from $1,400 a year to $1,800 and were raised again in 1924 to $2,100. Harding's first Postmaster General, Will H. Hayes, stated explicitly that the Post Office did not exist to make a profit but rather provided a service. Furthermore, Hayes wanted to "humanize" the postal industry, arguing that labor is not a commodity, which was a very Progressive sentiment. The result not only was higher wages, but an expansion in the Post Office's role. It expanded rural free delivery and established more city delivery offices. The Post Office also issued many more money orders and expanded its sales of savings bonds, an activity that began in 1917 and continued through 1931. Postal deficits in the 1920s are explained by the expansion of postal services and the provision of many services either without charge or considerably below cost, in addition to higher postal wages.

The deficits of the 1920s might be looked at as a return to the idea that because of its service to the public, postal deficits should not be considered objectionable. However, that sentiment stands in stark contrast to Postmaster Burleson's ideas, which were more in line with the contemporary vision of limited government and bureaucratic accountability and had been the status quo for eight years under the Democratic Wilson's administration. If the Harding-Coolidge administration was a return to limited government, it could have continued Wilson's businesslike stance. The Post Office under the Harding-Coolidge administration, however, shows a turn away from the conservative principles of the Wilson administration and a return to the Progressivism that preceded it.

Prohibition

Prohibition corresponds exactly with the Republican administrations of Harding, Coolidge, and Hoover. After the passage of the Eighteenth Amendment to the Constitution, Prohibition became effective in 1920 and continued until it was repealed in 1933 by the Twenty-First Amendment. While Prohibition itself predates the Harding administration slightly, its enforcement was a function of the executive branch of government. Prohibition's enforcement harkens to the Harrison Act of 1914, which regulated the use of narcotic drugs. Because taxes were supposed to be paid by the users of legal narcotics, compliance with the Harrison Act was delegated to the Bureau of Internal Revenue, housed within the Treasury Department. Because legal nonbeverage uses of alcohol (sacramental wines, for example) were allowable, the Bureau of Internal Revenue also was charged with enforcing Prohibition.

Expenditures to enforce Prohibition extended beyond the Bureau of Internal Revenue, because the Customs Service, the Coast Guard, and the Department of Justice also were involved. Federal law enforcement expenditures on Prohibition increased by more than 600 percent in the 1920s, more than quadrupling from 1920 to 1925, and then rising by more than 40 percent from 1925 to 1930. In 1920, a Prohibition Unit was established within the Bureau of Internal Revenue, and in 1927 a separate Bureau of Prohibition was created within the Treasury Department. The Treasury's Prohibition-related expenditures obviously were not intended to generate revenues. In no year did the Treasury Department collect more revenues from the enforcement of Prohibition than it expended in enforcement activities. By 1922, expenditures to enforce Prohibition were more than 50 percent higher than the revenues collected, and by 1930 expenditures were more than double revenues.[5]

The government's powers related to Prohibition expanded as rapidly as its spending; the creation of a separate Bureau of Prohibition was an initiative of the Coolidge administration to enforce Prohibition more effectively. That was yet another area in which the government expanded its powers during the 1920s, and it did so with the approval of the Coolidge administration.

Agriculture

In the 1920s the agricultural sector of the economy did not fare well, creating the impression of an agriculture versus industry antagonism and the impression that the Harding and Coolidge administrations favored industry over agriculture. Much of the blame for agricultural problems must be placed on greater worldwide production, which led to worldwide market gluts. The agricultural sector could have been allowed to adjust to market conditions, creating more transitory hardship among farmers, but such a laissez-faire public policy response was not in the political cards. With respect to governmental policy in the 1920s, higher tariffs on imported farm products were passed by Congress in 1921; the Capper-Volstead Act was passed in 1922, exempting agricultural cooperatives from the antitrust laws; and in 1926 the Division of Co-operative Marketing was set up in the Department of Agriculture with the warm endorsement of President Coolidge. The Agricultural Credits Act of 1923 made it easier for farmers to get loans immediately from the Federal Farm Loan Board.

Looking at the facts, one has to conclude that government intervention assisting the agricultural sector was significant in the 1920s, and in no case was any government protection or assistance to farmers repealed. But farmers wanted more than they got from Coolidge. After much debate and substantial controversy, the McNary-Haugen Bill passed in 1927, which would provide government support prices for agricultural commodities. Coolidge vetoed the bill, and it was rewritten and passed again the next year, but vetoed again by

---

5. Laurence F. Schmeckebier, *The Bureau of Prohibition: Its History, Activities, and Organization* (Washington, DC: Brookings Institution, 1929).

Coolidge. After Hoover's election, the Agricultural Marketing Act of 1929 was passed, creating a Federal Farm Board with the power to buy and store "any quantity" of agricultural commodities for the purpose of supporting prices.

The government did not treat farmers as generously as they wanted to be treated in the 1920s, but despite the "industry versus agriculture" impression that some historians have of the period, the 1920s saw no reversals of government policy to aid agriculture and new agricultural policies were enacted. The McNary-Haugen Bill, first introduced in 1924 might even represent the true beginning of the New Deal. Starting in 1924, legislation increasingly was designed to help control the economy and to support the economic interests of well-defined interest groups; farmers were major beneficiaries of those policy initiatives. In 1920, federal expenditures on agriculture amounted to approximately $17 million in 1930 prices and had increased by 193 percent (to $49 million) by 1930. Whether evaluated with regard to finances or programs, the 1920s saw considerable government growth in the agricultural sector and laid the foundation for more federal involvement that was to follow in the New Deal.

Antitrust

Expenditures are the easiest and most readily available measure of the size of government, but they only tell a part of the story of government growth. Government regulation also has a substantial impact but is harder to measure. Starting with the Sherman Act in 1890, the federal government began its antitrust activity supposedly to limit the economic power of businesses. Only 22 antitrust cases were brought before 1905, but the pace started picking up later in that decade, when 39 federal cases were filed between 1905 and 1909. From 1910 to 1919, a total of 134 cases were launched, representing more vigorous federal antitrust law enforcement efforts. Little slowdown in law enforcement efforts materialized in the 1920s, which saw a total of 125 cases instituted.[6]

One might anticipate, after an increase in the number of antitrust complaints issued, that firms would be more cautious in their business practices

---

6. Statistics from Richard A. Posner, "A Statistical Study of Antitrust Enforcement," *Journal of Law & Economics* 13, no. 2 (October 1970): 365–419.

to avoid antitrust cases being brought against them, but in the 1920s a large proportion of antitrust cases were brought against industries not normally regarded as being highly concentrated, which accounted for the steady stream of new cases. Antitrust enforcement in the 1920s was vigorous and increasingly broad in scope. That represents another dimension along which the federal government was flexing its muscles during the 1920s, despite the conventional wisdom of that decade as friendly to business.

Academic Influences

In a famous passage in his 1936 book, *The General Theory of Employment, Interest, and Money*, John Maynard Keynes remarked that "the ideas of economists and political philosophers, both when they are right and when they are wrong, are more powerful than is commonly understood. Indeed, the world is ruled by little else."[7] Reinforcing the ideas of Progressivism, the academic concept of scientific management was gaining currency in the early twentieth century and fostered interfaces between academic institutions and public policy. The creation of the National Bureau of Economic Research (NBER), which owes its origins to the Progressive technocratic reform movement that wanted to use government to improve the economy's ability to produce and distribute income, was one manifestation of an expanding influence of academic institutions on government.

With private funding and support from both public and private sectors, the NBER was established in 1920 with Wesley Clair Mitchell as its first director. Mitchell's goal was "to organize the bureau's research program around questions that were, first, of primary social importance, and second, capable of the statistical resolution needed to surmount social science's internal crisis of scientific legitimacy."[8] The NBER worked closely with the Department of Commerce and Secretary Hoover, who was very interested in making the government more actively involved in economic policymaking. Indeed, many of the Keynesian ideas of the 1930s were a part of the accepted wisdom of

---

7. John Maynard Keynes, *The General Theory of Employment, Interest, and Money* (New York: Harcourt, Brace, 1936), 383.

8. Guy Alchon, *The Invisible Hand of Planning: Capitalism, Social Science, and the State in the 1920s* (Princeton, NJ: Princeton University Press, 1985), 59.

American economists in the 1920s. The 1920s saw an alliance of academic institutions, private foundations, and government to create organizations like the NBER to further the scientific aspects of social science and provide data and ideas for government management of the economy.

Conclusion

The 1920s, falling between the Progressive Era and the New Deal and directly following World War I, may appear to be a decade of stable government sandwiched between major episodes of governmental growth. In a limited sense, that is true. Government expenditures were declining dramatically from their peak levels during the war, and Calvin Coolidge, president during most of the decade, was not acting aggressively to expand government. But in other ways the 1920s was a decade of increasing government activity—in expenditures, in regulation, and in attitude—as the federal government increasingly was willing to expand its role in the economic lives of its citizens. Indeed, the foundation of the New Deal was established in the programs of the 1920s, and it certainly would be wrong to conclude that were it not for the New Deal, government would have remained more confined later in the twentieth century. The New Deal really was an extension of the type of government growth that occurred in the 1920s.

Were it not for the Depression, government growth would have been slower in the 1930s, because it would not have been called upon to respond to a national economic crisis. But the government expanded its programs, its powers, and its budget during the 1920s, in the relatively passive presidential administration of Calvin Coolidge, which was consistent with the trend in government growth that had begun with the Progressive Era around the turn of the century. If the trends of the 1920s had continued, federal government growth would have been substantial with or without the Great Depression and with or without the New Deal. For Coolidge, being pro-business did not mean being antigovernment (or antilabor, or anti-agriculture), and he supported the expansion of government in almost every area, although not to the degree desired by some of his critics.

The seeds of government growth were sown in the Progressive Era prior to World War I, and the 1920s served to reinforce the principles of government established during the Progressive Era by continuing to expand the government's reach. The 1920s did not represent a plateau in government activity that was reversed by the New Deal; rather, the foundations of the New Deal were laid by the ever-expanding scope of federal government activity during the 1920s.

Well prior to the New Deal, several trends clearly were apparent in the evolution of American government. The most obvious—because it is the most easily quantified—was the growth in government expenditures. That expenditure growth was accompanied by growth in government regulatory activities and by a transition toward transfers of income, which were viewed as an illegitimate activity for government as late as the 1890s but were viewed as an integral part of the activities of a Progressive government by the early twentieth century. Government growth also brought with it greater centralization, as the federal government became more significant relative to state and local governments. Along with government growth came the snowballing democratization of government. The Progressive Era marks a turning point, as the fundamental principle directing public policy evolved from protecting individual liberty to furthering the will of the voting majority. Greater reliance on democracy as a guide to rights and to economic resource allocation supported the New Deal, but clearly predated it.

Prior to the Progressive Era, democracy was a method of political decision-making, but the limited government of the time had relatively little impact on people's economic affairs. In contrast, such policies as government regulation of business, antitrust laws that actually could force individuals to divest themselves of their property, higher taxes, and explicit transfer programs such as farm subsidies, were chosen democratically so as to replace market-based allocations of economic resources with politically determined ones. Democracy had evolved from a political decision-making process into one that would influence private market orderings decisively. That transformation predates the New Deal; the history of the 1920s shows that even in a period of relative normalcy the transformation continued to take place. The 1920s was a decade of growing government, in which government policy increasingly was determined by democracy rather than by the nation's founding bedrock principle of protecting individual liberty. It was a decade in which democracy increasingly became an integral part of the nation's economic system as well as of its political system.

IO

The New Deal and World War II

ONE OF THE TRADE-OFFS involved in the design of government is between consensus in collective decision-making and the scope of governmental activity. Because arriving at a consensus is costly and time-consuming, expansions in the size and scope of government typically bring with them a movement away from consensus, allowing government to act with less agreement and citizen approval. American constitutional history has seen continuous movement away from consensus in collective decision-making. The motivation for this movement away from consensus, toward majority rule, generally responded to a desire to increase the scope of governmental action. The Articles of Confederation were designed to unite the states and to give the federal government the power to gain independence from Britain. Although the states succeeded in accomplishing that goal, the Constitutional Convention was convened to broaden the powers of the federal government because the Founders thought that the activities of the federal government were too constrained by the Articles of Confederation. In the process, political decision-making moved further from consensus toward collective action based on the approval of a simple majority. The Great Depression and World War II were widely viewed as crises that required extensive government action in response, and the demand for a more active government brought with it a willingness among citizens to allow less consensus in the collective decision-making process to facilitate government's abilities to cope with those crises.

World War I had established a precedent for government action that went beyond the previously accepted limits of government power. During that war, businesses were nationalized, tax rates were increased substantially, citizens were drafted into military service, and federal policy pushed government into virtually every corner of the economy in furtherance of the war effort. Many of those increases in the scope of government remained in place after the war ended. When Franklin Delano Roosevelt (FDR) ascended to the presidency in March 1933, when the American economy hit bottom, the World War I experience provided precedent for government action to expand the scope of government and to narrow the reliance on consensus in collective decision-making. Ideological sentiments from the Progressive movement also contributed to citizens' sympathy with the idea that part of government's role is to look out for their economic well-being. Thus, the constitutional limits on the scope of government were eroded significantly during the New Deal and were eroded further because of US participation in World War II, a "good war" fought by what became known afterward as the "Greatest Generation."

An obvious effect of the New Deal and World War II was a substantial increase in the level of government expenditures and in the types of activities in which the federal government was involved. That growth in government programs and expenditures has been documented extensively and is well known to anyone with even a casual familiarity with the period, so rather than focus on those familiar facts, this chapter will focus on the erosion of the constitutional constraints on government during those two decades and on the replacement of constitutionally limited governmental powers as a guide to government action with the democratic idea of government policy designed in response to the desires of the majority. Government did get bigger during this period—much bigger. But the nature of government also changed in a fundamental way. The Progressive ideology that began to modify the role of the federal government in the 1890s had finally triumphed by the time Dwight D. Eisenhower assumed the presidency in the 1950s.

During the 1930s and 1940s, Americans ceded many of the constitutional limits on government power, allowing government to act more unilaterally, with less consensus, in exchange for expanding the scope of government to deal with the crises of world war and global depression. At mid-century, looking back, the major challenges the nation faced in the first half of the twentieth century were in the past. The Depression was over and the war had been won. Another looming crisis, in the form of the Cold War, cried out for continued strong government, but peace and prosperity also reigned following two decades of extraordinary growth in the scope of government. This chapter focuses on the ideological shifts that enabled those changes to occur. After World War I, Americans were more willing to increase the power of government to respond to crisis situations. After World War II, Americans were more willing to give government power over their lives in normal times, as a method of enhancing their economic well-being.

Partly that meant providing a safety net for society's least fortunate. More significant is that this meant giving the government the responsibility for maintaining an economic environment within which people can prosper. In the 1890s, that objective mostly entailed regulating the economic behavior of "big business" and others wielding concentrated economic power. In the 1950s, the goal meant regulating economic activity in general and providing a macroeconomic environment conducive to prosperity. Under the old ideology of liberty, government activity was limited to the protection of individual rights, allowing people to pursue prosperity on their own. Under the new ideology, if government is looking out for the economic well-being of its citizens, then those citizens find it important to have voices in determining the actions of government to ensure that government does not shortchange them in the process of furthering the economic well-being of others. Thus, democracy is a natural extension of government involvement in the economy.

Roosevelt's First One Hundred Days

When FDR's presidency began, the nation's economy was bordering on collapse. More than three years after the stock market crash of 1929, the economy continued its steep decline, and neither President Hoover nor Congress appeared to be capable of doing anything to stop the slide. Roosevelt was inaugurated on March 4, 1933, and on March 5 called a special session of Congress to meet on March 9, which began his First Hundred Days. On March 5, he ordered a national banking holiday and allowed banks to reopen their doors only after they had been individually inspected and their financial stability ensured. Even at that time, many argued that closing the banks was unnecessary and that it helped foster a crisis atmosphere. But by creating the appearance of a crisis and by taking decisive steps to deal with the crisis, Roosevelt accomplished two things. First, he burnished his reputation as a leader and a man of action, standing in contrast to Hoover and Congress, who appeared paralyzed in the face of the nation's economic problems. Second, the appearance of crisis conditions increased the popular demand for government action, making citizens more willing to accept Roosevelt's initiatives without waiting for some type of political consensus to affirm them.[1]

Roosevelt's inaugural address argued that the Depression was a crisis as serious as war and called for drastic measures to respond to the national emergency. His banking holiday served the dual purpose of showing strong leadership in responding to the emergency and of accentuating the crisis. Economic activity is much more difficult to undertake without banks. Roosevelt's quick and drastic action established his ability to lead the nation in crisis decisively and generated popular support. He created the foundations for the New Deal in his First Hundred Days, when he asked Congress to cooperate with him to pass fundamental New Deal legislation. Roosevelt succeeded with minimal opposition, and the New Deal was underway. Those Hundred Days saw the passage of foreign exchange controls, housing programs, new labor laws, the creation of the Civilian Conservation Corps and the Tennessee Valley Authority, and the passage of the Agricultural Adjustment Act and the National Industrial Recovery Act. The legislation itself is significant, but equally significant is the fact that it was supported so readily—almost without debate—by Congress and that the general public was so accepting of such broad expansions in governmental authority.

The Regulation of Banking and Finance

The onset of the Great Depression is normally placed at October 29, 1929, the date of the stock market's crash. From that initial meltdown of financial markets, the crisis spread throughout the rest of the economy. Part of the problem was that banks had made loans to individuals to buy stock on margin, and when the value of the stock fell, borrowers were unable to repay their loans. The problem was exacerbated by the nature of fractional reserve banking. Everyone knows that banks lend out the money they receive in deposit, so no

---

1. Robert Higgs, *Crisis and Leviathan (25th Anniversary Edition): Critical Episodes in the Growth of American Government* (Oakland, CA: Independent Institute, 2012), provides a good history of the New Deal and explains how the crisis atmosphere at the time enabled the expansion in the size and scope of government.

bank could possibly repay all of its depositors immediately. The system counts on the fact that most of the time deposits and withdrawals roughly balance each other out. But when depositors panic, as they did after the onset of the Depression, and many want their money right away, even the most solid bank will have to turn some depositors away.

The Federal Reserve Bank (Fed) was established in 1913 to mitigate just such a crisis, but for a number of reasons it failed to support the banking industry before or during the Depression. One reason was that the Fed was established as a lender of last resort for solvent banks. To borrow from the Fed, banks had to show that they had loans coming due in the future with which they could pay off their debt to the Fed. Bad loans did not count. Thus, if banks faced a temporary liquidity crisis, the Fed would help out, but if banks made bad loans and became insolvent, that was the bank's problem. Another problem the Fed faced was that the nation was still on a gold standard, and if it did prop up the banking system by creating new money the risk was that the new money would cause gold to flow overseas, undoing the Fed's policy and causing a loss of US gold at the same time. Perhaps the Fed could have acted to shore up the banking system and the economy, but it did not.[2]

The failure of the banking system led to a host of regulations on banking and finance. In 1933, the Glass-Steagall Act was passed, which separated commercial banking from investment banking. Thus, commercial banks, and the nation's money supply, would be insulated more substantially from problems that might arise in capital markets. To ensure the stability of the banking system further, the Federal Deposit Insurance Corporation (FDIC) was established in 1934 to provide federal insurance to depositors who kept their money in commercial banks. In addition, the Fed assumed much greater control over the banking industry, including instituting controls on allowable interest rates. It also became much more difficult to charter a bank, because the government did not want new banks entering the industry to threaten the stability of existing banks.

The Securities and Exchange Commission (SEC) also was created in 1933 as the agency to oversee the securities industry as specified in the Securities

---

2. Milton Friedman and Anna J. Schwartz, *A Monetary History of the United States* (Princeton, NJ: Princeton University Press, 1968), argue that the Fed could have, and should have, acted to prevent the monetary problems at the time from precipitating the Great Depression.

Act of 1933. Americans correctly viewed that speculation in the stock market in the 1920s had led to the crash of 1929, so found merit in regulating the issuance and trading of securities. While the cause of the speculation in stocks goes beyond the scope of this volume, it is worth remarking that many observers would place much of the blame on the Fed for allowing credit expansion that provided the money to engage in speculation, suggesting that the stock market crash was a failure of public policy rather than a breakdown of the market.[3] But it does not matter. The main issue here is the response to the stock market crash rather than its underlying causes. The SEC was given broad powers to require disclosure of substantial amounts of financial information at the time a security is issued. Furthermore, it was given substantial powers to regulate the types of bargaining that could take place in the securities industry and a mandate to prevent the insider trading of securities, which was made illegal.

The point here is not the effectiveness of the legislation, which has been debated, but rather the degree to which the public was eager to allow the federal government to dictate the terms of securities transactions. Whatever their benefits may have been, heavy regulations made it much harder to take a company public and reduced the freedom of individuals to undertake business in a mutually agreeable manner. Complete disclosure is important in publicly traded securities, beyond a doubt; financial markets could not operate effectively without it. Yet disclosure could be enforced through common-law rules against fraud or even through less restrictive regulation. But the public was, understandably, favorably disposed to heavy regulation of the securities industry, because the stock market crash was viewed, perhaps wrongly, as the initial cause of the Depression. Thus, people were happy to sacrifice some liberty to undertake financial transactions in exchange for more democratic control through federal regulation.

One aspect of this expanded regulation of banking and finance was the expansion of government power it entailed. But two more aspects of banking regulation are relevant also. First, the regulation was politically popular and serves as another example of public policy being determined based on the

---

3. Murray N. Rothbard, *America's Great Depression* (Kansas City: Sheed & Ward, 1963), argues that the Depression was caused by credit expansion in the 1920s that allowed too many investment projects that, in hindsight, proved unprofitable—a failure of public policy.

demands of the majority rather than on any reference to the constitutional limits on government power. Second, because banking stands as the central industry in any economy, acceptance of such far-reaching banking and financial regulation is evidence of further tolerance of the role that government should play in looking out for the economic well-being of the nation rather than merely protecting its liberty.

The Supreme Court and the Constitution

The US Constitution, with its three branches of government and a system of checks and balances, found itself overwhelmed by a charismatic president, a compliant Democratic-Party-controlled Congress, and popular opinion supporting a call to action. The Constitution, as originally written, provided the federal government with substantial insulation from popular opinion. The president was chosen by an Electoral College and by the House of Representatives (in the event of an electoral vote tie or the failure of any candidate to garner an Electoral College majority), the Senate was to be chosen by the state legislatures, and the members of the Supreme Court were chosen by the president with the Senate's advice and consent. The Founders intended that only members of the House of Representatives would be directly accountable to public opinion. By the 1930s, both the president and Congress were directly accountable to popular opinion, leaving only the Court insulated from the pressures of democracy. Accordingly, it was the Supreme Court that provided the biggest impediment to the New Deal.

The Supreme Court had advanced into the Progressive Era along with the rest of the nation and was not inclined to undo Progressive reforms or to turn back the clock to the earlier era of liberty. Thus, when a Minnesota law that mandated a moratorium on mortgage foreclosures was challenged, the Court ruled that the law was constitutional, and when New York established a board to regulate the milk industry and set legally mandated prices, the Court again ruled in favor of the state. Precedent for government intervention into the economic affairs of Americans had been set decades ago, and the Court was, if anything, willing to go beyond previous precedent in situations designed to mitigate the effects of the Depression. But the Court is, by design, a conservative institution, in the sense that its operation preserves the status quo and allows legal change to take place only slowly. Thus, the Court rejected many of the major parts of the New Deal.

In 1935, the Court signaled its skepticism toward New Deal programs by declaring legislation designed to give the president broad powers to regulate the petroleum industry unconstitutional. The law gave excessive power to the president, the Court ruled, and set the stage for further Court-produced setbacks for New Deal programs.[4] The Court's most severe blow to the New Deal came when it declared the National Industrial Recovery Act (NIRA) unconstitutional in a unanimous decision. The NIRA was a key part of Roosevelt's New Deal and was popular politically, supported by both business and labor interests and by Republicans as well as Democrats. The NIRA gave the president broad powers to design codes of fair competition, to be adhered to by industries, gave all employees the right to collective bargaining, and allowed the president to set minimum wages, maximum hours of work, and other conditions of employment. Those presidential powers were temporary, approved for only two years under the act, but they were far-reaching, and the Court decided that the NIRA delegated legislative powers to the executive branch, which violated the Constitution.

In 1936, the Supreme Court declared the Agricultural Adjustment Act (AAA), another key component of the New Deal, to be unconstitutional. The AAA was unconstitutional for two reasons, the Court determined, because it collected taxes from the population at large to finance a benefit to a specific group of individuals (farmers). In its decision, the Court addressed explicitly the general welfare clause of the Constitution and interpreted it liberally to state that it gave Congress the power to pass legislation to further the general welfare, over and above the enumerated powers granted in the Constitution. That liberal interpretation of the general welfare clause, written in the majority opinion, did seek to acknowledge the philosophy behind the New Deal. Nevertheless, the Court still found that the AAA exceeded the taxing powers granted in the Constitution.

In addition, during the first three years of the New Deal, the Supreme Court and lesser federal courts issued well over 1,000 rulings in opposition

---

4. See the discussion in Robert H. Jackson, *The Struggle for Judicial Supremacy: A Study of Crisis in American Power Politics* (New York: Alfred A. Knopf, 1941), 109–114.

to New Deal legislation.[5] The Court acted as a roadblock to many New Deal programs, which became a campaign issue for Roosevelt's opponents when Roosevelt ran for reelection in 1936. Roosevelt was trying to use his presidential power unconstitutionally, his opponents argued, using the Supreme Court decisions that went against him as evidence. Roosevelt himself had little to say about the Court in his campaign, but popular opinion was with him, as he won his bid for reelection in a landslide. In his State of the Union message to Congress on January 6, 1937, he mentioned the need for judicial reform to enable more progress to be made against the problems confronting the nation.

Roosevelt believed that the problem he faced with the Court was not so much the legal system itself, but that the Court was populated by enough conservative justices to thwart his initiatives. Even though the Court was aging, the justices seemed intent on keeping their seats in order to oppose Roosevelt. During his first four years in office, no justice stepped down, preventing Roosevelt from making any appointments to the Court. On February 5, 1937, Roosevelt took action against the Court by sending a message to Congress suggesting that he be able to add justices to the Court to ease their workload. Roosevelt noted that many of the justices were older than the "retirement age" of 70 and suggested that he should be able to appoint an additional justice to the Court for each justice older than 70 who had not retired. Roosevelt's proposal could have added as many as six new Supreme Court justices, enough to give his backers a majority on the Court.

Roosevelt's plan met with immediate opposition from the Court. The justices spoke publicly against it and testified before Congress. Of course, new justices could not be appointed without the approval of Congress, and Roosevelt's bold initiative died. Roosevelt failed in his attempt to pack the Court, but he won the larger battle. The Court seemed more willing to approve New Deal programs during Roosevelt's second term. The retirement of a justice early in Roosevelt's second term did allow him a new appointment, but more significant is that the existing justices seemed more willing to go along with Roosevelt's New Deal. In 1937, the Court handed down a host of decisions that reversed its previous opposition to New Deal legislation. The court sustained the constitutionality of an amended Railway Labor Act, which it had declared

---

5. Higgs, *Crisis and Leviathan (25th Anniversary Edition)*, 180.

completely unconstitutional previously; it reversed its previous opinion on a revised Frazier-Lemke Act, which provided debt relief to farmers; and it reversed earlier decisions to declare minimum wage laws unconstitutional. While the Court earlier had ruled that such laws interfered with freedom of contract, Chief Justice Hughes declared, "The Constitution does not speak of freedom of contract. It speaks of liberty and prohibits the depravation of liberty without due process of law."[6] Thus, the Court underwent a remarkable transformation in 1937, enabling the New Deal to move ahead largely without the judicial opposition it had faced in its first four years.

What caused the Court to reverse its course and support the New Deal? Undoubtedly the justices continued to be motivated to put their duty to the Constitution ahead of politics, but the Constitution always has been subject to interpretation, and several factors weighed in favor of the Court's movement. One was that the nation's economic problems continued, and there might have been some merit in the argument that a more modern interpretation of the Constitution would help the government deal with the nation's problems more effectively. Another factor was the demonstrated popularity of Roosevelt's initiatives after his strong victory in the presidential election of 1936. Surely popular opinion sided with Roosevelt's New Deal initiatives, if not his Court-packing plan. And although Roosevelt's attempt to pack the Court failed, the justices may have sensed that hostility toward their opposition to New Deal programs threatened the viability of the Court. Along those lines the Court's ideological change has been referred to as "the switch in time that saved nine."[7] Yet another factor was the reality that the existing justices eventually would be replaced by others more sympathetic to the president, even if the aging justices were determined to hold onto their seats until death. Indeed, Roosevelt appointed five new justices by 1940, before the end of his second term, and a total of eight during his full, three-plus-term presidency. Only George Washington had appointed more Supreme Court justices. Whatever the reasons for the Court's reversals, the end result was a Court more inclined

---

6. Jackson, *Struggle for Judicial Supremacy*, 209.

7. Henry J. Abraham, *Justices and Presidents: A Political History of Appointments to the Supreme Court* (New York: Oxford University Press, 1992), 211.

to take into account popular opinion in its rendering of its decisions. Thus, in the 1930s the Supreme Court made a major shift from liberty to democracy.[8]

Social Security

The erosion of constitutional constraints on the power of the federal government occurred gradually and began well before the New Deal. Yet the New Deal remains significant because it so firmly established the role of the federal government in promoting the nation's economic well-being. Many of the New Deal's programs were temporary, however, and explicitly of an emergency nature. While it might be difficult to assign one New Deal program with the responsibility for fundamentally transforming the historical, constitutional role of the federal government, the single program that would make the most persuasive candidate is Social Security. Unlike some entitlement programs, such as Aid to Families with Dependent Children (which was created as a part of the Social Security program) or food stamps (now "SNAP"), Social Security is not aimed at the needy, despite the tendency of the elderly to be poor in the 1930s. Unlike other entitlement programs, such as farm price supports, Social Security was not aimed at the regulation of commerce. It was designed as a compulsory retirement system, pure and simple. People were not forced to retire, of course, but they were forced to participate in the publicly funded retirement system. The Tenth Amendment to the Constitution plainly states, "The powers not delegated to the United States by the Constitution, nor prohibited by it to the States, are reserved to the States respectively, or to the people." Nowhere in the Constitution is there the slightest hint that the federal government has any power to establish a compulsory retirement program, yet the Supreme Court ruled it constitutional. If the Constitution, thus interpreted, gives the federal government the power to run a compulsory retirement program, it is difficult to see any constitutional limits on the programs that the federal government is permitted to undertake.

---

8. The Court's change has been referred to as legal realism, which is oriented toward interpreting law more so that government can enable individuals to accomplish their ends rather than just looking at law as a set of prohibited actions. See Paul L. Murphy, *The Constitution's Crisis Times: 1918–1969* (New York: Harper & Row, 1972), 103–107.

If the Supreme Court had not changed course in 1937, Social Security never would have survived judicial scrutiny. In 1934, Congress passed the Railroad Retirement Act, which created a mandatory pension system for railroad workers. In 1935, the Supreme Court ruled it unconstitutional, not on the basis of any specific provisions of the act but rather on the grounds that Congress did not have the power to pass any compulsory retirement system to cover railroad workers. In a dissenting opinion, Chief Justice Charles Evans Hughes argued that the Court's ruling was too extreme because it prevented Congress from remedying any defects in the existing retirement system and from creating any type of railroad pension program. But the majority of the justices clearly believed that a compulsory federal retirement system overstepped the federal government's constitutional limits.

In light of the judicial challenges that New Deal programs had faced in the past, Congress tried to design the Social Security program to withstand judicial scrutiny. Social Security was designed with three separate components, with the thought that if parts of the law were declared unconstitutional the remainder of the program might survive.[9] First, the program provided old age and survivors benefits to those who had paid into the system. Second, it provided aid to dependent children and to other needy individuals. Third, it created a federal unemployment compensation program with the option to allow states to run their own programs instead. Despite the fears of the president and Congress, the Court supported the Social Security program in its entirety and rendered three decisions favorable to Social Security on May 24, 1937.

In its decisions, the Court ruled that the compulsory Social Security payroll tax used to finance retirement benefits was a legitimate exercise of the power of Congress to tax to promote the general welfare, that Congress could provide money from the general Treasury for those in need, and that its unemployment compensation program did not unduly infringe on states' rights. While the Court's earlier ruling on the Agricultural Adjustment Act went against Roosevelt, that decision did expand the notion of the general welfare beyond the powers of government enumerated in the Constitution, opening

---

9. See C. Gordon Post, Frances P. DeLancy, and Fredric R. Darby, eds., *Basic Constitutional Cases* (New York: Oxford University Press, 1948), 239–241.

the door for a favorable ruling on Social Security. Thus, the general welfare, as referenced in the Constitution, had evolved to mean that whatever Congress thought was in the best interest of the citizens. The Constitution had been completely transformed.

New Deal Expenditures and Democracy

When the reach of governmental power extends beyond protecting the rights of individuals and into looking out for their economic well-being, it becomes important for citizens to be represented in the political process, because economic benefits are likely to flow toward political power. New Deal programs were to a substantial degree designed to provide economic relief to those hardest hit by the Depression, but the evidence shows that while resources did tend to flow toward those whose economic conditions were worst, benefits also went toward those areas of the country that had senior senators and representatives, that had representation on key oversight committees, and that had supported the New Deal in their popular voting.[10] In other words, New Deal expenditures had a substantial component of special-interest benefits.

It is not hard to see why this might be the case. For some types of expenditures, much discretion exists as to where, exactly, the money should be spent. For example, New Deal expenditures included highway expenditures that could have been made anywhere in the nation. Because the location at which such expenditures will be made is a political decision, it is not surprising that political power played a role in determining the allocation of that spending. Stepping back to look at the larger picture, many types of relief programs could have been funded. Obviously, representatives from rural areas would be more in favor of farm relief, while those from urban areas would prefer unemployment compensation and aid aimed at specific industries located in their districts. Much discretion existed as to how New Deal expenditures would be undertaken, primarily placed in the hands of Harry Hopkins, one of FDR's key advisers, and political power played a significant role in determining the geographical distribution of New Deal expenditures.

---

10. Gary M. Anderson and Robert D. Tollison, "Congressional Influence and Patterns of New Deal Spending, 1933–1939," *Journal of Law & Economics* 34, no. 1 (April 1991): 161–75.

The substantial increase in government programs, government expenditures, and especially government monetary transfers during the New Deal tends to be the focus of attention for both the New Deal's supporters and its detractors. Less noticed is the way in which the New Deal transformed how the nation's collective decisions were made. During the 1930s not only had the Progressive idea that the government should look out for the economic interests of its citizens become more firmly entrenched, but the idea that democratic decision-making was an appropriate way to determine public policy was also established. In part, this move toward democracy came because of the popular support for Roosevelt's initiatives that greatly expanded the economic role of government, and in part this move came from the acquiescence of the Supreme Court to the opinions of the popular majority. Thus, by the time World War II arrived, the idea that it was appropriate to determine public policy based on the will of the majority had become firmly established.

The Rise of the Federal Government

When the nation was founded, the federal government was a federation of state governments, and the intent of the Founding Fathers was to leave most of government's activities at the state or local level. The federal government would deal with issues involving the interactions of the nation with other nations and the interactions of states with each other. Limits on the federal government were put in place both by having the Constitution enumerate the government's powers and, with the Tenth Amendment, by limiting the government's actions only to those enumerated powers. By design, the federal government was subordinate to the states. That subordinate position clearly was reversed as a result of the War Between the States, but in many ways the federal government remained a minor presence in the lives of its citizens until the twentieth century.

Before the New Deal, the role of the federal government began to expand because of Progressive ideology, because of the leap forward in government programs during World War I, and because the federal income tax provided a new source of revenues to fund that expansion. Still, at the beginning of the New Deal, local government expenditures were substantially larger than either federal or state government expenditures. By 1940, federal government expenditures exceeded those of the subordinate governments and continue to do so.

The War Economy

The entry of the United States into World War II after the Japanese attack at Pearl Harbor on December 7, 1941, was much more popular than the nation's entry into World War I, and understandably so. But the nation also was well-prepared to enter the war prior to the Japanese attack. The Selective Training and Service Act of 1940 required all males from ages 21 to 35 to register for the draft and gave the president authority to draft individuals into uniform regardless of whether the nation was at war. The act went further than just enabling the draft; it also allowed the president to place orders for military materials and equipment that would take precedence over other business and allowed the government to seize any noncomplying facility.[11] While the nation was not at war, it was clear that in deference to popular sentiment Congress was willing to legislate substantial sacrifices of individual liberty to further the nation's collective goals.

After the United States entered the war, Congress granted considerably more power to allow the executive branch of government to direct the economy to further the war effort. The First War Powers Act was passed on December 18, 1941, and gave the president authority to enter into any contracts he saw fit to facilitate the nation's involvement in the war, including making advance payments to contractors and amending and modifying contracts in any way he determined. The Second War Powers Act, passed on March 17, 1942, gave the executive branch even more far-reaching economic powers, including authority to take possession of any property that might advance the war effort, either by purchase or by outright appropriation. If the president foresaw a shortage of any material, the act gave him the right to procure it as he saw fit; the law also created a link between the Treasury and the Federal Reserve Bank that essentially would allow for the printing up of new money to finance the war.

Price Controls and Rationing

As the nation entered the war, inflation started heating up, prompting Congress to pass legislation to control wages, rents, and prices in January 1942.

---

11. Higgs, *Crisis and Leviathan (25th Anniversary Edition)*, 200–201.

Congress did so by establishing the Office of Price Administration (OPA), run under the direction of an appointed administrator, John Kenneth Galbraith. Congress offered two justifications for the price control legislation. First, controlled wages and prices would make sure that defense appropriations were not eaten up by rising prices. This meant that sellers would be required to help subsidize the war effort, but this should seem like a small sacrifice to those working in the civilian economy, considering that others had been drafted to fight a dangerous war overseas. The second justification was to try to protect people whose incomes were fixed or relatively limited. Once again, the government was following the Progressive principle of looking out for the economic well-being of its citizens. With price controls, it is clear that if one person pays a lower price, another person receives a smaller income, so the effect is clearly redistributive. It is telling that this second justification did not have to be offered at all. Why not just justify the controls based on the war effort? Yet the role of the government to protect economic interests was offered, despite the policy's clearly redistributive nature. Again, this observation emphasizes the importance of democratic representation in a nation that adopts policies according to the voting majority's preferences, as expressed in election results.

Exceptions were made to the authority of the OPA's administrator, and two major exceptions are telling. Employee compensation was exempted partially, as were agricultural product prices. Thus, the political power of labor unions and the farm lobby was evident. Organized labor had close ties to the Democratic Party, which helped their cause, and agriculture always has been disproportionately represented as an economic sector, because of lobbying by the Farm Bureau and other groups representing the interests of farmers. This is because many congressional districts are primarily were rural and agricultural, whereas few other districts are so heavily represented by one industry. Again one sees that when economic resources are allocated democratically, the success of a group depends on how well its interests are represented in the political process.

Wage and price controls rapidly brought with them shortages because with prices held down, purchasers wanted to buy more of almost everything than sellers wanted to sell. The result was a potentially inequitable allocation of goods as merchants saved items for their friends or allocated them in other ways besides selling them to whomever placed the highest value on them. As a result, the OPA began rationing a number of necessities and organized the rationing program by establishing thousands of local boards to administer the allocation of artificially scarce items. Despite substantial regulations and red tape, this program merely transferred the authority to sell from the sellers to a board, and the results were generally unsatisfactory. The price controls had eliminated market prices as signals of how to allocate resources, and the economy increasingly became chaotic as a result. Seeing the problems, President Roosevelt argued, much as he had in his first term, for ever more broad presidential powers to set prices and wages, including those that had been exempt under the legislation passed the previous year.

The wage and price controls and the accompanying rationing system was a wartime program, of course, and was accepted as such by Americans. But it set a precedent, and when President Nixon mandated wage and price controls on August 15, 1971, this move was very popular. Roosevelt's price controls provided the precedent, but Nixon's price controls came only in response to rising inflation, without any other associated crisis. A move that was justified by war in 1942 was justified only because it was popular in 1971, despite the fact that such controls clearly limit freedom of contract and exchange and thus compromise the liberty of the nation's citizens. The widespread acceptance of Nixon's wage and price controls clearly shows the triumph of democracy over liberty.

Withholding and the Income Tax

War-related expenditures affected an incredibly large share of the economy, and the government worked to finance them every way it could. It borrowed and implied that it was the patriotic duty of citizens to buy war bonds, it printed up new money with the compliance of the Fed, and it increased taxes substantially. In 1939, most Americans did not pay income taxes because the personal exemption was high enough to exclude most people from income tax liability. That ended with the onset of the war, when the personal exemption was lowered substantially and tax rates were increased dramatically. The personal exemption in 1939 was $1,000, meaning that a family of four would have $4,000 of income shielded from income taxation, which was well above the national median income in 1939. In addition, the lowest tax bracket in 1939 was 4 percent, so even if that family earned a bit more than the exemption, they paid only 4 percent of any additional income above the threshold in taxes. By 1944, the personal exemption had been cut in half, to $500, and the lowest income tax bracket had been raised to 23 percent.

Even with this substantial increase in income tax rates, the federal government still ran a large budget deficit and was looking for ways to raise additional revenues. One initiative to do so was to institute income tax withholding. Prior to World War II those citizens whose incomes were high enough to be taxed were supposed to make quarterly income tax payments based on their previous year's annual incomes. While this system had satisfactory results prior to the war, the increase in tax rates and the reduction in the personal exemption created some problems for income tax collections. First, because the newly covered taxpayers were less well off than those who paid income taxes before the war, it was more likely that they would have trouble putting together the money needed to pay their taxes on a quarterly basis because it would require saving over a period of three months to make those quarterly payments. If they underestimated their tax liabilities, this could create the additional hardship of trying to put together enough money to make up the difference on tax day, April 15. It is easy to imagine that as more people were liable for income tax payments, some people with average incomes would not have the financial discipline to set aside enough money to pay their taxes. The problem was aggravated further by the much higher marginal tax rates that the lowest-income taxpayers faced. Surely, without withholding, many taxpayers would have found themselves financially unable to meet their tax liabilities because they would not have had the financial discipline to save enough to pay them.

Another smaller, but real advantage to withholding was that it provided a steady stream of revenues into the Treasury. Rather than waiting several months for quarterly tax payments, the Treasury would receive the revenues almost as soon as the money was earned by employees. In a government strapped for funds, any little bit helped, and withholding reduced somewhat the need for the Treasury to borrow.

Withholding also had the major advantage of providing the federal government with a method of monitoring taxpayer compliance.[12] When the lowest tax bracket was 4 percent and most taxpayers did not even make enough to owe any income tax, cheating was not a big problem. For those well enough off to pay income taxes, sending 4 percent of their taxable income to the federal government was not a major financial burden, so compliance was likely to be high. Even if some people cheated, the rate was low enough that except for very high-income cheaters (who were more likely to be spotted and so less likely to cheat), the Treasury would not lose much revenue anyway. With higher tax rates and the addition of lower-income taxpayers into the tax base, there was both a bigger incentive for cheating and a bigger potential revenue loss to the Treasury.

The requirement that employers withhold tax payments from employee paychecks provides a good mechanism for controlling noncompliance among employees. The employers have no incentive to disregard the law. To do so would bring legal penalties on them without giving them anything in return. Surely an employer could not offer to pay employees a little less in exchange for not withholding taxes, because the knowledge of this would be widespread enough that the employer would be found out. It would only take one disgruntled employee to report the violation. Once the income is withheld, the Treasury knows the identity of the taxpayer, so it is better able to make sure that taxpayers file returns and pay any additional taxes they owe.

The creation of withholding has greatly enhanced the federal government's ability to collect income taxes for several reasons. First, it created a system of monitoring that cut down on cheating. Second, it provided a mechanism of forced saving so that taxpayers had no choice but to set aside sufficient funds to meet their tax liabilities. Surely many taxpayers who want to comply would find themselves unable to do so without withholding. This leads to a third advantage of withholding. By creating the impression that most taxpayers are complying with the system, it encourages other taxpayers to go along and pay their taxes.[13] If, in contrast, people had the impression that cheating was

---

12. Charlotte Twight, "Evolution of Federal Income Tax Withholding: The Machinery of Institutional Change," *Cato Journal* 14, no. 3 (Winter 1995): 359–95.

13. Carolyn C. Jones, "Mass-Based Income Taxation: Creating a Taxpaying Culture, 1940–1952," in *Funding the Modern American State, 1941–1995: The Rise and Fall of the Era of*

widespread, individuals who were paying would be more tempted to cheat, thinking that they had no moral obligation to pay when many others were evading their tax payments. In wartime, when patriotic sentiments are strong, this surely is the case, but it applies any time people have ideological commitments to their government. Even US citizens who dislike the income tax and the Internal Revenue Service typically still have patriotic affinities to American government ideals, and those people will be encouraged to pay taxes if only because they view the tax system as a legitimate product of the democratic institutions that are at the nation's foundation.

The evolution of the federal income tax during World War II had several significant effects on the development of American democracy after the war. First, it provided stronger and more predictable flows of revenues into the federal government's coffers. Tax rates remained much higher in the 1950s than they were in the 1930s, and it is unlikely that Congress would have been able to enact such tax increases in the absence of a major crisis. Second, it made most Americans income-taxpayers for the first time. Those who were paying into the system would have felt that they should have some say in how the resulting revenues were spent, and rightly so. Prior to World War II, any democratic decision on how to spend the nation's income tax revenues would have been a decision on how revenues collected from the nation's upper-income elites should be spent. After World War II, any decision on how those revenues should be allocated was a decision on the part of voters on how the money they themselves contributed should be spent. Because it was their money, they had every right to have a say in how it would be used.

Other factors with regard to the income tax were the greater ability of the government to keep track of the financial affairs of Americans, the presumption in tax law that one is guilty until proven innocent, and the acceptance of the idea that the federal government could garnish everyone's wages in anticipation of their future income tax liabilities. The scope of government power, democratically authorized by Congress, had increased substantially and generally was accepted by Americans. Surely this was the result of a willingness on the part of Americans to give up some of their liberties to support the war effort, but those liberties were not restored after the war. In contrast,

---

Easy Finance, ed. W. Elliot Brownlee (Cambridge: Cambridge University Press, 1996), 107–47.

several attempts in the 1980s to institute income tax withholding on interest and dividend payments were proposed, but all of them failed to be approved through the political process. Most interest and dividend income is earned by upper-income individuals, so one could envision support for the proposal among many Americans who would not be affected by the legislation, yet the same type of withholding with which every wage earner must comply as a legacy of World War II was rejected for interest and dividend earners when no crisis was underway.

In the process of collecting income taxes, the Internal Revenue Service also collects a substantial amount of information on the business affairs of every American. While libertarians might view this as an invasion of privacy, it apparently does not constitute an unreasonable search "of persons, houses, paper, and effects," following the language of the Fourth Amendment to the Constitution, at least according to popular opinion and the learned judgement of the Supreme Court. Furthermore, when taxpayers are challenged by the Internal Revenue Service, they must prove their innocence rather than leave the burden of proof of guilt to the IRS. While it is generally recognized that this is one area of law in which the accused is presumed guilty until proven innocent, again that policy stance appears to be generally accepted by Congress, the Supreme Court, and the population at large. One could make a convincing argument that were this not so, the federal government would not be able to collect nearly as much in income tax revenue as it does and that noncompliance would be rampant. This is perhaps true, but this perversion of the law shows the willingness of a democratic society to sacrifice liberty in response to the demands of the majority.

The Roosevelt Era

When President Roosevelt died in 1945, the US government differed significantly from the one he had taken command of in 1933. The growth in the scope and power of the federal government and the expansion of government programs during the Roosevelt era are well-known. Perhaps because of this growth of government, the transformation in ideology supporting government has been neglected by-and-large. In response to the Great Depression and World War II, Americans willingly turned over to democratic control substantial liberties that formerly had been guaranteed by the Constitution and that had been a part of the American ideology. The changes that occurred were extensions of those begun during the Progressive Era and sustained during the 1920s. Americans had bought into the Progressive idea that it was appropriate for their government to look out for their economic well-being in addition to protecting their rights, and the Depression was a period during which their economic well-being was threatened. Thus, Americans accepted greater government control through the regulation of the economy, through taxation in order to spend more on government programs, and through restrictions on individual liberties for the good of the nation, as determined by the desires of the majority.

The government's extended scope in response to crisis is one thing. The increasingly democratic ideology that developed along with growing government is a related but different phenomenon. For more than a decade, Americans had become acclimated to greater democratic control of their society, giving up individual liberty in exchange for policies designed to aid their economic well-being and to protect the nation and the world. By 1945, the Depression was over, and the United States had emerged victorious. The government had faced two major crises and after substantial struggle had won both. Despite any lingering Jeffersonian ideals, Americans wanted a government that would continue to intervene in their lives when it could have a positive influence.

The Employment Act of 1946

Any doubt about the government's responsibility to promote the economic well-being of its citizens was erased by the passage of the Employment Act of 1946. The Great Depression had not ended until after the United States entered World War II, and the common view was that it was the government's demand for military output that finally pulled the economy out of its slump. With the war over, there was the real fear that the economy would slip back into its prewar depression. But it did not have to do so, according to some of the nation's academic economists. Through active aggregate demand management, the federal government had the power to maintain full employment with low inflation. The intellectual foundation for the idea appeared in John Maynard Keynes's *The General Theory of Employment, Interest, and Money*, published in 1936, and by the end of World War II Keynes's ideas had been adopted enthusiastically by the nation's leading academic economists and policymakers.

The Employment Act of 1946 states,

> The Congress hereby declares that it is the continuing policy and re-sponsibility of the Federal Government to use all practicable means consistent with its needs and obligations and other essential consider-ations of national policy, with the assistance and cooperation of indus-try, agriculture, labor, and State and local governments, to coordinate and utilize all its plans, functions, and resources for the purpose of crea-ting and maintaining, in a manner calculated to foster and promote free competitive enterprise and the general welfare, conditions under which there will be afforded useful employment opportunities, includ-ing self-employment, for those able, willing, and seeking to work and promote maximum employment, production, and purchasing power.

The act tries to cover many bases and is vague about what, exactly, the government might do to promote maximum employment, but this vague-ness is explained both by the potential for disagreements regarding what the appropriate policy would be and the uncertainty about whether the govern-ment really has the power to do anything to prevent unemployment anyway.

The Employment Act of 1946 may be more symbolic than anything, but what it symbolizes is a wholesale acceptance of the Progressive ideology as a part of federal government policy. The act states plainly that it is the re-sponsibility of the federal government to promote maximum employment, production, and purchasing power, and the tenets of the law have remained a part of the basic ideas of economics ever since. Students are taught in their college economics classes how federal government policy can be used to keep the economy near full employment and with low inflation. Armed with this knowledge, citizens continue to adhere to the idea that the federal govern-ment is responsible for keeping the economy healthy and for promoting their economic welfare. In response to the crises of war and depression, Americans accepted an expansion in democratic control over their lives and a result-ing sacrifice in their liberties. The Employment Act of 1946 symbolizes the extension of this acceptance from crisis times into the post-crisis era. Thus, the events of the Great Depression and World War II further facilitated the transformation of the national ideology from liberty to democracy.

Conclusion

The presidency of FDR, encompassing both the Great Depression and World War II, has the popular reputation of being both an era of substantial government growth and the era in which the welfare state was born. The creation of major transfer programs, such as Social Security and Aid to Families with Dependent Children, justifies that reputation, but the impact of the era on the future of American government is understated if one focuses only on the growth in government programs, taxes, and expenditures. That era witnessed the rising acceptance of democracy as a principle upon which to base government policy and a corresponding decline in the principle of liberty. People were ever more willing to give up their personal liberties in exchange for government programs aimed at securing their economic well-being, and people increasingly viewed democratic decision-making as the mechanism for determining appropriate public policy. Democracy in a time of crisis, when the scope of government was growing, also meant a move away from consensus in collective decision-making. FDR was elected democratically, and the popular mandate registered in democratic elections enabled Roosevelt to implement public programs without further democratic input, except from a complaisant Congress. The underlying principle was democracy, not consensus, and even though the majority went along, a vocal discontented minority always could be heard.

Increasingly, American democracy became an economic system in addition to a political decision-making mechanism. The major changes made during the period included more regulation of private commerce, government restrictions on private contracts, a massive expansion in government transfer programs, increases in taxation, and income tax withholding. The Supreme Court, final guardian of the Constitution, was at first reluctant to go along with the sacrifices in liberty that accompanied Roosevelt's interventions, but in his second term, the Court was more agreeable and in the process changed America's constitutional rules substantially. The United States, still predominantly a market economy, moved unmistakably in the direction of economic democracy, wherein economic resources are allocated according to the will of the majority rather than to the principles of liberty that had been the economy's foundation in the previous century. The nation was in dire straits when Roosevelt took office. When he died, the nation was prosperous again and victorious in war. Americans did not want to give up those gains. Government had grown, but Americans saw some security in a big government that was charged with looking out for their well-being, and because of that belief they willingly accepted the further shift from liberty to democracy.

11

Democracy Triumphs
The Great Society

THE "RATCHET HYPOTHESIS" of government expansion argues that government grows in response to crises but after a crisis has passed never shrinks down to its pre-crisis level. Thus, government growth is an intermittent process whereby a crisis appears and government ratchets up in response, shrinking somewhat after the crisis but remaining forever larger than before the crisis. Then another crisis comes along, ratcheting government up again. The process continues, and the government grows in response to each crisis. The hypothesis is credible and finds support in academic research.[1] More cynical observers have even argued that those with government power engineer crises to aggrandize the state. Indeed, much of the transformation from liberty to democracy over the history of the United States has been in response to crises. The War Between the States was the major crisis in the nineteenth century. The twentieth century was one of almost continual crisis, with two world wars, the Great Depression, and a cold war that lingered for more than half a century. The twenty-first century's war on terror has the appearance of a never-ending crisis, with perpetual government policies and programs that sap individual liberty. Lyndon Johnson's Great Society programs, launched in the mid-1960s, stand in stark contrast. Those programs were initiated by popular demand, not because of a crisis, but despite one.

---

1. See, for examples, Alan T. Peacock and Jack Wiseman, *The Growth of Public Expenditure in the United Kingdom* (Princeton, NJ: Princeton University Press, 1961); Robert Higgs, *Crisis and Leviathan (25th Anniversary Edition)* (Oakland, CA: Independent Institute, 2012); and Karen A. Rassler and William R. Thompson, "War Making and State Making: Government Expenditures, Tax Revenues, and Global Wars," *American Political Science Review* 79, no. 2 (June 1985): 491–507.

Johnson's Great Society was a triumph of democracy because after a long transformation, public policy was founded not on constitutional principles but rather on democratic ones. Programs were proposed and implemented in response to the general public's demand. Unlike the New Deal programs spawned during the Great Depression, no crisis propelled the government into action. Indeed, if a crisis existed during the period, it was the Cold War and its hotter subcomponent, the Vietnam War, and the Great Society's programs actually diverted resources away from those crises. The Great Society's programs were aimed at helping those at the lower end of the income distribution, but at a time when poverty was declining and the poor were becoming better off anyway. They were aimed at improving access to healthcare and educational opportunities, but at a time when the population increasingly was healthy and increasingly well-educated anyway. Race relations were a prominent issue, but even here, following *Brown v. Board of Education* in 1954, some progress was being made, although it was painfully slow. In all of the areas addressed by the Great Society's programs, things were getting better. The Great Society's programs were not responses to a crisis, as could be argued about the New Deal programs, but rather were initiated even though the problems they were addressing were diminishing on their own. Unlike past initiatives of a similar scale, they were initiated because of their popular appeal, as a response of a democratic government to the desires of its citizens.

While one might make a similar argument about the Progressive movement, major changes were occurring at that time owing to America's increasing industrialization and urbanization. Those changes supported the argument that American society was undergoing a major transformation and that the role of government should change in response. The greater concentration of wealth and economic power in the hands of a few industrialists and financiers alarmed many people and prompted a demand for government action. Furthermore, individuals and groups with political power rationally would try to maintain their power by curtailing the growing economic power of a group of people they could rightly view as competing for the leading roles in American society. Things were completely different in the 1960s. The Cold War presented a crisis in the international arena and the Vietnam War created unrest at home, but as the 1960s began the nation was prosperous and optimistic.

Economic policy turned from trying to stabilize the economy and create an environment for full employment toward using the gains of prosperity to achieve public goals in addition to private goals. This was the contemporary liberal ideology endorsed by President Kennedy and increasingly supported by public opinion, especially among the nation's youth.

The Transition to the 1960s

The presidential election of 1960 pitted John F. Kennedy, a liberal senator from Massachusetts, against Richard Nixon, who had served as vice president during Eisenhower's two terms in the White House. The two candidates represented sharply contrasting political ideologies. Nixon represented a continuation of the conservatism of the Eisenhower years. Eisenhower was elected in 1952, when the nation still labored under a cloud of uncertainty about the future. As the nation's top general during World War II, Eisenhower was a hero and had a reputation as a strong leader. The Depression was slipping into the nation's memory, although concern remained even into the 1960s that a repeat of the 1930s could someday be on the horizon, partly because people still did not have a clear understanding about what caused the economic problems of the 1930s. World War II also was a memory, but the Korean conflict was underway as a part of the larger Cold War that would pit the United States and its allies against the Soviet Union and its allies for decades to come. In light of the international situation, having a general at the nation's helm was reassuring.

On the economic front, the nation was experiencing unparalleled growth and prosperity during the 1950s. As automobile ownership became more common, Americans moved to the suburbs. America's love affair with the automobile was never greater than in the 1950s and 1960s, when owning a car came within the reach of most American families. In 1950, 40 million passenger cars were registered in the United States, up from 26 million in 1945. By 1960, 62 million passenger cars had been registered, an increase of 55 percent since 1950, representing an average of more than one car per family. American automakers changed styles every year, and because Americans always wanted the latest model it was common to trade in a car well before it was worn out, just to get the newer model. That behavior provided a ready source of used cars for those who could not quite afford a new one.

The automobile was not the only major lifestyle change that occurred during the 1950s. Television was rare in American households in 1950 but was common by 1960. In 1949, only 50 television stations broadcast in the entire nation. That number nearly doubled in the next year, to 97 stations in 1950, and increased to 517 stations in 1960, putting at least one television station within reach of most Americans. By 1960, 88 percent of American households had a television set, up from 67 percent just a few years earlier in 1955. The greater wealth of the 1950s brought about not only a higher standard of living, but a major change in lifestyles for many people, with the automobile, the television, and migration to the suburbs leading the way. The economic strength of the United States, coupled with its military victories in the world wars, established it unquestionably as the world's leading nation. America was brimmingly optimistic, with the Cold War providing the only significant cloud on the horizon.

Despite that prosperity, few Americans would attribute their good fortune to the policies of President Eisenhower. While Eisenhower was well liked, he had a reputation for being relatively passive in the public policy arena, in stark contrast to Roosevelt, who had guided the nation through two decades of crisis. Eisenhower favored minimal government involvement in the economy and warned of the "military-industrial complex" that threatened to dominate the nation. If Nixon were elected in 1960, the nation could expect more of the same. Nixon had an advantage in the Cold War era of looking more experienced in dealing with international affairs, but when faced with the choice, the nation chose Kennedy by the slimmest of margins. The popular vote count gave Kennedy 34.2 million votes to Nixon's 34.1 million, but once in office Kennedy was ready to push his agenda for American progress. What Kennedy lacked in international experience he made up for with a vision of a grander America at home. Working together, he argued, the nation would be able to do good things with its newfound prosperity. "Ask not what your country can do for you," Kennedy told his fellow citizens, "but what you can do for your country." It would be difficult to think of a phrase that is more out of tune with John Locke's view of government as a servant of the people than Kennedy's call for Americans to serve their government.

The Kennedy-Johnson Years

President Kennedy saw his administration as a significant enough break from the past to call it a "New Frontier," evoking images of Roosevelt's New Deal but at the same time using terminology implying that progress was on the horizon. Americans were used to progress in the private sector. After adjusting for inflation, average earnings had risen by 26 percent from 1950 to 1960, but while the previous decade had shown substantial progress in the private sector, not much had changed in the public sector. It was easy to argue that some of the nation's newfound wealth should be put into financing public amenities to enhance the quality of life and to help out those who truly were needy. Kennedy, a Harvard man both by education and by philosophy, drew inspiration from prominent liberal Harvard faculty members. Those ideas included empowering the government to make social change and to use new techniques of economic policy to engineer the economy to full employment and low inflation.

Despite the passage of the Employment Act of 1946, government policy toward employment had changed little when Kennedy took office. Until the 1960s, the conventional wisdom on fiscal policy was that, except during emergencies, the government's budget should be balanced, and during the Eisenhower years the conventional wisdom ruled. Any budget deficits were small and unintentional. But the conventional wisdom already had been overthrown in academic economics, where Keynesian ideas had firmly taken hold and dominated the thinking on macroeconomic policy. The government could stabilize the economy by using functional finance, which meant running budget deficits when unemployment threatened, to stimulate the economy and keep it close to full employment, and running budget surpluses when inflation threatened, to rein in excess aggregate demand and prevent the economy from overheating. Kennedy brought in a new set of economic advisers who preached the Keynesian gospel. The first major policy move was the tax cut of 1964, designed specifically to stimulate an economy that appeared to be sliding into a recession.

While the effectiveness of this tax cut can be debated, for present purposes it is more important to note that even the magnitudes of government taxes and expenditures were now being calculated to enhance the nation's economic well-being. Before 1960, federal taxes were viewed as a method of financing federal expenditures. The new view depicted them as a crucial tool for managing the economy to create full employment with low inflation. A look at any introductory economics textbook from the 1960s can confirm that conclusion. The discussion of federal taxes and expenditures takes place mostly under the heading of macroeconomics, where they are shown to be critical elements of aggregate demand that determine whether the nation will have unemployment or inflation. The textbooks explain how taxes and expenditures can be adjusted to produce full employment, without ever considering what the government buys. In textbook Keynesian analysis, what government buys with its expenditures largely is irrelevant. The Employment Act of 1946 was based on these Keynesian ideas, but it was not until a decade and a half after the law's passage that the nation's voters chose policymakers who truly were committed to placing the ideas expressed in the law at the center of national economic policy.

Kennedy's New Frontier barely had time to get off the ground before he was felled by an assassin's bullet on November 22, 1963. On the international front, he had been distracted by the Cuban missile crisis the year before and the failed Bay of Pigs invasion to try to oust Fidel Castro from power. On the other side of the world, the Vietnam War was escalating. Meanwhile, at home, recession threatened, causing Kennedy to focus on macroeconomic policy more than microeconomic policy. But Kennedy had ideas. In 1961, Congress passed the Area Redevelopment Act, targeting funds to the most impoverished regions of the United States, and in 1962 the Manpower Development and Training Act was passed. Both bills were supported by Kennedy as federal programs that would address directly the economic well-being of the least well-off Americans. Kennedy's vision of a greater America, propelled by federal government programs to enhance the nation's well-being, was picked up by his successor. Kennedy and Johnson were not friends, as was well known, and during Kennedy's brief presidency Vice President Johnson stood in Kennedy's shadow. As president, Johnson was determined to rise above his predecessor, and he formulated his Great Society programs to eclipse Kennedy's New Frontier and to expand the programs the Democrats had established during the New Deal.[2]

Johnson had his distractions, to be sure. The war in Vietnam was escalating out of control, and Johnson was at a loss as to how to deal with it. The Civil Rights Movement was a component of the Great Society, as Johnson made an effort to extend to all Americans the same rights enjoyed by whites. But progress was slower than some would have liked, and the demonstrators and rioters, sensing an opportunity, protested both the nation's racial problems and its involvement in the Vietnam War. The nuclear arms race continued, and the Cold War remained a serious concern. The space race was also on in response to the Soviet Union's launching of a satellite into space in 1957, ahead of the United States. The Soviet Union continued its dominance in 1961 by being the first nation to put a man into orbit. President Kennedy pledged to land a man on the moon before 1970, and Johnson supported that effort as well. Johnson had a full policy agenda handed to him but added to it his Great Society programs in an effort to transform the role of the federal government further, extending Progressivism and the New Deal.

The Great Society

In March 1964, a few months after assuming the presidency, Johnson initiated a cornerstone of his Great Society by calling for a "war on poverty."[3] The War on Poverty was optimistic in its outlook. While income transfers had been at the heart of most poverty programs, the War on Poverty envisioned providing economic opportunities to poor people. Job training would help them earn their own incomes, and investment in health, nutrition, and education

---

2. Philip Reed Rulon, in chapter 8 of *The Compassionate Samaritan: The Life of Lyndon Baines Johnson* (Chicago: Nelson-Hall, 1981), describes Johnson as "in the shadow of the New Frontier."

3. James T. Patterson, *America's Struggle Against Poverty: 1900–1985* (Cambridge, MA: Harvard University Press, 1986), 134.

programs for the children of the poor would enable them to rise out of poverty to join mainstream America. The Office of Economic Opportunity was created, and a host of new programs with optimistic titles like Upward Bound, Job Corps, and Head Start were launched to change the culture of poverty and to bring the advantages of a thriving economy to every American. The philosophy behind the War on Poverty was built on the Progressive idea that through scientific management the findings of social science can be applied to attack the causes of poverty at its roots and that as the programs succeeded the need for them in the future would be reduced. The War on Poverty, it goes without saying, is an example of government working to enhance the economic well-being of its citizens, not to protect their liberties.[4]

One of the key elements in the War on Poverty was the provision of enhanced educational opportunities for everyone. The poor could benefit, obviously, but a more educated society could improve everyone's well-being. Thus, Johnson formally introduced his Great Society at the University of Michigan in a speech he gave on May 22, 1964. He had tested the term on smaller audiences previously, but in Michigan he used it in a major policy speech that defined the ideas of his presidency and created his own identity, separate from his predecessor. Johnson reorganized the Department of Health, Education, and Welfare; passed legislation to provide federal funding for education in Appalachia; provided federal funding for vocational education; increased the budget of the National Science Foundation sharply; created federal scholarships for students; and opened the doors for college students to get federally guaranteed student loans. Despite wartime distractions and domestic unrest during Johnson's presidency, he continued to push successfully for additional federal aid to education. Education was important because it was the key to economic opportunity, and the Great Society was all about enhancing the economic well-being of Americans.

Perhaps the greatest legacies of the Great Society are Medicare and Medicaid, two federal healthcare programs designed to extend government financing of medical care to the elderly and to the poor, respectively. At the time, the United States was alone among industrialized nations in having neither

---

4. In hindsight the Great Society did not live up to its promises. See Vaughn Davis Bornet, *The Presidency of Lyndon Johnson* (Lawrence: University Press of Kansas, 1983). But any disappointment in its results does not affect the political foundation upon which it was built.

socialized medicine nor some form of national health insurance. Attempts had been made previously to create a similar program in the United States, but the American Medical Association (AMA) opposed the efforts. Franklin Delano Roosevelt wanted to include socialized medicine along with the Social Security program but foresaw that political opposition would threaten the whole program. An attempt was made in 1950 to create national health insurance, but that too failed. During the Eisenhower years no new initiatives were floated, but Johnson saw an opportunity to make national healthcare part of the Great Society.

The AMA adamantly was opposed to any government involvement in healthcare, and health insurers understandably were concerned that the government was going to drive them out of business. On the other side, organized labor, headed by the AFL-CIO, was strongly in favor of national healthcare. Johnson believed that such a program would be politically viable if it was limited to providing healthcare to the poor and the elderly. The poor lacked health insurance anyway, lessening some of the political opposition, and the elderly were a high-risk group for insurers. The insurance industry mounted little protest, and despite the AMA's opposition both programs were passed in 1965. The Great Society was underway.

The Great Society and Democracy

A major force behind the Great Society was the Civil Rights Movement, and, in particular, the legislation that was passed to eliminate discrimination based on race. Despite the ideal of liberty that was at the foundation of the Revolution, slavery is explicitly recognized in the Constitution, and in its first two centuries the nation's progress in eliminating differential legal treatment based on race had been painfully slow. Progress accelerated in the 1960s, which was one way the Great Society unambiguously furthered the ideal of liberty. One must keep in mind, however, that much of the discrimination based on race that existed as the 1960s began was sanctioned legally and even mandated by law. The Supreme Court had begun dismantling the vestiges of segregation, most notably with the landmark *Brown v. Board of Education* case in 1954, but the Court is by its nature a conservative institution and can modify the law only in response to cases brought to it. Congress, under President Kennedy's leadership, passed the Civil Rights Act of 1964 to speed the progress. It mandated desegregation of public education and required that all accommodations open to the public, including restaurants, motels, stores, and places of entertainment, could not discriminate based on race.[5]

In addition to other provisions, the Civil Rights Act mandated that completion of the sixth grade was sufficient proof of literacy for purposes of voting in federal elections. The voting component of the act was intended to reduce the barriers that discouraged blacks from voting, but Johnson viewed it as insufficient and the next year pushed the Voting Rights Act of 1965 through Congress. Because the Civil Rights Act had been passed only the year before, the Voting Rights Act cannot be viewed as a response to any demonstrated failure of that law. Rather, it took additional measures to try to increase black voter turnout, including suspending literacy tests altogether in counties where less than 50 percent of those eligible to vote were registered and extending the act's provisions to all elections, not just federal elections. In addition, poll taxes that discouraged minority voters were made unconstitutional after the passage of the Twenty-Fourth Amendment, ratified in 1964. Johnson's attempt to extend voting rights to all Americans must be applauded, but his actions had a political element in them that also must be recognized.

Especially in the southern states, whites went to great lengths to discourage black voters, both by legal means like poll taxes and literacy tests, and by more subtle means. Everybody recognized that blacks who were discouraged from voting were a natural constituency of Johnson's Democratic Party. Johnson's push for civil rights, his War on Poverty, and indeed his more general vision of the Great Society made blacks a natural constituency, and anything Johnson could do to increase voter turnout among blacks surely would increase his political support. While the principle of liberty may have been at the foundation of much of the Great Society's civil rights efforts, the principle of democracy was at work in the 1965 Voting Rights Act, because Johnson and supporters of the Great Society realized that they could help their political agenda by extending the franchise to those who would rally behind their programs. With

---

5. Irving Bernstein, *Guns or Butter? The Presidency of Lyndon Johnson* (New York: Oxford University Press, 1996), discusses the Civil Rights Act of 1964 in detail.

public policy determined by public opinion, the object of the Voting Rights Act ultimately was to attract more voter support for Johnson's initiatives.

This link between voting and the support of Progressive social programs also was recognized by the nation's largest charitable foundations, who were strongly supportive of the War on Poverty. The Ford Foundation, in particular, funded voter registration drives in the 1960s aimed specifically at registering blacks for the purpose of expanding the political constituency for the programs it supported. A Ford Foundation voter registration drive undertaken exclusively in black neighborhoods has been credited with electing Carl Stokes, Cleveland's first black mayor. Because of the overtly political nature of some foundation activities, Congress passed legislation in 1969 to limit the ability of foundations to engage in political advocacy.[6] The ideology of democracy had taken firm root, and individuals on all sides recognized that public policy would be determined based on the demands of voters, not the principles underlying the Constitution.

The Legacy of the Great Society

President Johnson was committed to pushing forward his Great Society programs, but the nation's attention was focused in large part on the war in Vietnam. Civil rights struggles were reported on the daily news as well, but it is not hard to imagine that President Johnson could have let his domestic agenda slide to focus on international issues. Indeed, that is not hard to imagine because Nixon, Johnson's successor, did just that. Nixon's response to vocal protestors on civil rights policy and the Vietnam War was to say that his policies were aimed at the "silent majority" rather than the vocal minority of disenchanted Americans. Johnson, however, pushed ahead with his Great Society.

One of the problems the Vietnam War posed for Johnson was that military resources diverted to the war were resources that would not be available to further his domestic policy agenda, which in itself imposed a constraint on Johnson's ability to implement the Great Society fully. In 1960, military

---

6. The role foundations played in activist social policy is discussed in Randall G. Holcombe, *Writing Off Ideas: The Effect of Tax Laws on America's Non-Profit Foundations* (New Brunswick, NJ: Transaction for the Independent Institute, 1999).

expenditures consumed half of the federal government's budget and outlays on human resources—which include Social Security and other income security programs, health programs, education, and veterans benefits—represented 28.4 percent of the federal budget. By 1968, defense expenditures had fallen slightly to 46 percent of the budget and human resource expenditures were up to 33.3 percent of the budget. If the share of the budget going to human resources is used as a measure of the degree to which Johnson had been able to establish his Great Society, only slight evidence of the Great Society can be found. But Johnson was able to get the Great Society legislation through Congress, laying the foundation for subsequent growth of the Great Society's programs.

After Johnson left office, President Nixon focused his attention more on international affairs than on domestic policy. With a Democratic congress and the winding down of the Vietnam War, by 1975 defense spending had declined to 26 percent of the federal budget, while expenditures on human resources had risen to 52.1 percent, almost the reverse of the percentages in 1960. The major increases in Great Society expenditures came in Nixon's administration, not in Johnson's. That was not because Nixon supported the Great Society, but because he was powerless to stop it. The programs already were in place. Congress wanted to allocate more federal expenditures to human resources, and the end of the Vietnam War provided a source of revenues to do so.

The expansion of the federal government was not limited to social programs or income redistribution. Rather, government programs expanded to fill all areas of the nation's economy. The Environmental Protection Agency (EPA) was established in 1970, following the National Environmental Policy Act of 1969, which required any public or private institution that received federal funds to file an environmental impact statement prior to the beginning of any construction project. The National Highway Traffic Safety Administration was created in 1970 to set safety requirements for automobiles, and the Consumer Product Safety Commission was created the same year and given substantial powers to regulate the safety of consumer products. The Occupational Safety and Health Administration (OSHA) also was created in 1970 to regulate workplace safety. The idea that government was responsible both for looking out for the economic well-being of its citizens and for protecting them from being harmed by business, as workers and as consumers, readily was accepted by the general public, and democracy was extended further from a method for making political decisions to a method for determining the allocation of economic resources.

The Reagan revolution applied a temporary brake to Great Society expenditures. Reagan wanted a stronger national defense, and defense expenditures grew from 22.7 percent of federal expenditures in 1980, the year Reagan was elected, to 26.6 percent in 1989, the year he left office. Meanwhile, human resource expenditures fell only slightly, from 53 percent of the budget to 49.7 percent. If the change in the allocation of government expenditures is used to judge revolutions, it would be more fitting to talk of a Nixon revolution that shifted expenditures from defense to human resources than of a Reagan revolution, which changed the status quo only modestly. But in 1989, Reagan left office and the Berlin Wall fell, signaling the end of the Cold War. During the presidencies of the senior Bush and Bill Clinton, defense expenditures fell to just 16.4 percent of federal spending by 1997, while expenditures on human resources rose to 62.5 percent of the budget. The expansion in Great Society expenditures took a breather during the Reagan years but resumed its climb after Reagan left office.

The Triumph of Democracy

How does a nation determine what activities its government will undertake? Different nations may use different mechanisms. Dictatorships place ultimate authority in the dictator, for example. And the same nation may use different mechanisms at different times in its history. In the United States, the original principle upon which the activities of government were determined was liberty, but by the time the end of the twentieth century had arrived, the principle upon which American government rested was democracy. The government undertakes those activities that a majority of the citizens want it to undertake, and the preferences of the majority are measured through the electoral process.

In 1993, President Clinton, along with First Lady Hillary Rodham Clinton undertook a campaign to try to create a system of national health insurance. The Clintons argued that their plan should be enacted because the American people wanted the kind of health security that it would provide. Their opponents claimed that their plan would not work as advertised, but more tellingly, also claimed that the Clintons were mistaken about the plan's popular appeal and that most Americans opposed it. That debate on national health insurance revealed as much about the principles of American politics by what was not said as by what was said. The issue ultimately came down to one of popularity. Did Americans want it or not? Never was the issue of whether the program was within the constitutional bounds of the federal government considered, and never was the issue considered of whether it would have an impact on the liberty of Americans. The old constitutional principles had gone by the wayside, and the issue simply was one of determining democratically what public healthcare policy Americans wanted.

The issue played out similarly in 2009 with President Obama's healthcare proposals, albeit with a different outcome. President Obama and the Democratic Congress behind him enacted the Affordable Care Act of 2009 because of the mandate they claimed from their 2008 electoral victory. Obama and other Democrats campaigned on it and passed it because they said their election showed that the people wanted it. Its constitutionality and its effect on liberty never were debated. Its constitutionality was challenged on several grounds, and in *National Federation of Independent Business et al. v. Sebelious, Secretary of Health and Human Services et al.* (2012) and in *King v. Burwell* (2015), the Supreme Court found most of it to be constitutional. The Court's rulings were controversial, but it was clear that much like the Social Security decisions in 1937, the Court went out of its way to rule in support of the legislation. If one reads the Constitution literally, it is difficult to find mandated health insurance among the federal government's enumerated powers, but that criterion was abandoned more than half a century ago, replaced by the broader criterion of furthering the general welfare, as measured by democratic political processes.

In a democratic political system, those running for election must cater to the opinion of the majority, because if they do not the electorate will choose someone else. The result of this electoral competition is public policy aimed at voters who are at the center of public opinion. But to abandon the principle of liberty in favor of democracy, democratic opinion must be viewed as representative of the public interest. Thus, democracy has expanded in two dimensions. First, the franchise has been extended continuously. Partly this is because if public policy is determined democratically, it is important for individuals to have the right to vote so that their economic interests are represented. In addition, if democratic decisions are to claim some legitimacy as representative of the public interest, they must represent the interests of everybody rather than a select few. Democracy has been expanded in a second dimension, as a larger share of the federal government has been subject to direct democratic oversight by moving to popular voting for both the president and for senators.

The Great Society represents the ultimate triumph of democracy because for the first time a major expansion in the scope of government was based on the demands of the electorate, with no extenuating circumstances. The Progressive movement, which explicitly called for a shift in the role of government, asking the government to look out for the economic well-being of its citizens in addition to protecting their rights, arose in response to substantial concentrations of economic power toward the end of the nineteenth century. Progressives argued that the nation was not the same one the Founders envisioned governing more than a century before and that changes in government were required to respond to changes in the character of the nation. The old Jeffersonian ideal of limited government should be retired, they argued, and instead the Hamiltonian vision of more expansive government power should be adopted. Changes that the nation was undergoing demanded changes in the nation's government. In the twentieth century, the two world wars and the Great Depression represented national emergencies that created the demand for more government action in response. Despite the philosophical undertones, government action was a pragmatic response to conditions rather than an acceptance of the fact that the role of government had changed.

The Great Society was different. Its declaration of a War on Poverty and a commitment to civil rights came despite the fact that progress was being made on both fronts. Calls for securing and protecting civil rights already were being heard and the incidence of poverty had been falling for two decades prior to Johnson's Great Society programs. The progress was too slow for many, of course, which is why Johnson initiated the Great Society. But unlike the New Deal, which was launched to counteract the setbacks and misfortunes that had befallen many Americans, the Great Society was designed to further assist those whose fortunes were already improving. There was no crisis and no emergency, unless one wants to count the protests, riots, and demonstrations of those who wanted government policy to go their way. But even those demonstrations help prove the larger point. By appealing to popular sentiment and making the intensity of their desires known, the demonstrators hoped to push the democratic decision-making process further to advance their own interests.

Before the Great Society, federal government policy had sacrificed some liberty to further the will of the majority. But past sacrifices of liberty had been in response to changes that threatened the well-being of Americans, and the government's response was intended to push American society back toward the prior status quo by offsetting the effects of recent events. The Great Society was an attempt to change the status quo in response to the demands of the electorate. Some people were in favor and some opposed, but the issue came down to what the majority wanted, not whether the liberty of Americans was threatened. When Barry Goldwater ran for president against Johnson in 1964, he was labeled as an extremist and retorted, "Extremism in the defense of liberty is no vice." The American electorate did not buy it, and Goldwater was trounced solidly by Johnson. In a nation run on the principle of democracy, extremism on any issue is a political vice, because public policy is determined by the demands of the majority. President Nixon, who won two presidential elections, had a better read on the American political system when he said he was aiming his policies at the "silent majority." In a democracy, the majority rules.

In the twenty-first century an ongoing debate exists about the proper scope of government in the United States and around the world. Some people want more government, others want less, and some are content with the status quo. But democracy has won out over liberty, and the issue is not what type of government would best preserve the liberty of Americans, but rather what type of government the majority favors. The Great Society established democracy firmly as the underlying principle of American government by promoting its programs as a response to public demand. Of course, President Johnson believed that his Great Society was the right thing for America, but not because it promoted the liberty that the Founders created the nation to protect. Much of the Great Society—Medicare, Medicaid, the jobs programs, and the educational initiatives—worked against the concept of liberty as envisioned by the Founders. Rather, with public opinion on his side, Johnson pushed the Great Society to enhance the economic well-being of Americans, following the Progressive ideology.

In response to crises, it had been demonstrated previously that Americans would sacrifice their liberty in exchange for government action to try to regain the status quo. Government action in response to crises had to be designed, aimed, and controlled by some process, and that process was democracy. In Jacksonian terms, democratic control of public policy was the way to protect against government programs run for the benefit of the elite. When crises arose, Americans would allow the demands of the majority for government action to dominate the concept of liberty. The Great Society demonstrated that during normal, prosperous times, democracy remained the underlying principle of American government. Indeed, if crises emerged during the 1960s, they were the Cold War and the Vietnam War, and the Great Society forged ahead not because of these crises, but in spite of them. International events were not a sufficient distraction to disrupt the Great Society, and President Johnson's unpopularity owing to the Vietnam War was not enough to derail the Great Society programs that the majority wanted.

Conclusion

Perhaps the continual inroads that democracy made over liberty during times of the crises during the twentieth century enabled it to be accepted unconsciously as a replacement for the principle of liberty, or perhaps Americans were satisfied with the way democracy had worked during crises and were willing to entrust themselves even more to the will of the majority. In the twenty-first century, the term *liberty* has an almost quaint ring to it, and the liberties that Americans still enjoy often are taken for granted. No, worse. A utilitarian undercurrent has arisen in the nation that is willing to weigh the costs of sacrificing a little more liberty in exchange for other goals. Liberty is not taken for granted; it is willingly sacrificed. Democracy and prosperity are the goals promoted by the American ideology, not liberty. The Great Society signaled the final acceptance of democracy as the fundamental principle of American government.

12

The Dangers of Democracy

BY 1980, DEMOCRACY had completely replaced liberty as the fundamental principle of American government. Liberty remained as something valued by Americans and worth protecting only to the extent that it met with the approval of the majority. Lyndon Johnson's Great Society brought with it a sense of optimism about what government could accomplish if only the nation would be willing to devote sufficient resources to it. A decade and a half later, Ronald Reagan questioned the efficacy of the government to solve the nation's problems, and public opinion on the desirability of government intervention fell, largely because the actual experience of government intervention did not live up to its promises. The Reagan revolution, as it was then called, was brought about not by an ideological or philosophical change in the American people, but rather by the realization that government intervention did not work as well as advertised.

The proponents of smaller government objected to wasteful programs that were unable to achieve their goals and to taxation and regulation that interfered with the productivity of the private sector, making everyone poorer as a result. The objections to government were pragmatic and utilitarian, based on the argument that government intervention did not work as its proponents had hoped. And it was democratic. Taxation and regulation were attacked because most people thought they were overtaxed and overregulated. Unlike the revolution in 1776, which was based on the principle of liberty, the so-called Reagan revolution was based on the principle of democracy and moved forward because most people favored less government intervention. The argument was not that government should be reduced to further the cause of liberty, but that it should be downsized because the majority wanted smaller government.

The governments of Margaret Thatcher in Britain and Ronald Reagan in the United States were turning points in the sense that both were based on the policy goal of limiting the scope and power of government. But they did not change the underlying democratic philosophy of government. Any retrenchment during the Reagan and Thatcher eras was because popular opinion favored it, not because people wanted to reclaim liberty as the underlying philosophy of American government. The retrenchment was even more substantial during Bill Clinton's presidency, even though Clinton clearly was Progressive in his ideological orientation, because popular opinion in the 1990s weighed against big government. But because the backlash against big government was pragmatic rather than ideological, the ideology of democracy remained, and the minor retrenchment during the Reagan and Clinton administrations was reversed in the twenty-first century administrations of George W. Bush and Barack Obama.

The ascendancy of democracy as the fundamental principle of American government raises important questions about whether democracy is a political system capable of ensuring a stable government and a prosperous economy, or whether democracy itself is even capable of surviving over the long term. Francis Fukuyama, in his 1992 book *The End of History and the Last Man*, argued that the ascendancy of democratic government and the market economy signaled the end of history in the sense that political democracy will be the final form of government and the market economy will be the end point in the evolution of economic systems. Fukuyama's view contrasts with Joseph Schumpeter's argument a half-century earlier, in *Capitalism, Socialism, and Democracy*, that democracy plants the seeds of its own destruction, because it allows people to vote away their freedoms. People are more inclined to engage their governments to get special-interest benefits rather than to preserve the system that made them prosperous. While one might argue that the case for democracy is strong, because it has survived for more than two centuries in the United States and that by the end of the twentieth century it was spreading around the world, the history recounted in this volume suggests that the evidence is not as strong as it first appears.

Democracy in the United States always has been tempered by a constitutionally limited government, and even in the twenty-first century constitutional constraints still retain some force. Furthermore, it has only been since the 1960s that democracy has become firmly entrenched as the fundamental principle of American government. Earlier in the twentieth century, concessions were made to the principle of liberty in response to the crises of wars and depression, and only more recently did Americans demonstrate that they were willing to agree to give up some liberty to further the desires of the majority during normal times. The United States has not experienced two centuries of democratic government. Rather, the United States began, in 1776, as a government dedicated to the principle of liberty, with a very limited role for democracy. Until the Progressive Era that began at the end of the nineteenth century, one could easily claim that democracy was a means to an end, but by the end of the twentieth century it had become an end in itself. In addition, until the Progressive Era, democracy played the limited role of a political decision-making mechanism, but starting with the Progressive Era democracy increasingly has supplanted the market economy as a method of allocating economic resources. Democracy in its current incarnation is relatively new and relatively untested, but it is easy to see how, once the constitutional constraints on government action have eroded, it becomes inevitable that democracy will play an ever larger role in the economic system. People have a natural tendency to use their political power to try to secure economic gains for themselves at others' expense.

Andrew Jackson, a strong democrat, supported democracy as a means of controlling the power of political elites and of curbing the growth of government. Despite his hope that democracy would be a tool to limit the power of government, Jackson's democratic ideals were used to expand government. The right to vote was viewed as important enough after the War Between the States to be embodied in a constitutional amendment, but it was the Populists and Progressives who turned democracy philosophically from a means to an end into an end in itself, promoting the idea that public policy should be determined by the will of the majority and that the government should expand its role to protect the economic well-being of its citizens. Even in the twentieth century, the expansion of democracy came largely as a response to the crises of wars and depression, only emerging finally in the 1960s as a principle of government that stood on its own. In that sense, American democracy at the end of the twentieth century was less than half a century old and the nation's experience with true democratic government is limited.

Problems with Democracy

The problems with democracy fall into two categories. First, as a method of making group decisions, democracy is most likely to fail when it is most needed. Democracy is a great system for making collective decisions when a substantial consensus of opinion exists among those in the decision-making group, but it tends to break down when there is no general agreement. Second, as a method of allocating resources, democratic allocation is inefficient. If democracy creates problems as a political system, it creates even more problems as an economic system. With private property in a market economy, where owners of economic resources are free to determine how those resources are deployed, individuals pursuing their own interests are led by an invisible hand to do what is best for everyone, as Adam Smith observed in *The Wealth of Nations* more than two centuries ago. When resources are allocated democratically, everyone has a potential claim on the productivity of everyone else, enticing some to use the political process to take resources from others and forcing them to enter politics to protect the wealth they have produced. When public policy is determined by the will of the majority, political democracy brings with it economic democracy, because it allows government to design policies that redistribute wealth and reallocate economic resources.

When everyone is given a say in how resources are allocated through the democratic decision-making process, private ownership is transformed into collective ownership and the incentives to preserve and enhance the value of a nation's resources are destroyed. After the fall of the Berlin Wall, the advantages of market economies over centrally planned economies—and private ownership over government ownership—were well recognized. What was not so well recognized is that the mandates of democratic governments—whether they were zoning laws or land use regulations that dictate how property owners can develop their property, or regulations restricting certain types of products from being sold, or regulations requiring products to have certain characteristics and features, or labor laws that dictate some of the terms under which people can exchange their time for money—all take a step toward collective ownership of resources. Freedom of exchange is replaced by government mandate. As the Founders envisioned it, democracy was a component in the political decision-making process, not a method for determining how people can use their economic resources.

Agreement in Politics and in Markets

In politics, one must be careful about choosing alliances, because people who have common interests on some issues may find themselves disagreeing on others. Thus, when choosing with whom to cooperate, it is important to consider the views of potential allies on all issues, not just issues on which views are held in common. For almost everybody, supporting one candidate or one platform over another will be a compromise in which the supporter agrees with the candidate or platform on many issues but not on all of them. Supporting a candidate because one agrees with the candidate on many issues also helps the candidate promote issues with which the supporter disagrees. One may agree with a candidate's views on taxation, for example, but may not support the candidate because of the candidate's views on abortion. A supporter, therefore, must evaluate potential candidates and parties not based on whether they share opinions on one issue, but rather how close their views are on all issues. That circumstance creates an obvious source of conflict, because party supporters who agree with their colleagues on many issues will always have the incentive to try to push for a change in party position on issues that supporters are in disagreement with their party. Politics, by its very nature, fosters conflict, even among people who agree about almost everything.

In markets the situation is just the opposite. People cooperate only when they gain from trade on some specific good or service. When a person buys gasoline at a filling station, for example, whether the gas station attendant favors higher or lower taxes is irrelevant to the transaction. Similarly, nobody enters a transaction at a department store contingent on whether the cashier has the same views on abortion as the purchaser. The only relevant issues are whether the purchaser wants to make the particular purchase and whether the seller is willing to sell. Nobody asks, or even cares, about the political views of those with whom they do business. Their interests simply are to complete the transaction as easily as possible. Market exchange, by its very nature, fosters cooperation, even among people who disagree about almost everything.

In the market, purchasers are free to support the Coca-Cola Company by buying Sprite, if they prefer it to other lemon-lime soft drinks, but they are also free to support the Pepsi-Cola Company by buying Pepsi, if they prefer it to Coke. They are free to buy from both companies, or only one, or neither. Similarly, purchasers can buy their vans from the Ford Motor Company and their sedans from General Motors, if that is what they prefer, supporting only those offerings of a company they actually prefer. In politics, however, supporting a party means supporting all of the party's positions. As long as substantial consensus exists, that may not be a problem, but when consensus cannot be found, disagreements can arise that cause the collective decision-making process to function less smoothly. In other words, the more important it becomes to make collective decisions to resolve disagreement, the less well democracy is able to function as a collective decision-making mechanism.

In the market, people can disagree about most things and yet still cooperate in areas where they agree, typically without even being aware of areas of disagreement, because any areas of disagreement are of no consequence to the transaction at hand. That is not so in politics. Supporting a candidate on one issue strengthens that candidate's impact on all issues, leaving much room for conflict even among people who agree about most things. Market decision-making is designed to find common ground and to limit controversy and conflict. Political decision-making highlights differences among people and fosters controversy and conflict.

The Founders designed a limited government to protect the liberty of its citizens, a goal that elicits broad support because everyone wants to have their rights protected. The scope of government has expanded beyond the protection of rights into areas where people's views have less in common and has brought with it more political conflict because the ideology of democracy implies imposing the will of the majority on everyone else, regardless of whether or not they agree.

Consensus and Democracy

When a group of people are in agreement about most things, democratic decision-making works well but is of minor importance. Democratic decision-making will produce decisions that reflect the opinion of the group, but this would also be the case if all of the group's decisions were made by one of its members or if a small committee made all collective decisions for the larger group. In groups where people join together for a common purpose, such as clubs or homeowners' associations, democratic decision-making is a sensible way of assessing the group's opinion, because the group is designed so that the interests of their members largely are homogeneous and the scope of collective decision-making is very limited. However, when members of a group have homogeneous interests, it is relatively unimportant how that group arrives at its collective decisions. Everyone has the same goals.

When consensus does not exist among a group's members, democratic decision-making is likely to break down as various factions compete to assemble a majority to impose their preferences on the rest, and is unlikely to be a good reflection of the group's preferences. Thus, as a mechanism for making group decisions, democratic decision-making has the flaw that it is most likely to break down precisely when it is most needed.[1] When areas of disagreement surface in a collective decision-making group, it is natural for members of the group to ally themselves with others in the group who have similar views, creating factions within the group. But because people who are allies on one issue may well disagree on others, tensions are created even within allied factions, which impedes the collective decision-making process.

With heterogeneous views, any outcome will be less than completely satisfactory. One side or the other wins, leaving some people dissatisfied. And very likely, people satisfied on some issues will be dissatisfied on others. Alternatively, the outcome could be a compromise, in which case nobody is completely satisfied and everybody has an incentive to continue the political conflict to push the outcome a little more toward their own preferences. The problem is that political decisions are imposed on everyone in the group. In contrast, market transactions occur only among those who agree to them, so nobody is forced to participate in a market exchange if for any reason the person does not view it as satisfactory. Some commentators have observed that politics has become more polarized in the twenty-first century. If this is the case, one

---

1. This point is insightfully discussed by Russell Hardin, "Democracy on the Margin," in *Understanding Democracy: Economic and Political Perspectives*, ed., Albert Breton et al. (Cambridge: Cambridge University Press, 1997), 249–66.

reason may be that more interpersonal interactions have been shifted from markets, which foster cooperation, to politics, which foster conflict.

This problem with democracy can be limited somewhat by requiring more consensus in collective decision-making. Two-thirds majorities could be required, or separate approval by more subgroups could be mandated. What if state legislatures had the power to nullify the federal laws they opposed? But requiring more consensus means limiting the scope of collective decision-making, thus reducing the role of democracy. Consensus can be enlarged by limiting the scope of collective action, as the Founders intended to do by designing a constitutionally limited government. Their idea was that democratic decision-making would not be strained by creating a government that only undertook actions that produced benefits for everyone.

One can also create more consensus by subdividing groups into smaller, more homogeneous units, keeping more collective actions at the local rather than the national level, but the evolution of American government has gone the opposite way. National decision-making has replaced state and local decision-making on many issues, and the constitutional limits on the scope of government have been eroded so that government deals with more issues on which a diversity of opinion exists. Thus, democracy has become a less satisfactory way of making collective decisions because the scope of democratic decision-making has expanded beyond those areas on which a substantial consensus of opinion can be found.

When consensus exists, almost any collective decision-making procedure will arrive at a satisfactory outcome. When no consensus exists, democracy tends to break down, just when the need for a satisfactory collective decision-making procedure is the greatest.

Problems with Majority Voting

Democracy, as a political system, is much more than just simple majority rule voting. Still, majority rule decision-making is at the foundation of contemporary democracy and also is at the foundation of popular opinion about the way democracy operates as a governing principle. Majority rule voting is subject to a number of problems as a mechanism for making decisions for a group.

The first problem with collective action determined by majority rule is that those in the minority must accept the outcome preferred by the majority. If a group is voting on whether to drink Coke or Pepsi, if a majority votes for Coke, then those who prefer Pepsi get Coke. If the decision were left to the market, those who want Pepsi get Pepsi, those who want Dr Pepper get Dr Pepper, and those who want 7UP get 7UP. If a democratic government is deciding on the characteristics of public schools, the preferences of the majority are imposed on the minority. In a market system that produced schools in the private sector, there is no reason to think that the variety of schools would be any less great than the variety of soft drinks the market produces, allowing those in the minority to have their preferences satisfied too.

A second problem with majority voting is that it does not allow for voters to register their preference intensities. Thus, a majority may prefer one alternative only slightly, whereas a minority strongly prefers another alternative. When decisions are made through voting, an intense minority cannot pay a mostly indifferent majority to change their votes; indeed, it would be considered antidemocratic if they could. Under majority rule, the majority could easily impose costs on the minority that exceed the benefits reaped by the majority. The majority rules even if the benefits to the majority are less than the costs imposed on the minority.

A third problem with majority rule decision-making is that the collective decision-making procedure itself is costly. Of course, market exchange also is costly, but market exchange eliminates the necessity of having to get a group of people to agree to an outcome that will be only partially satisfactory to them in any event. In market exchange, transactions take place between parties who have a mutual interest and can reap the gains of their exchange without having to convince others that it is a good idea.

A more vexing problem is that in many circumstances no single outcome may command approval by a majority of voters against all other possible outcomes. In its simplest form this problem is called the cyclical majority, which is illustrated by the hypothetical example in the table below. Three voters, numbered 1, 2, and 3 decide, and the table shows their rank-order preferences for three alternatives *A, B,* and *C.* For example, voter 1 prefers *A* to *B,* and *B* to *C.* Now consider a majority rule vote to determine whether the group will choose *A*, *B*, or *C*. If *A* is voted on against *B*, then *A* gets the votes of voters 1 and 3, so *A* defeats *B*. If *C* is voted on against *A*, then *C* gets the votes of voters 2 and 3, so *C* defeats *A*. But in an election of *B* against *C*, *B* gets the votes of voters 1 and 2 to defeat *C*. Thus, *B* defeats *C*, *A* defeats *B*, but *C* defeats *A*. No matter which outcome is chosen, there is another that is preferred to it by a majority. A majority defeats every option.

Voter Preferences That Produce a Cyclical Majority

Voter 1	Voter 2	Voter 3
A	B	C
B	C	A
C	A	B

This example shows that in some cases majority rule voting has no rational way of choosing which outcome is most preferred by a group of voters. There is no guarantee that majority rule will produce any particular outcome, let alone the one that voters value most highly.[2]

If the preferences of the voters are equally intense, it would not matter (except to the individual voters) which outcome was chosen, because no one would be more valuable than another. But what if voter 1, for example, had strong preferences for *A*, but the other two voters were close to being indifferent among the three options? Then *A* would be the most highly valued choice, but majority rule voting would not identify it as such.

For many reasons, when there is no consensus of opinion, majority rule voting is not an effective mechanism for selecting a group preference. In many cases it will not choose the alternative the group values most highly, and in some cases majority rule voting will produce an arbitrary result. When opinions are diverse, simple majority rule can lead to political instability. The cyclical majority provides a simple example in which no matter which outcome is chosen, a majority would prefer something else. Majority rule decision-

---

2. This cyclical majority problem is discussed by Kenneth J. Arrow, *Social Choice and Individual Values* (New Haven: Yale University Press, 1951); Duncan Black, *The Theory of Committees and Elections* (Cambridge, CT: Cambridge University Press, 1958); and many others before and since those books. It is a well-known problem in political theory.

making also imposes the preferences of a majority on the minority. Of course, if everyone agrees on which outcome is best, that outcome will be selected by majority rule, but also by any other political decision-making mechanism. Problems arise when a consensus cannot be found, pointing to the conclusion that democracy fares worst when it is needed the most.

Democratic Institutions

Democratic decision-making is more complex than simply taking a majority vote on issues that arise. Previous chapters emphasized the influence of the congressional committee system on the types of legislation produced by Congress, and on the ways in which the interactions among Congress, the president, and the courts have influenced public policy. Democracy means more than just majority rule voting, and political institutions have a substantial impact on the outcomes of democratic processes and the activities undertaken by democratic governments. One major institutional change has been the greater democratic accountability of the executive and legislative branches of government. The Founders tried to insulate public policy decision-making from the pressures of democracy, but from the very beginning American political institutions have evolved to become more democratic.

If Congress were a deliberative body insulated from democratic pressures and relied on the Constitution as its first guide for public-policy making, its decisions would be much different from the situation in the twenty-first century, where legislators think of their elected offices as lifetime occupations and therefore the actions they take must always be made with an eye toward reelection to keep their jobs. This means that democratic pressures are always an important motivation behind legislative decision-making. Similarly, if the chief executive were selected by an Electoral College insulated from popular opinion, as originally intended by the Founders, the president would be sheltered from democratic pressures rather than directly accountable to the electorate, as has been the case throughout most of American history. Not only would this change the incentives facing the president, it is likely that a different type of individual would be selected if the choice were made by a well-informed Electoral College and House of Representatives rather than by popular voting by the electorate.

While democratic accountability—the quest for popular support—drives the political decision-making process, most voters have only the vaguest notion about most of the decisions legislators make, and rationally so. Even legislators themselves are unaware of many of the details of the legislation on which they vote, relying on their staffs to evaluate the merits of legislation they must consider. Too much legislation is proposed and passed for any one person, no matter how dedicated, to be aware of all of its details. Indeed, some people in the private sector have full-time jobs just trying to keep abreast of small fractions of the legislative agenda, such as tax law or environmental law. It would not be possible for a voter to be knowledgeable about most of it.

Not only would it not be possible, it would not be rational. An individual voter has a negligible impact on the legislative process. People rationally concentrate their efforts on doing their own jobs and on allocating the incomes they earn from their work. Voters who take some time to understand the differences among local restaurants or the differences among makes of automobiles can improve their lives by making more informed choices. Voters who take the time to understand the details of various trade agreements may be better informed, but the government will make the same decisions on trade agreements regardless of what any one individual voter thinks. Similarly, because elections—even close ones—always are determined by more than one vote, a voter has almost no chance of changing an election's outcome. Voters collect information about political candidates because they are interested, just as they collect information about sports teams, but that information has a negligible impact on the outcome of an election or the determination of any issue. Thus, a large proportion of voters remain rationally ignorant about most of what the government does.[3]

Elected officials preach the message that every vote counts and that citizens have a patriotic duty to vote because those in elected positions have an incentive to get high voter turnout. Higher voter turnout implies more support for elected officials and so imparts more legitimacy to an election result. Could elected officials claim citizen support for their policies if only a small fraction of eligible voters actually voted? Thus, government officials encourage

---

3. Rational ignorance of voters in democratic elections was emphasized by Anthony Downs, *An Economic Theory of Democracy* (New York: Harper & Row, 1957).

people to vote, even though they know that they are encouraging the turnout of relatively uninformed citizens.

In contrast to the electorate, interest groups are well informed about those issues that affect their interests directly. Farmers are informed about farm policy, waterway shippers are informed about policies that affect navigable waterways, and business and industry associations are informed about tax, regulatory, and other issues that affect their industries specifically. Interest groups support candidates based on their positions on issues that affect their group directly and pay little attention to candidates' positions on other issues. Meanwhile, the general public is rationally uninformed about most of what government does. Thus, a strong bias exists for legislation that delivers benefits to special interests over the general public interest. How can one make sense of a federal government that claims a policy goal of curtailing tobacco use by its citizens yet subsidizes tobacco farmers? It makes complete sense if one recognizes that tobacco farmers are an interest group that has an incentive to promote its interests before the legislature while the general public has at best a slight interest in becoming informed on the issue.

Democratic institutions act as a filter on public opinion, sifting out small costs and benefits that are spread among the population at large and focusing instead on concentrated costs and benefits that have large impacts on narrow interests. For this reason, democratic political institutions favor policies that impose small costs on most people, who are rationally ignorant about the policies, to finance large benefits to smaller groups. Thus, despite potential problems with majority rule voting, political institutions that distort the process even more so than the preferences that are transmitted through the democratic political process to the legislature are not those of the general public—the majority—but rather those of narrow concentrated interest groups.

Support for a politician on one issue strengthens that politician's position on all issues, and because political issues are bundled to parties and candidates, it is difficult to identify support on one issue from support on other issues. If people choose to support candidates based on their positions on issues that are of special interest to them, then the support-maximizing politician will choose to side with concentrated special interests on all issues rather than the more diluted general interest. Modern democratic politics favors special interests more than the general public interest. Democracy demands it.

Economic Liberty Versus Economic Democracy

The Industrial Revolution brought with it such wealth that Americans almost take it for granted. The persistent question among those who study poverty is, "Why are some people poor?" Yet prior to the Industrial Revolution almost everybody was poor, and Thomas Robert Malthus, writing in 1798, believed that poverty was destined to be the normal state of affairs for most people throughout time.[4] The more appropriate question is, "Why are so many people rich?" If one could figure out why many people are rich and apply this answer to the poor, the problem of poverty could be lessened. The answer clearly has to do with nations, not individuals. Poor people in the wealthiest nations are materially much better off than most people in the poorest nations.

The answer to this question has been known for hundreds of years. Adam Smith, in his book *The Wealth of Nations*, published in 1776, explained how a system of economic liberty, characterized by private ownership of property, freedom of exchange, and limited government, guides individuals who pursue their own interests to be led by an invisible hand to benefit the entire society. Economic liberty produces the wealth of nations. In the twenty-first century it is common to view economic liberty as a situation in which everyone has a certain level of economic wealth or income, but to view it this way neglects the fact that wealth is difficult to produce and that to give income to some means to taking it from others. Taking from some to give to others reduces the incentive to produce wealth and makes everybody poorer. To see economic liberty as guaranteeing people the property rights to the products of their own labor, and the right to exchange their property voluntarily with others, leads to an economic system based on voluntary agreement and exchange, rather than mandates and coercion.

Economic democracy, in contrast, gives everybody some say in how all people are able to own and use economic resources. It compromises economic liberty because people are no longer able to determine how the fruits of their labor are allocated. The result is that resources are distributed by public opinion rather than by the desires of the owners of those resources. Political allocation blunts the motivation to be productive and creates the incentive for

---

4. Thomas Robert Malthus, *An Essay on Population* (1798; repr. New York: E.P. Dutton, 1914).

some people to try to control the production of others through the political process. The United States still allows resource owners considerable latitude to determine how the resources they own are used, but the ideology of democracy constantly is pushing public policy toward greater economic democracy.

An economic system of liberty has generated growth and prosperity in nations that have adopted it for 250 years. Economic democracy is much more recent, but in nations where economic liberty has been displaced by economic democracy, people's economic well-being has suffered. The idea that American democracy has proven itself from more than two centuries of good performance is, in an important sense, wrong. American democracy as it had evolved by the end of the twentieth century is a relatively recent phenomenon. Liberty, rather than democracy, was the fundamental principle of American government until the twentieth century, and democracy as the fundamental principle of American government was not firmly established until the 1960s.

Production Versus Predation

The essential differences between economic liberty and economic democracy lie in the differences in the incentives the two systems provide for production versus predation. People can obtain income in two ways. They can produce goods and services, adding to the stock of wealth available to be consumed, or they can take goods and services from others, redistributing income but adding nothing to total production. Economic liberty provides the incentive for production because the only way people can enhance their economic well-being is by supplying goods and services that others want. Economic democracy provides the incentive for predation because it allows people to use the democratic political process to assert claims to the economic production of others. Despite the inroads made by the ideology of democracy, a substantial amount of economic liberty remains. But a look at the nation's political history shows that economic liberty has often been eroded and rarely been restored. And because democracy has been so thoroughly accepted as a principle, the liberty that remains is threatened. If economic democracy were to completely displace economic liberty, nobody would have an incentive to produce anything, because anything they produced would be subject to appropriation by the majority.

The American Founders recognized that if government becomes too powerful, it might violate the rights of individuals and appropriate their property. The American colonists, in the Declaration of Independence, claimed that they were rebelling against just such a government. The American Founders objected to the excessive government infringement on their liberties by the British Crown, but democratic governments likewise have the same capacity to infringe the liberties of their citizens. The democratic government that Americans now take for granted was the very type of democracy that the American Founders were trying to prevent. The Founders wanted to create a limited government that would protect the liberty of its citizens from the oppression they perceived from the British, and they wanted to limit the scope of their new government so that it would not become predatory and infringe on the liberty of its citizens. They did not intend to create a democracy in which some people could use the political process to appropriate the production of others or to dictate the conditions under which people could use or exchange resources they owned.

As an economic system, the danger of democracy is that it creates incentives for people to gain wealth by using the political process for predation rather than creating wealth through production. The Founders wanted to create a government that prevented predation, but the democratic system that came to govern the United States in the twentieth century increasingly encouraged predation. When some people have the ability to take the resources of others by political means, whether the predators are kings or members of some political majority, the stability of the political system and the productivity of the economic system are threatened. Those are the dangers of democracy.

The Ideology of Democracy

Contemporary American political ideology views the role of government as transforming the preferences of its citizens into public policy. As its citizens view it, American government is a democracy in which those with political power implement the policies that citizens request through the political process. The message of this chapter is that democracy is severely limited in its potential both as a political system and as an economic system. For democracy to work as a long-term component of government, its role must strictly be limited, as the Founders intended. There is tendency to view criticism of democracy as anti-American, but an analysis of American political history shows that its Founders tried to prevent the creation of the type of democracy that characterizes twenty-first-century American government.

American democracy was substantially different at the end of the twentieth century from what it was at the beginning, so any claim that American democracy has proven itself because of its long record of success would be inaccurate. In fact, potential hazards have been created by the transformation of the fundamental principle of American government from liberty to democracy. While the American Founders attempted to insulate their new government from the democratic pressures, much of the insulation they created has been removed over the subsequent two centuries.

Conclusion

The United States became an independent nation because the Founders believed they were being oppressed by the British government, and they declared their independence to protect the liberty of Americans. To them, liberty meant freedom from government oppression, because the clearest threat to liberty in those times came from government. The US government was created as a limited one to protect against the threats of more oppressive governments. The Founders recognized that their newly created government had the same potential to threaten liberty as did the British government they were trying to escape, so they imposed constitutional limits on the power of government to protect the liberty of its citizens and deliberately insulated the government from the democratic pressures of popular opinion. The insulation is now gone, and popular opinion drives the public policy process, partly because of conscious decisions that changed the nature of government and partly because popular opinion holds democracy in higher esteem as a political value than liberty. The dangers of democracy are not as readily apparent as the dangers of dictatorship, but they are just as menacing. Unfortunately, many Americans do not appear to fully understand these dangers as they continue to push the foundations of their government away from liberty and toward democracy.

Bibliography

Abraham, Henry J. *Justices and Presidents: A Political History of Appointments to the Supreme Court*. New York: Oxford University Press, 1992.

Alchon, Guy. *The Invisible Hand of Planning: Capitalism, Social Science, and the State in the 1920s*. Princeton, NJ: Princeton University Press, 1985.

Anderson, Gary M., and Robert D. Tollison. "Congressional Influence and Patterns of New Deal Spending, 1933–1939." *Journal of Law & Economics* 34, no. 1 (April 1991): 161–75.

Anderson, Terry L., and Peter J. Hill. *The Birth of a Transfer Society*. Stanford, CA: Hoover Institution Press, 1980.

Arrow, Kenneth J. *Social Choice and Individual Values*. New Haven, CT: Yale University Press, 1951.

Baye, Michael R., and Dennis W. Jansen. *Money, Banking, and Financial Markets*. Boston: Houghton Mifflin, 1995.

Beard, Charles A. *An Economic Interpretation of the Constitution of the United States*. New York: Macmillan, 1913.

Berman, Harold J. *Law and Revolution: The Formation of Western Legal Tradition*. Cambridge, MA: Harvard University Press, 1983.

Bernstein, Irving. *Guns or Butter? The Presidency of Lyndon Johnson*. New York: Oxford University Press, 1996.

Black, Duncan. *The Theory of Committees and Elections*. Cambridge: Cambridge University Press, 1958.

Bornet, Vaughn Davis. *The Presidency of Lyndon Johnson*. Lawrence: University Press of Kansas, 1983.

Buchanan, James M. *The Limits of Liberty: Between Anarchy and Leviathan*. Chicago: University of Chicago Press, 1975.

Buchanan, James M., and Gordon Tullock. *The Calculus of Consent.* Ann Arbor: University of Michigan Press, 1962.

Cole, Donald B. *The Presidency of Andrew Jackson.* Lawrence: University of Kansas Press, 1993.

Croly, Herbert. *Progressive Democracy.* New York: Macmillan, 1915.

Cullinan, Gerald. *The Post Office Department.* New York: Praeger, 1968.

Donald, David. *The Politics of Reconstruction, 1863–1867.* Baton Rouge: Louisiana State University Press, 1965.

Downs, Anthony. *An Economic Theory of Democracy.* New York: Harper & Row, 1957.

Eidelbereg, Paul. *The Philosophy of the American Constitution: A Reinterpretation of the Intentions of the Founding Fathers.* New York: Free Press, 1968.

Edelman, Murray. *The Symbolic Uses of Politics.* Urbana: University of Illinois Press, 1964.

Farrand, Max. *The Records of the Federal Convention of 1787.* rev. ed. New Haven, CT: Yale University Press, 1937.

Fenton, William N., ed. *Parker on the Iroquois.* Syracuse, NY: Syracuse University Press, 1968.

Friedman, Milton. *Capitalism and Freedom.* Chicago: University of Chicago Press, 1962.

Friedman, Milton, and Anna J. Schwartz, *A Monetary History of the United States.* Princeton, NJ: Princeton University Press, 1968.

Friedrich, Carl J. *Constitutional Government and Democracy.* rev. ed. Boston: Ginn, 1950.

Fukuyama, Francis. *The End of History and the Last Man.* New York: Free Press, 1992.

Glasson, William Henry. *History of Military Pension Legislation in the United States.* New York: Columbia University Press, 1900.

Gould, Lewis L. *Reform and Regulation: American Politics from Roosevelt to Wilson.* 2nd ed. New York: Alfred A. Knopf, 1986.

Grindle, Donald A. *The Iroquois and the Founding of the American Nation.* San Francisco: Indian Historian Press, 1977.

Hamilton, Alexander, John Jay, and James Madison. *The Federalist.* Reprint. Washington, DC: National Home Library, 1937.

Hardin, Russell. "Democracy on the Margin." In *Understanding Democracy: Economic and Political Perspectives,* edited by Albert Breton, Gianluigi Galeotti, Pierre Salmon, and Ronald Wintrobe, 249–66. Cambridge: Cambridge University Press, 1997.

Hayek, Friedrich A. *The Constitution of Liberty*. Chicago: University of Chicago Press, 1960.

———. "The Use of Knowledge in Society." *American Economic Review* 35 (September 1945): 519–30.

Hicks, John D. *The Populist Revolt: A Story of the Farmers' Alliance and the People's Party*. Minneapolis: University of Minnesota Press, 1931.

Higgs, Robert. *Crisis and Leviathan (25th Anniversary Edition): Critical Episodes in the Growth of American Government*. Oakland, CA: Independent Institute, 2012.

———. *Depression, War, and Cold War: Challenging the Myths of Conflict and Prosperity*. Oakland, CA: Independent Institute, 2009.

———. *Neither Liberty nor Safety: Fear, Ideology, and the Growth of Government*. Oakland, CA: Independent Institute, 2007.

Historical Statistics of the United States from Colonial Times to 1970. Washington: Department of Commerce, 1976.

Hobbes, Thomas. *Leviathan*. 1651. Reprint. New York: E. P. Dutton, 1950.

Hofstadter, Richard. *The Age of Reform: From Bryan to F.D.R.* New York: Alfred A. Knopf, 1969.

Holcombe, Randall G. "The Growth of the Federal Government in the 1920s." *Cato Journal* 16, no. 2 (Fall 1996): 175–99.

———. "Veterans Interests and the Transition to Government Growth: 1870–1915." *Public Choice* 99, nos. 3/4 (June 1999): 311–26.

———. *Writing Off Ideas: The Effect of Tax Laws on America's Non-Profit Foundations*. New Brunswick, NJ: Transaction for the Independent Institute, 1999.

Hughes, Jonathan R. T. *The Governmental Habit: Economic Controls from Colonial Times to the Present*. New York: Basic Books, 1977.

Hummel, Jeffrey Rogers. *Emancipating Slaves, Enslaving Free Men: A History of the American Civil War*. Chicago: Open Court Press, 1996.

Jackson, Robert H. *The Struggle for Judicial Supremacy: A Study of Crisis in American Power Politics*. New York: Alfred A. Knopf, 1941.

Johansen, Bruce E. *Forgotten Founders: Benjamin Franklin, the Iroquois, and the Rationale for the American Revolution*. Ipswich, MA: Gambit, 1982.

Jones, Carolyn C. "Mass-Based Income Taxation: Creating a Taxpaying Culture, 1940–1952." In *Funding the Modern American State, 1941–1995: The Rise and Fall of the Era of Easy Finance*, edited by W. Elliot Brownlee, 107–47. Cambridge: Cambridge University Press, 1996.

Kelly, Clyde. *United States Postal Policy*. New York: D. Appleton, 1932.

Ketcham, Ralph. *Presidents Above Party: The First American Presidency, 1789–1829*. Chapel Hill: University of North Carolina Press, 1984.

Keynes, John Maynard. *The General Theory of Employment, Interest, and Money.* New York: Harcourt, Brace, 1936.

Kolko, Gabriel. *Railroads and Regulation, 1877–1916.* Princeton, NJ: Princeton University Press, 1965.

Lee, Jr., Charles Robert. *The Confederate Constitutions.* Chapel Hill: University of North Carolina Press, 1963.

Locke, John. *Two Treatises on Government.* 1690. Reprint. Cambridge: Cambridge University Press, 1967.

Malthus, Thomas Robert. *An Essay on Population.* 1798. Reprint. New York: E.P. Dutton, 1914.

Martis, Kenneth C. *The Historical Atlas of United States Congressional Districts, 1789–1983.* New York: Free Press, 1982.

McConnell, Grant. *Private Power and American Democracy.* New York: Alfred A. Knopf, 1966.

McMath, Jr., Robert C. *American Populism: A Social History, 1877–1898.* New York: Hill & Wang, 1993.

Mises, Ludwig von. *Socialism.* New Haven, CT: Yale University Press, 1951.

Murphy, Paul L. *The Constitution's Crisis Times, 1918–1969.* New York: Harper & Row, 1972.

Murray, Robert K. *The Politics of Normalcy: Government in Theory and Practice in the Harding-Coolidge Era.* New York: W. W. Norton, 1973.

North, Douglass C. "Ideology and Political/Economic Institutions." *Cato Journal* 8 (Spring/Summer 1988): 15–28.

———. *Structure and Change in Economic History.* New York: W. W. Norton, 1981.

Patterson, James T. *America's Struggle Against Poverty, 1900–1985.* Cambridge, MA: Harvard University Press, 1986.

Peacock, Alan T., and Jack Wiseman. *The Growth of Public Expenditure in the United Kingdom.* Princeton, NJ: Princeton University Press, 1961.

Posner, Richard A. "A Statistical Study of Antitrust Enforcement." *Journal of Law & Economics* 13, no. 2 (October 1970): 365–419.

Post, C. Gordon, Frances P. DeLancy, and Fredric R. Darby, eds. *Basic Constitutional Cases.* New York: Oxford University Press, 1948.

Quynn, Russell Hoover. *The Constitutions of Abraham Lincoln and Jefferson Davis.* New York: Exposition, 1959.

Rassler, Karen A., and William R. Thompson. "War Making and State Making: Government Expenditures, Tax Revenues, and Global Wars." *American Political Science Review* 79, no. 2 (June 1985): 491–507.

Rawls, John. *A Theory of Justice.* Cambridge, MA: Belknap Press, 1971.

Rothbard, Murray N. *America's Great Depression.* Kansas City: Sheed & Ward, 1963.

Rulon, Philip Reed. *The Compassionate Samaritan: The Life of Lyndon Baines Johnson.* Chicago: Nelson-Hall, 1981.

Samuelson, Paul A. *Economics.* 9th ed. New York: McGraw-Hill, 1973.

Schlesinger, Jr., Arthur A. *The Age of Jackson.* Boston: Little, Brown and Company, 1945.

Schmeckebier, Laurence F. *The Bureau of Prohibition: Its History, Activities, and Organization.* Washington, DC: Brookings Institution, 1929.

Schumpeter, Joseph A. *Capitalism, Socialism, and Democracy.* 3rd ed. New York: Harper & Row, 1950.

Severo, Richard, and Lewis Milford. *The Wages of War: When America's Soldiers Came Home—From Valley Forge to Vietnam.* New York: Simon and Schuster, 1989.

Skocpol, Theda. *Protecting Soldiers and Mothers: The Political Origins of Social Policy in the United States.* Cambridge, MA: Belknap, 1992.

Skowronek, Stephen. *Building a New American State: The Expansion of National Administrative Capabilities, 1877–1920.* New York: Cambridge University Press, 1982.

Smith, Adam. *The Wealth of Nations.* 1776. Reprint. New York: Random House, Modern Library, 1937.

Tocqueville, Alexis de. *Democracy in America.* 1835. Reprint. New York: Alfred A. Knopf, 1963.

Trenchard, John, and Thomas Gordon. *Cato's Letters, Or Essays on Liberty, Civil and Religious, and Other Important Subjects.* Indianapolis, IN: Liberty Fund, 1995.

Twight, Charlotte. "Evolution of Federal Income Tax Withholding: The Machinery of Institutional Change." *Cato Journal* 14, no. 3 (Winter 1995): 359–95.

Warren, Charles. *The Making of the Constitution.* Cambridge, MA: Harvard University Press, 1937.

Watkins, William J., Jr. *Crossroads for Liberty: Recovering the Anti-federalist Values of Americas First Constitution.* Oakland, CA: Independent Institute, 2017.

———. *Reclaiming the American Revolution: The Kentucky and Virginia Resolutions and Their Legacy.* New York: Palgrave/Macmillan for the Independent Institute, 2008.

White, Richard. *Railroaded: The Transcontinentals and the Making of Modern America.* New York: W. W. Norton, 2011.

White, William Allen, *The Old Order Changeth: A View of American Democracy.* New York: Macmillan, 1910.

Woddy, Carroll H. *The Growth of the Federal Government, 1915–1932.* New York: McGraw-Hill, 1934.

Index

About the Author

RANDALL G. HOLCOMBE is the DeVoe Moore Professor of Economics at Florida State University, a Research Fellow at the Independent Institute, past President of the Public Choice Society, and past President of the Society for the Development of Austrian Economics. He is also Senior Fellow at the James Madison Institute and was a member of the Florida Governor's Council of Economic Advisors.

Dr. Holcombe is the author of twelve books, a contributing author to forty volumes and the author of more than 100 articles in academic and professional journals. Among his books are *The Economic Foundations of Government*, *Public Policy and the Quality of Life*, *Smarter Growth* (ed. with S. Staley), *From Liberty to Democracy*, *Writing Off Ideas*, *Public Sector Economics*, *Public Finance and the Political Process*, and *Entrepreneurship and Economic Progress*. His primary areas of research are public finance and the economic analysis of public policy issues.

He received his Ph.D. in economics from Virginia Polytechnic Institute and State University, and has taught at Texas A&M University and Auburn University.

Independent Institute Studies in Political Economy

Independent Institute Studies in Political Economy

NATURE UNBOUND |
by Randy T Simmons, Ryan M. Yonk, and Kenneth J. Sim

NEITHER LIBERTY NOR SAFETY | *by Robert Higgs*

THE NEW HOLY WARS | *by Robert H. Nelson*

NO WAR FOR OIL | *by Ivan Eland*

OPPOSING THE CRUSADER STATE |
edited by Robert Higgs & Carl P. Close

OUT OF WORK |
by Richard K. Vedder & Lowell E. Gallaway

PARTITIONING FOR PEACE | *by Ivan Eland*

PATENT TROLLS | *by William J. Watkins, Jr.*

PLOWSHARES AND PORK BARRELS |
by E. C. Pasour, Jr. & Randal R. Rucker

POPE FRANCIS AND THE CARING SOCIETY |
edited by Robert M. Whaples

A POVERTY OF REASON | *by Wilfred Beckerman*

THE POWER OF HABEAS CORPUS IN AMERICA |
by Anthony Gregory

PRICELESS | *by John C. Goodman*

PROPERTY RIGHTS | *edited by Bruce L. Benson*

THE PURSUIT OF JUSTICE | *edited by Edward J. López*

RACE & LIBERTY IN AMERICA |
edited by Jonathan Bean

RECARVING RUSHMORE | *by Ivan Eland*

RECLAIMING THE AMERICAN REVOLUTION |
by William J. Watkins, Jr.

REGULATION AND THE REAGAN ERA |
edited by Roger E. Meiners & Bruce Yandle

RESTORING FREE SPEECH AND LIBERTY ON
CAMPUS | *by Donald A. Downs*

RESTORING THE PROMISE | *by Richard K. Vedder*

RESURGENCE OF THE WARFARE STATE |
by Robert Higgs

RE-THINKING GREEN | *edited by Robert Higgs
& Carl P. Close*

RISKY BUSINESS | *edited by Lawrence S. Powell*

SECURING CIVIL RIGHTS | *by Stephen P. Halbrook*

STRANGE BREW | *by Douglas Glen Whitman*

STREET SMART | *edited by Gabriel Roth*

TAKING A STAND | *by Robert Higgs*

TAXING CHOICE | *edited by William F. Shughart II*

THE TERRIBLE 10 | *by Burton A. Abrams*

THAT EVERY MAN BE ARMED |
by Stephen P. Halbrook

TO SERVE AND PROTECT | *by Bruce L. Benson*

T.R.M. HOWARD |
by David T. Beito and Linda Royster Beito

VIETNAM RISING | *by William Ratliff*

THE VOLUNTARY CITY | *edited by David T. Beito,
Peter Gordon, & Alexander Tabarrok*

WAR AND THE ROGUE PRESIDENCY |
by Ivan Eland

WINNERS, LOSERS & MICROSOFT |
by Stan J. Liebowitz & Stephen E. Margolis

WRITING OFF IDEAS | *by Randall G. Holcombe*

INDEPENDENT
I N S T I T U T E

100 SWAN WAY, OAKLAND, CA 94621-1428

For further information:
510-632-1366 • orders@independent.org • http://www.independent.org/publications/books/